Players

AND

Pawns

HOW CHESS BUILDS
COMMUNITY
AND CULTURE

Gary Alan Fine

The University of Chicago Press   CHICAGO AND LONDON

GARY ALAN FINE is John Evans Professor of Sociology at
Northwestern University. He is the author of numerous books,
including *Difficult Reputations: Collective Memories of the Evil,
Inept, and Controversial; Authors of the Storm: Meteorologists and
the Culture of Prediction; Everyday Genius: Self-Taught Art and the
Culture of Authenticity; With the Boys: Little League Baseball and
Preadolescent Culture;* and *Shared Fantasy: Role-Playing Games as
Social Worlds,* all published by the University of Chicago Press.

The University of Chicago Press, Chicago 60637
The University of Chicago Press, Ltd., London
© 2015 by The University of Chicago
All rights reserved. Published 2015.
Printed in the United States of America

24 23 22 21 20 19 18 17 16 15   1 2 3 4 5

ISBN-13: 978-0-226-26498-1 (cloth)
ISBN-13: 978-0-226-26503-2 (e-book)
DOI: 10.7208/chicago/9780226265032.001.0001

Library of Congress Cataloging-in-Publication Data

Fine, Gary Alan, author.
  Players and pawns : how chess builds community and culture /
Gary Alan Fine.
      pages   cm
  Includes bibliographical references and index.
  ISBN 978-0-226-26498-1 (hardcover : alk. paper) — ISBN
978-0-226-26503-2 (e-book)   1. Chess—Psychological aspects.
2. Chess—Social aspects.   3. Chess—Tournaments.   I. Title.
  GV1448.F55 2015
  794.101′9—dc23

                                              2014033248

♾ This paper meets the requirements of ANSI/NISO Z39.48–1992
(Permanence of Paper).

To two psychoanalysts

BERNARD FINE (1917–1992)
My father, who taught me to play chess

REUBEN FINE (1914–1993)
American grandmaster

CONTENTS

Prologue

A TOURNAMENT
REVEALED

On a chilly Friday the week before Christmas, 150 adults and children drift into a pleasant if undistinguished Sheraton hotel in Atlantic City to spend the weekend in common cause. The diversity is impressive. First graders mingle with octogenarians. Present are college students, doctors, and those who, to judge from their clothing, are homeless. Some are dressed in coats and ties, and a few reveal their admiration for hip-hop; many wear T-shirts and jeans. Attendees are black, Hispanic, white, and Asian. A few are women. This is the opening of the inaugural Atlantic City International Chess Tournament ("Imagine Your Dreams on the Board and on the Boardwalk"). These gamers play six rounds over three days, and in the gaps in the schedule some stroll to local casinos, trying their skills in poker, a pastime at which many strategically minded chess players excel.

For each tournament game, a player is allocated two hours, although those with digital clocks receive 115 minutes with a five-second delay before the clock starts counting, allowing more time in the endgame's rush. The organizers rented a ballroom for the formal games and a smaller "skittles" room for informal play. Some of those decamped in the skittles room do not enter the tournament, finding the bets laid down in "street chess" more lucrative. A few men are chess hustlers like those at Washington Square. Organizers have also set up a bookstore, selling magazines, chess sets, and trinkets, and there is a tournament room where the organizers establish game pairings and resolve disputes over rules and judges' decisions that inevitably arise.

This is the tournament's inaugural year, and I have been permitted to watch the planning from the start. The organizers, two well-established tournament directors from Chicago, are nervous about attendance.[1] They dream of five hundred and fear one hundred. Winter storms hold off, but the timing a week before Christmas dampens attendance. Choosing Atlantic City, a rough-hewn gambling town, might have dissuaded cautious parents. The final numbers, slightly more than 160, are a real disappointment and a financial blow (the deficit is slightly above $20,000, not pocket change), given the prize money and advertisements. The organizers revel in dark humor about their misfortune, speculating on the responses of their families. Fortunately players book enough rooms to meet the contractual obligations with the hotel, so the Sheraton does not levy a penalty. The tournament promises $50,000 based on five hundred players, one of the larger prize funds of the year, but, as at many tournaments, the organizers carefully promise only $30,000 if the number of entries does not meet expectations. The tournament was not held the following year.

But tournaments are not about accounting; they are about community, friendship, and rough competition. On Thursday evening, the organizers have arranged a "simul" (simultaneous demonstration) with Gata Kamsky, a challenger for the world championship and the second-highest-rated American player. In a simul, a chess star plays all comers, making rapid moves as he visits each board in turn, giving less talented opponents time to consider their moves. Perhaps as a result of the low attendance, Kamsky, sometimes seen as shy or aloof, jokes, gives personal advice to each of his eight opponents, and describes classic games. He is charming, and his opponents clearly enjoy the attention, even though the low attendance means that he will not receive much for the evening; he retains all registration fees for the event. Tonight there are no upsets, and Kamsky triumphs in his competition and chooses to play in the tournament. Simuls are a means by which lower-level players can touch the stars, and these events are a drawing card for many players. One can play (and lose to) a man who might someday be crowned the best in the world. World champions such as Garry Kasparov and Anatoly Karpov fill their simuls, but Kamsky is not a sufficient draw to encourage players to stay an extra night on the Jersey shore, even if rooms are a modest ninety-nine dollars.

Most players arrive on Friday morning as the communal feeling slowly builds. The first game starts on time at 11:00 a.m. Between rounds attendees greet friends, gossip about mutual acquaintances, review games with past opponents (sharing disappointments and startling victories), play rapid and informal contests, sightsee, or study. Many parents bring children, and some analyze the children's games, generally with good grace. Some children travel with siblings or school friends, resulting in running and wrestling, but no more than mild boisterousness. Still, this is an adult tournament; most children have attended similar tournaments and conduct themselves with dignity.

Once chess tournaments were infamous for delayed rounds,[2] but with the advent of computer programs, most events run smoothly unless complaints arise about pairings. Players often guess their opponent, given their rating and record, and become distressed (or delighted) if they guess wrong. They also expect to switch the color of their pieces. Most players prefer white, which according to one study wins 58 percent of decided games.[3] The major complaints this weekend involve color assignment, although some players object to playing those with greater or fewer victories. At the Atlantic City tournament, complaints only occur, as they often do, prior to the final round when the results directly affect the final outcome.

Most tournaments are not a single event, but, as in the case of the Atlantic City tournament, multiple tournaments run in parallel. Each is limited to players of a particular strength level. The elite competition is the open section for the top players, although anyone can register. When other players complete their games, they drift to the tables in the open section, where they watch the marquee players. Other sections are for players with ratings under 2200, under 2000, under 1800, under 1600, under 1400, and under 1200. Open section matchups are based on ratings from the World Chess Federation; the others use ratings from the United States Chess Federation, figured differently and slightly more generous. Thirty-three players participate in the open division, including eight grandmasters (players with a World Chess Federation rating over 2500 and at least three tournament "norms," or strong results) and six international masters (excellent players who have not yet achieved sufficient ratings and norms to be grandmasters). The outcome is as expected, as the two top-rated grandmasters, Gata Kamsky and the Dutch star Loek van Wely, tie for first (splitting $3,600). Often chess tournaments conclude without a single champion. There are no major upsets, but players can watch chess at its highest level, comparable to a contest at an elite international tournament. Their prizes are neither glorious nor insignificant. As grandmasters they don't pay an entry fee, but a fee is deducted from their winnings (seven of the eight grandmasters win money this weekend). Because of how the rounds are paired, Kamsky and van Wely played in the third round, rather than in a climatic sixth round, although the final round was tense, as it was clear that the order of finish would be determined by these contests. However, at some tournaments the two top players face each other during the final round for the cash prize and bragging rights. On these occasions the table is surrounded by those less gifted whose games have concluded. The top six boards at which those players with the most wins and highest ratings compete are set on individual tables set apart from the other boards, which are placed on long tables. This supports the concentration of top players. Yet, at the end of the final round attendees crane to see the top boards, edging as close as possible. This is where the action is. As the clocks tick down in the deciding game at some tournaments, the players rush to move with a whir of hands and a clattering of pieces, but more often these games end anticlimactically with a resignation by one player who can see the end in sight or an agreement to a gentlemanly draw, dividing the prize.

Leaders of other sections also receive monetary prizes, less lucrative than the open division. While all games are played in the same ballroom, spectators rarely observe the lower-rated sections. The lower the rating of players, the more likely their games will end quickly. The ballroom empties from back to front. As at many tournaments where players fight for cash prizes, those with weak records often withdraw from the final rounds, seeing no point in playing for its own sake. This is so common that excuses are not necessary. Nine of the thirty-three players in the open division depart before the final round, an indication of the financial considerations of chess competition.

The most emotionally intense moment is the late-night blitz competition in which twenty-one players compete in a rapid-fire event in which each player has five minutes to make all his moves, and in which many games end with a player running out of time. In contrast to the deliberate silence of the main event, blitz is a bodily rush, slamming of clocks, and a wash of good fellowship. Sometimes this fellowship is forgotten—I have seen pieces and boards thrown after particularly distressing defeats. Each competitor plays an opponent twice, once as white and once as black, for a total of ten games. Blitz competition, now found in most multiday tournaments, is a collective favorite that seems more like video games than thoughtful deliberation. The fact that these competitions are held late in the evening adds pungency, separating day from night. While success in blitz correlates with skill in traditional chess, some players are renowned for their skill in speed chess.

On Sunday evening the final games end, checks are distributed, and players depart. The Atlantic City tournament did not have a concluding drama of a battle between two champions or the cachet of leading events: the World Open in Philadelphia, the National Open in Las Vegas, or the United States Open. Yet joy and quiet sadness were evident, along with restraint and decorum. At minor tournaments few stories enter chess lore. The expected players win, and the upsets are not so dramatic as to reveal a new chess star.

This tournament typified most midsize events. People networked, but there was sufficient diversity of backgrounds, abilities, and interests that not all participants belonged to one community. Even top players did not know more than a few dozen others. While the tournament seemed a single event, in fact it was a collection of nodes, bound together on this occasion. The eight grandmasters and other titled players had competed against each other, but many players knew only a few others. The world of competitive chess is built on clusters of tiny publics, wispy groups that appear for a pleasant weekend and vanish like the snow.

Introduction

FIRST MOVES

I am not related to Reuben Fine. This statement, of little interest to sociological readers or to the common patzer, matters for serious chess players who treasure the genealogy of the game. The name Fine is honored within the world of American chess. Reuben Fine was an international grandmaster, won the United States Open seven times, and could have competed for the world championship if he chose. Based on his subsequent psychiatric training, Reuben Fine is known for his book *The Psychology of the Chess Player*.[1] Not surprisingly, given its psychoanalytic thrust, the book is highly controversial. As a prolific chess writer, Reuben Fine published on openings and endgames, analyses that were more conventional. My father, Bernard, and Reuben Fine shared a profession, practicing a few blocks from each other in Manhattan, where they knew each other casually. I never met my famous namesake, even though I played chess as a child.

The history of chess is broad, deep, and treasured. Aside from religion and medicine, some say more books have been published on chess than on any other topic. Although I am skeptical of such claims, the literature on chess is indeed vast. It overwhelms the literature on bridge, checkers, and poker. Active participants often maintain extensive libraries, treating their collection as central to their identity.[2]

Given this profusion of texts, what justifies another volume? This book has two distinctions, neither of which may prove to be much of a recommendation. First, this is the first volume that claims the sociology of chess as its subject matter. My goal is not to psychoanalyze chess players, to examine the politics of chess, or to critique the literature on chess, but to see chess as a system—actually several systems—of activity: a social world[3] with history, rules, practices, emotions, status, power, organization, and boundaries. By "social world" I refer to a community that is meaningful for its participants, that provides a social order, and that permits a sense of self and a public identity. Through the idea of a *social world* sociologists distinguish salient subgroups from a more extensive, more complex society at large in which many subgroups (or worlds) abut each other. A social world provides a local order in which shared interests are linked to social relations. Activities often depend on sociability. Further, a widely known activity might have several social worlds associated with it, as networks of relations do not always overlap. As a result, chess depends on intersecting leisure worlds and common metaphors, similar to other social worlds on which I have conducted studies—Little League baseball, Dungeons & Dragons, mushrooming, high school debate, and art collecting.

The second distinction is that this book is arguably written by the weakest player who has ever spent years analyzing the world of chess: a patzer among patzers, a fish in a school of sharks, a committed pencil pusher but not a dedicated wood pusher.

As the head of Boston's Boylston Chess Club explained to me, "A tournament player is a chess player. Someone who plays with his family or on long vacation trips is not a chess player." To be a chess player is to participate in the chess community. By this measure, I am not a chess player but at best a tourist. I have no rating and have never played in a rated tournament. The zenith of my chess life was in summer camp when I was ten, when I won the chess competition in our "Color War." I spent a few evenings as a preadolescent in some Manhattan chess clubs. Although I enjoyed chess, I enjoyed the intuitive side of the game: my play was all tactics, no strategy. It was when I learned about the existence of openings, something to study, that I packed up my pawns. I picked them up twenty-five years later when my oldest son was at an age (six) when he could learn the game. We played about four years until I became an easy victim (or, as he called me, "roadkill"). I even organized a chess club at his elementary school, and we held a small school tournament in Atlanta. My son played twice at the National Elementary School Tournament, winning more games than he lost and reaching a United States Chess Federation rating of nearly 1300. Fifteen years later, Caissa, the goddess of chess, whispered for me to return.

As a sociologist who observes groups and communities, I was unconcerned about my ignorance of the nuances of chess. Knowing too much can be a disadvantage, forcing the observer to see the action "from the inside," distracted by the content of the match, rather than by its social meaning. This book is not about how to play chess well but about how chess as a community is organized. Not having an expert's rating takes my mind off the board and allows me to observe everything that surrounds it. This is a book by an outsider who was a guest in this absorbing, complex, feisty world, a world of brilliancies, of commitment, and of conflict. My fundamental argument is that chess as a shared action space—as a leisure world—is *eternally social*, building on group ties. Even if we lionize the champion and suggest that chess is a game of the mind, as an activity it depends on groups acting in concert. I return to the issue of social worlds at the end of this introduction.

The World of Chess

Chess is not the oldest game of humankind. That honor goes to an Egyptian board game dating back to 3500–4000 BC.[4] But chess's longevity is remarkable. While claims of the true beginnings of chess are various and the origins are shrouded in mystery, consensus exists that the game as we recognize it began on the Indian subcontinent in approximately 700 AD, although Persia shaped the early game as well.[5] As with so many origin stories, one can find political motives. For instance, some claim that chess originated in Uzbekistan or even in China.[6]

Chess is considered a war game, or at least a game that models warfare or prepares soldiers, although some legendary origins (Myanmar or Sri Lanka) suggest in a more pacifist fashion that the game was developed to provide a less bloody equivalent to conflict.[7] Given the passion of Napoleon for the game, such sublimation was not inevitably effective. When the game spread to the Islamic world, which rejected gambling and gaming, chess was permitted because it was considered preparation for war. In the Soviet Union, the game was treated not as a bourgeois diversion but a form of proletariat culture.[8]

Over the years, the rules of chess evolved. By the Middle Ages, chess had gained admirers in Europe. Its popularity is evident in writings about chess as morality by Pope Innocent III and Rabbi ben

Ezra, both around 1200 AD.[9] The second book printed in English, *The Game and Playe of the Chesse* (translated from the French), addressed chess as morality. The medieval attention to chess is evident in that the names and movement of the chess pieces changed substantially during this period. The most salient change was to increase the power of the vizier, making it the most powerful piece on the board. This transformation, first labeling the piece the queen and then increasing her range, occurred between the twelfth and fifteenth centuries. Some suggest that this change reflects the authority of women in medieval and Renaissance Europe.[10] Perhaps these explanations are shaped by scholarly wishful thinking, but it is clear that chess changed substantially during the late Middle Ages, and as a result, games prior to the introduction of the powerful queen are rarely studied. Although chess has continued to evolve, a game played after the introduction of the powerful queen is essentially the same game that we play today. The first international tournament was organized in 1851,[11] and by 1886 the world had its first undisputed chess champion, Wilhelm Steinitz.

Depending on one's definition, today there are many chess players or a great many. A large proportion of Americans, although surely nowhere close to a majority, can play chess at some level. According to Susan Polgar, a prominent grandmaster, there are forty-five million chess players in the United States.[12] Other estimates are slightly lower, but most hover around forty million.[13] In chess hot spots such as Russia, eastern Europe, Iceland, Cuba, and Argentina, the proportion is far higher. Polgar guesses that there are seven hundred million players worldwide. Some skepticism of that figure is warranted, but chess is indeed a global game.

We must distinguish between those who are knowledgeable about the basic rules and those who have a commitment to the game: those who play chess and those who participate in the *chessworld*. Here the numbers diminish. Though we do not have firm figures for the number of serious players, as of 2010 the United States Chess Federation (USCF) had a membership of approximately eighty thousand. Some of these members are not active, and many others play chess outside the auspices of the organization (particularly in scholastic chess, where some state and city organizations run their own tournaments). The USCF claims that there are approximately ninety thousand active tournament players. In the last fifteen years, there has been substantial growth in the number of young (scholastic) chess players. Chess is now treated as an activity that provides cultural capital. Playing the game is said to increase a child's cognitive development. In an age in which many parents wish to cultivate their children, chess is treated as a valued training ground, even if it is not perceived as one of those life skills that will continue into adulthood.[14] Estimates of the number of children playing chess run as high as thirty million. But whatever the number, it is striking that the largest number of members of the USCF are third and fourth graders. According to one source, 60 percent of the members of the USCF are age fourteen or younger.[15] While the politics of the organization are set by adult members (one must be sixteen to vote in federation elections), many of the organizational resources are contributed by scholastic members. As a result, it is not surprising that battles have been fought over whether to use resources for high-visibility adult chess or the more popular scholastic chess. Some scholastic chess tournaments are profitable, and the growth of youth chess provides employment for adult teachers.

On many demographic dimensions chess holds up well. A visit to a large tournament finds an impressive number of African Americans, South Asians, East Asians, Hispanics, and eastern European immigrants. A large tournament has the feel of a United Nations of leisure. Such diversity is rare in leisure or voluntary activities. While chess is largely a middle-class pastime, some participants hold working-class jobs or are from working-class homes. And many children participate at adult tournaments. It is common to find a nine-year-old playing—and crushing—a sixty-nine-year-old, an oft-remarked reality that leads to adults being reluctant to play children, who are often better than their ratings suggest. One tournament I attended had participants from five to eighty-seven, a range that was not especially remarkable. The only exception to this demographic diversity is gender. Chess has long been—and still is—male dominated, and the participation of women declines with age and with rated ability. In elementary school as many as 40 percent of players are girls, but there is only one woman in the top one hundred US chess players. In most domains, at least 90 percent of chess players are male, an even greater percentage than in Little League baseball, Dungeons & Dragons, or high school debate. Because of the highly gendered structure of chess and to avoid awkward syntax, I use the male pronoun. Perhaps before too long, readers will find my pronoun usage odd and inappropriate.

The Metaphors of Chess

When one examines any activity, an inevitable question emerges: what kind of thing is this? Put another way, what is the "cultural logic" of chess? What framework of meaning explains this community? What conventions are embraced? In what domain of activity do we place it? This is the human desire for labeling and categorization.[16] Compared to other games, chess is incredibly deep. No two games are the same,[17] and the seemingly unending choices have lured many players. Chess edges close to infinite possibility. The number of legal positions in chess has been estimated at 10^{40} (the number of stars in the universe is estimated at 10^{24}), the number of possible games is 10^{120}, and chess databases contain over 3.5 million games.[18]

Is chess so multifaceted? Why and how do these figures resonate with chess players? In the diversity of metaphors, chess exemplifies generic features of human association, including focus and attention, affiliation, beauty, status, collective memory, consumption, and competition. These are topics to which I return.

Perhaps the most obvious metaphor, and hence the one that I address least, is that chess is a game, a form of voluntary activity, grounded on rules and on rivalrous competition. One might say that "game" is not a metaphor but a description. Its voluntarism links chess, like all games, to play, but games have a structured organization that "pure play" lacks. The model of human activity as game, a common metaphor, suggests a strategic approach to everyday life.[19] Chess is a game of strategy and tactics. But it goes beyond the domain of the game, even if other activities (sex, business, or politics) can be treated as symbolic games because of their strategic dimensions.

While chess is a game—a minor aspect of life—it can be treated as much else. Metaphors abound. In a riot of metaphors, Pal Benko and Burt Hochberg argue that the game takes many forms, depending on style.[20] Chess can be a fight, an art, a sport, a life, or a war. Folklorists Marci Reaven and Steve Zeitlin, touring public chess spaces in New York City, found competing visions of chess: an unsolved mathematic problem, a language, a search for truth, a dream, and even "a ball of yarn."[21] Some speak of chess as a race and the chessboard as a piano. The personification of pieces is common, particularly in scholastic chess. Pawns desire friends, pieces are runners, they look for a job or are unhappy and crying (field notes). The range of cultural images that define this pastime is extensive. Such diversity suggests that activities do not have a singular meaning but can be framed in multiple ways to connect with the needs of the speaker and desires of the audience.[22]

Treating chess as a game of war[23] leads to military metaphors. In one account, the rook is a panzer unit, the knight a spy, the bishop a reconnaissance officer.[24] As the population of chess players is overwhelmingly male, violent and sexual metaphors are common, as when the defeated are judged as weak, soft, or effeminate. Opponents are pinned, hit, stomped, crushed, sacked, or killed. More explicit is the claim of world champion Alexander Alekhine that during a match "a chess master should be a combination of a beast of prey and a monk."[25] While not many chess players speak so graphically, grandmaster Nigel Short was not alone when he remarked, "I want to rape and mate [my opponent]."[26] In his rant, Short provides support for a Freudian analysis of chess as a sublimated form of homosexual eros and parricide.[27]

Freudians believe that the unconscious appeal of chess results from oedipal dynamics, leading to sexual and aggressive themes.[28] Reuben Fine pondered why many strong chess players display psychiatric disorders, seeing danger in the metaphorical dynamics of the game.[29] Fine argued that chess is often learned by boys at puberty or earlier and that the pieces represent a symbolic keying of ego development (the king is a phallic symbol representing castration anxiety; the queen represents the mother). Those drawn to chess are said to have difficulty balancing aggressive and sexual impulses because of a weakly developed superego. Players are susceptible to developing neurotic traits, echoing grandmaster Viktor Korchnoi's observation that "no Chess Grandmaster is normal; they only differ in the extent of their madness."[30] Others point to unconscious aggressive and sexual themes.[31] Any competitive chess player knows the stories of madness, including those of Paul Morphy ("the pride and sorrow of chess") and Bobby Fischer. However, these examples do not tell the whole story. Focusing on atypical cases such as Morphy's or Fischer's paranoia is an inadequate basis for generalization.[32] Much psychoanalysis of chess is based on speculative Freudian assumptions with little empirical support;[33] perhaps this is related to the fact that many psychoanalysts, notably Reuben Fine, are serious chess players. The evidence is more literary confection than systematic proof.

Besides these tendentious images, others build on morality or images of the state. The great Dutch historian of play, Johan Huizinga, argued that "civilization arises and unfolds in and as play."[34] His assertion applies to the vast array of political metaphors of chess. Chess reveals not only sexual and aggressive dynamics, but social order. This is one reason that authors select chess as a background (or foreground) for understanding human relations: Nabokov, Cervantes, Borges, Tolstoy, Ezra Pound, Edgar Allan Poe, and Woody Allen. As early as 1862, the well-known chess editor Willard Fiske, writing as B. K. Rook, connected pieces and society:

> We [rooks] are generally considered as the most upright and straightforward of all the denizens of Chessland, from our habit of moving.... We have long been the fast friends of the Kings.... Of the Bishops there is little to relate. Each of the chess races possesses two individuals of this name, and yet so strong is the hatred of those belonging to the same stock that one of them can never be induced to go into a house that has been occupied by the other.... The most erratic members of our state are undoubtedly the Knights.... The Pawns are the most numerous members of our body politic.[35]

Lewis Carroll's imaginings in *Through the Looking-Glass* have something of the same flavor. The twelfth-century Persian poet Omar Khayyam proclaimed, "We are in truth but pieces on this chess board of life."[36] To Pope Innocent III (1161–1216), a chess player himself, was attributed a morality on chess (now thought to be written by John of Wales) that asserts, "This whole world is nearly like a Chess-board, one point of which is white, the other black, because of the double state of life and death, grace and sin. The *familia* of the Chess-board are like mankind; they all come out of one bag, and are placed in different stations."[37] Harry, a well-regarded teacher of my acquaintance, expressed the same theme: "The thing I love about chess is that at the beginning of the game, everyone is equal. Everyone is a citizen, and then through the game, we see what they can do. Chess represents our democratic values. It provides a metaphor of society" (field notes). Pieces stand for political positions—whether democratic or monarchical—in a way easily recognized by children and adults.

As a result, *chess* is used metaphorically, by the public as well as players. Away from the chessboard, we speak metaphorically of a stalemate, selecting a gambit, or keeping an opponent in check. The political metaphors were even more extensive in medieval and Renaissance Europe. Jenny Adams emphasizes how the game extended politics, reflecting a medieval social hierarchy, sometimes considered an instrument of reform.[38] The English playwright Thomas Middleton in his drama *A Game at Chess* satirized abortive marriage negotiations between Charles, the son of James I, and Donna Maria, the sister of Philip IV of Spain.[39]

Nowhere is the sociopolitical culture of chess more evident than in the names of the pieces. Chess is a global game in which the pieces have had different meanings over time and in various languages. The names of chess pieces in English and other western European languages were changed from their Middle Eastern designations, as medieval society treated the game as a mirror. The vizier became a queen, the horse a knight, and the elephant a bishop.[40] The allegories of chess were revised. In contrast, even today Russian mirrors the Arabic; there is no queen, but a "ferz," a counselor. While Russian chess has a "king," the word used for *king* is *korol*, not *czar*. Perhaps the most problematic example of political labeling is the bishop, borrowed from the Catholic hierarchy. In Russia and throughout much of Asia, the bishop is an "elephant" (borrowed from Indian tradition); in Hebrew and in Dutch the bishop is a "runner," and in France, the bishop is the *fou* or "fool." An account of the naming of chess pieces reveals much about the societies in which they are used.[41] At moments of transition, as in the Middle Ages, names are "in play." At the time of the American Revolution there was an attempt to rename king, queen, and pawn as governor, general, and pioneer. After their revolution Soviets wanted to use the name commissar and to turn black into red, with its pieces representing the proletariat.[42] Such changes, however, could not overturn the inertia of collective knowledge. These fights over metaphors indicate how tightly linked chess is to the social structure of its location and how its location affects its image.

Art, Science, Sport

While some activities fall neatly into human categories—sculpture is art, chemistry is science, tennis is sport—chess can plausibly be seen as all three,[43] each with its own conventions, like any established and collectively recognized social world. Conventions—norms of proper activity—are to be found in all institutionalized domains.[44] Chess action can be striking, systematic, or strategic. The former world champion Anatoly Karpov claimed in an oft-quoted remark that "chess is everything—art, science, and sport." Perhaps chess is not everything, but each of these categories has been treated as the primary basis of the game.

CHESS AS ART

The rhetoric of chess as constituting an art form is extensive. There are styles and schools of chess, and beautiful moves and combinations. World champion Emanuel Lasker asserted, "There is magic in the creative faculty such as great poets and philosophers conspicuously possess, and equally in the creative chessmaster."[45] The brilliant Ukrainian grandmaster David Bronstein wrote, "Chess is a fortunate art form. It does not live only in the minds of its witnesses. It is retained in the best games of masters, and does not disappear from memory when the masters leave the stage."[46] Discussions of symmetry and beauty are seen not only in the writings of masters but in descriptions by amateurs: "It's kind of hard to see, but there's beauty in it. The symmetry of the pieces and the idea of threatening, sometimes it all just comes together and it gets distracting at points, but sometimes I really just sit back and go 'Wow, look at this game.' It's like a perfect balance, an absolutely perfect piece of art ... for instance the idea of a checkmate that's six moves away is just beautiful."[47] In simpler words, a high school player remarked, "I like chess because of the way it flows together and it's like meticulous and artistic. And [my friend] said that's why he liked music" (interview). I have heard players liken chess to improvisational jazz in the way that combinations of pieces emerge over the course of a game. The rhetoric of competition as art is hardly unique to chess. In examining lifestyle sports, such as surfing, skateboarding, or windsurfing, Belinda Wheaton points to activities linked to the participants' sense of self. She notes a similar attention to artistic expression, stylistic nuance, and creative invention.[48] For those in the upper echelon, chess also constitutes a lifestyle community, although one with less threat of injury than so-called extreme sports.

Much beauty is found in the elegance of a perfect and inescapable solution to a complex problem. As William James posited, solving problems is deeply gratifying and reveals aesthetic satisfaction.[49] If beauty exists in a competitive environment, it cannot be an individual achievement but must be relational. The philosopher Stuart Rachels observes: "Great chess games are breathtaking works of art.... Perfect play, however, cannot guarantee a beautiful game. For one thing, it is not enough that you play perfectly; your opponent must also play well."[50] Another player writes, "It only takes one brilliant mind to conjure up a brilliancy, but it takes two minds ... to produce the position in which the fireworks can be let off."[51] The challenge of a patzer does not produce beauty for the skilled player.

The specific metaphor used by chess players to describe a moment of artistry is *brilliancy*: a cut diamond on a square board. Brilliancy results from the awe experienced from a simple and perfect answer to a daunting and complex problem—a victory, but not *only* a victory. The concept is so central to the world of chess that many elite tournaments award a "brilliancy" prize for the game or position with the greatest aesthetic appeal.[52] Brilliancies result from a novel combination of pieces that produces a position that colleagues find startling, even spiritual.[53] Each piece supports and defends other pieces of that color while attacking the opponent's pieces. As Reuben Fine remarked, "Combinations have always been the most intriguing aspect of Chess. The masters look for them, the public applauds them, the critics praise them.... They are the poetry of the game; they are to Chess what melody is to music."[54]

Often the brilliancy derives from the victor's sacrificing or placing a piece in danger; only later do observers recognize that the stratagem led to victory. "The bigger the sacrifice, the more beautiful."[55] It is because of his willingness to sacrifice his queen that thirteen-year-old Bobby Fischer's defeat of former United States Open champion Donald Byrne at the Rosenwald Memorial Tournament in New York is called "the game of the century." The brilliancy was not recognized when the move was first made but only after the game was analyzed and revealed in time.

How is the beauty of chess experienced? How do players become engrossed in chess play? Part of the beauty of chess is its experienced quality. Mihaly Csikszentmihalyi speaks of "flow" to capture the capacity of people to focus on an activity so closely that they lose awareness of time, external surroundings, and self-consciousness.[56] Such experiences become *autotelic*, as the boundaries between self and activity fade. This is when we are most creative, productive, and satisfied in our work, leisure, and personal lives. Csikszentmihalyi selected chess as a key example of a focused activity. Players report performing best when the flow experience is maximized and they "dig in" to the game.[57] It is not only the logic of pieces on the board that contributes to treating chess as art, but experienced emotions. Liquid moves replace concrete choices.

CHESS AS SCIENCE

Players commonly view chess as a science, and many of the greatest chess players (as well as those less gifted) have jobs in technical or scientific fields.[58] Adolf Anderssen, Emanuel Lasker, and Max Euwe were mathematicians; Mikhail Botvinnik was an engineer, and José Raúl Capablanca also studied engineering. As one player explained, "They are all math guys." Reuben Fine estimated that about half of the greatest players had mathematical or scientific backgrounds.[59]

The metaphor of chess as science relies on the commonsense image of science as value-free, objective, and rigorous. In chess some assert that there is always one best move in a given position. For these players, worrying about "chess psychology" is wasted time if the proper move can be found through rational deliberation. As one informant explained, players review their games because "they are looking for the truth." At any point there is only "one truth in the position" (field notes). For many players and some philosophers there is "truth in chess."[60] Computer programs such as Rybka or Fritz are popular in that they support this comforting illusion, no matter the action of an opponent. From this perspective one should play the board, not the opponent. Bobby Fischer was a leading exponent of this view, avowing, "I don't believe in psychology. I believe in good moves." His position has a powerful logic. The rhetoric of science proclaims that long-term strategies and short-term tactics can be developed through close study of the *principles* of chess. Aron Nimzowitsch's *Chess Praxis* treats chess as a science by stressing fundamental principles, such as "centralization" and "over-protection."[61] Such a systematic presentation of *chess theory* emphasizes logic and objectivity, training the mind to apply general principles to vaguely defined situations. Chess is a game of *perfect information*, in which chance or information unequally distributed among the players should not play a role (as in poker or bridge), and this enshrines science. Each player has the *opportunity* to see the same things, even if background or training does not permit that seeing.

Chess theory has evolved over time in fits and starts. Of course, much theory cannot be easily detached from stylistic preferences or accepted conventions of play, tied to local chess cultures. Innovation is necessary for grandmasters to dethrone their predecessors; the tactical and strategic answers that worked in previous models are translated into an approach that is alleged to be objectively superior. As games are won and lost, newly "correct" and "objective" approaches to the game are discovered, and advice is reframed. This model suggests that chess theory is metaphorically likened to a science with experimental tests. However, as scholars of science studies indicate, a simple-truth model of scientific progress is not persuasive. Science advances through changes in practices that are defined as legitimate and embedded in social relations. The rational and objective basis of science cannot be separated from cultural context, politics, and scientific reputations and is often contested[62] as chess styles rise and fall.

Max Euwe and John Nunn note that "succeeding generations of experts have contributed to the development of chess play, but it was the style of some outstanding individual which moulded the thinking and style of play of his time."[63] Perhaps this lays too much emphasis on the genius, rather than the community of competitors, but they rightly indicate the dynamics of change. This is what international master Anthony Saidy terms "the battle of chess ideas."[64]

Styles of play did not develop steadily and cumulatively but often advanced in revolutionary paradigm shifts that served as strategic replies to dominant paradigms. The objectivity of theoretical principles is often blurred by the confounding factor of creative genius and calculative ability found in the best players. Further, chess theory, like scientific knowledge generally, is in part "Whig history," a theory of continual progress that interprets the past in light of the choices that characterize the activity in the present.

In the chessworld, as in science, knowledge is acquired socially. Advancement depends on challenges over the board. Players participate in local and extended networks of knowledge, but always based on the recognition of community. Chess is a set not just of ideas but of ideas that become recognized through social relations and shared practices.

CHESS AS SPORT

Chess games are competitive, like the world of sports. While the more prestigious images of chess as art or science are common, the agonistic aspects of sport are also evident. As the *Great Soviet Encyclopedia* suggests, chess is "a sport masquerading as an art."[65] Chess can be symbolically "bloody," as pieces live and die. This reality thrills players, motivates improvement, and shapes status hierarchies. Many players attribute their love for chess to the cutthroat competition. Former world champion Anatoly Karpov remarked, "Chess is a cruel type of sport. In it the weight of victory and defeat lies on the shoulders of one man.... When you play well and lose, it's terrible."[66] Indeed, *checkmate* is derived from the Persian for "the king is dead." As a master-level player describes the hypercompetitive approach of top players at a local club, "The masters at the top ... [are] very competitive, and [have] big egos.... Their whole attitude ... [is] that I am going to crush you. And I will be extremely rude. And I will do whatever is necessary to crush you."[67] Another player explained to me, "Chess is like hand-to-hand combat. It's so visceral. How can I hurt you?" (field notes). Such metaphors are so common as to be unremarkable.

Why is chess so competitive? The answer is found largely in the institutional framework by which club play is organized. In Britain chess had been funded by the Sports Council, intercollegiate chess at Harvard was once overseen by the Department of Athletics, and in Chicago public schools, scholastic chess is administered by the Department of Sports Administration.[68] Some high schools offer athletic letters for chess players. To capture the fan loyalty of sports, entrepreneurs organized the United States Chess League in 2005 and receive funding from poker websites. Sixteen teams of strong players, including grandmasters, play each other in competitive but unrated matches. Teams include the New York Knights and the Saint Louis Arch Bishops. Of course, chess is often a simple pastime for fathers and sons or friends on lazy afternoons, merely a more complex version of Candyland, a board game for preschoolers. While casual games are part of the subculture, they are markedly different from tournament play, where the logic of chess as sport is evident.

Local clubs and tournaments are organized under rules established by national organizations such as the USCF. Players in tournaments can gain or lose rating points that measure their skill in comparison to other players. Ratings range from zero (novices start with an assumed rating of 600 but can lose rating points) to over 2800 for a top grandmaster. As of 2004, the average rating for a member of the USCF (including the many scholastic and occasional players) was 1068. Ratings are perhaps the primary motivating factor of organized play and serve as a form of identification. A rating locates one in a competitive hierarchy and determines in which tournaments one can participate and in which division one can play. The outcomes of tournaments affect ratings, based on a complex and changing mathematical computation. Rating points are assumed to be generally accurate, reliable, and universal indicators of a player's chess skill, even though, as I discuss in chapter 6, they can be misleading. But in practice, ratings translate into status, prestige, and respect.

The chess rating system is distinctive among leisure worlds in shaping player identities, organizing status rankings, and encouraging or dissuading participation. Comparing chess to other organized sports helps decipher the effects of different evaluative systems. For example, baseball players are judged by a set of statistics (batting average, home runs, runs batted in, fielding percentage, stolen bases) that describe their competence in different skill sets. These sorts of statistics diminish competition among teammates, since they emphasize specialization. Chess does not create separate measures for different facets of the game, but players are assigned a single rating. This is a powerful example of "commensuration," or "the transformation of different entities into a common metric,"[69] affecting personal investment, social comparison, and status competition. Often, as in ice skating, the determination of these measures is altered to achieve what members of the community consider a "fair" distribution.[70]

Chess is famously an activity of the mind, with only the slightest movement of light wood pieces. Yet lengthy games may involve bodily stress, and players are known for lacking physical fitness, even if prior to long matches some adopt exercise regimes. As I discuss in chapter 1, chess is a game of body as well as mind. To play chess requires an awareness of body, and even if competitors do not require muscle, endurance is essential.

Still, *sport* has multiple meanings, and chess can, at times, fit the metaphor of sport. The patterns of play suggest an aesthetic appeal that links chess to art worlds. If it is neither quite a material art nor a performance art, the beauty of a well-played game is recognized.

Likewise, we link chess to science. Over the centuries, chess has developed a body of systematic knowledge labeled "chess theory." As in Thomas Kuhn's scientific paradigms, there are periods of revolution, periods of active incorporation, and periods of normal play.[71] Finally, chess involves brutal competition. Ultimately chess depends on embracing a culture and a status system based on uncertain outcomes in the form of victories and defeats. While we may speak of chess as a leisure world, ignoring those professionals who earn a living from the activity, it creates solidarity, a desire to demonstrate commitment to a local community.

Observing Chess

My investigation builds on five years of observation of various chess scenes from 2006 to 2010, coupled with fifty interviews and reading of the extensive literature. While I have conducted ethnographic observations of many activities, this study is different. Most of my research focused on one or several similar groups. For instance, when I examined Little League baseball, the research was based on close observation of ten Little League baseball teams in five locations.[72] While each team had its own distinctive culture, the teams had similar structures. This was true of the three offices of the National Weather Service as I examined cultures of forecasting.[73] However, part of my desire to observe the world of chess related directly to its diversity. I wished to examine a differentiated cultural field. My goal is to understand how community is established in a world of status divisions and varied involvements. This required that I immerse myself, not in the *world* of chess but in the *worlds* of chess. Examining five high school teams would not have allowed me to understand the range of chessworlds.

Specifically, I observed chessworlds in the following settings:

· the Marshall Chess Club on West Tenth Street in Greenwich Village for periods in both 2006 and 2010, a total of six observations
· the open chess tables in Washington Square Park in Greenwich Village on four occasions in 2006
· several elementary school programs in New York and Chicago on six occasions in 2006 and 2008
· weekly meetings of a suburban chess club during 2006 and 2007 and several matches and lessons at the Touch Move Chess Center

in Chicago during 2008 and at the North Shore Chess Center in 2010
- biweekly meetings of a suburban Illinois high school team for a season, from September 2007 to April 2008
- weekly meetings of a collegiate team for ten weeks during fall 2008
- six private lessons in 2008
- weekly meetings of a private adolescent chess group, taught by a grandmaster, for ten weeks in 2009
- ten weekly matches of one of the professional teams in the United States Chess League during 2009
- during 2006–2010, several dozen tournaments, including the World Open; several years of the Chicago Open and United States Open; the Illinois State High School Chess Championship; the National Youth Action Tournament; the Atlantic City International Tournament; the National High School Tournament; the Super Nationals (a five-thousand-person tournament in Nashville, held every third year for children and adolescents in high school, junior high school, and elementary school); matches in the Chicago Industrial Chess League; the Pan-American Intercollegiate Championship; a simul and lecture conducted by former world champion Anatoly Karpov; high school matches and tournaments; and local tournaments sponsored by the Renaissance Knights in the Chicago area.

Over the years, I met a dozen of the top one hundred American players and became friends with several. In addition I relied on my memory of my time as a chess parent in the late 1980s and early 1990s, when I took my older son to elementary school tournaments and for two years organized a club at my son's elementary school.

Ethnography among chess players is invigorating but also challenging. The greatest challenge is that tournament games are silent. While a game is in progress, it may seem as if nothing happens. The ethnographic eye is in reality an *ethnographic ear*. We rely on words. Fortunately, before and after games one can observe meals, meetings, and lectures and read website posts. The visual is enriched by language. Many players are well educated, and they are often articulate and, not coincidentally, opinionated. At times, participants expressed opinions with "piss and vinegar."

A further complication is that my chess abilities are limited. I was often asked the simple question "Are you a chess player?" Was I an insider or outsider? It was a question that I could readily answer in my study of meteorologists. But here the proper answer eluded me. I know the rules. I can play the game and even had modest pre-adolescent success. I taught my sons to play chess, and I played regularly with my older son. But when I was asked, the questioner typically meant "Are you good? Are you serious? Do you play in tournaments? Do you play in a club? Do you study chess games?" These questions I must answer in the negative.

While my lack of knowledge forces me to see the world with fresh eyes, I needed guidance to understand the events before me. Occasionally I was invited to play. I joined to the best of my ability. One evening I was asked to serve as the "tournament director" for the professional chess team that I observed to certify that no cheating occurred. At one tournament I volunteered to work registration and help in the back room, learning the practical organization of tournaments.

I conducted in-depth interviews with fifty players at various skill levels, from grandmasters to players of modest abilities. I interviewed adults, collegians, and high school players. Interviews lasted from forty-five minutes to three hours. I also scanned several public Internet sites, including discussion boards operated by the USCF and real-time discussion boards during major chess matches, operated by the Internet Chess Club. I followed several chess blogs, notably Brad Rosen's *64 Square Jungle*, relating his experience as the parent of a talented teenager.

I also read chess literature extensively, focusing on discussions about the game itself rather than particular games or styles of play. I read the USCF's *Chess Life* and the international *New in Chess*. I also spent three days at the John G. White Collection of Chess Literature at the Cleveland Public Library, examining works from the nineteenth century. Antony Puddephatt, a sociologist at Lakehead University and chess player, shared his ethnographic field notes from several Canadian tournaments and club meetings and approximately a dozen interviews with tournament-level Canadian players.

In the past I have humorously referred to "Fine's Law of Shared Madness." Every community brought together by a shared activity believes that outsiders see them as "crazy," not recognizing the internal logics of their actions and believing that unexpected actions of their colleagues characterize the activity to outsiders. A jocular rhetoric of shared madness is common in the world of chess, where oddity is known and even venerated. One chess player explained, "I'm going into psychology. In our case, abnormal." Another remarked: "It's too bad that you're not a psychiatrist." Still another reported while meeting me for the first time, "We're all crazy" (field notes). Perhaps they, like members of other communities, exaggerate, as many were most agreeable companions: men and a few women from whom I have learned much.

Understanding Chessworlds

Leisure worlds invariably develop community and culture, and chess is no exception. Yet, as I observed local clubs, high school teams and tournaments, collegiate teams, elementary school matches and tournaments, players in public parks, and high-level tournaments, I recognized the diversity and differentiation of chess and, by extension, the diversity of other social worlds. Leisure communities are not homogeneous but have internal boundaries and complex status systems. They link to other domains, as many participants are cultural omnivores, enjoying varied voluntary activities.[74] I attempt to understand these local worlds in light of status, history, boundaries, and resources.

Local worlds, including the worlds of chess, are social spaces that build on interaction, shared values, common feelings, and communal culture. While chess appears to be based on silent contemplation and private feelings, essential to the public image of chess, the presence of others shapes thought, emotion, and action. Chess play arises through meanings that develop from social relations. Like other domains, chess is a form of *collective action*, a world that could not exist without the coordination with others. The images of cool cognition and hot emotion associated with chess occur within the context of a social institution that builds on an interaction order,[75] a world in which shared expectations and collective responses shape what minds conclude and bodies feel. Chess involves common references and recognized status hierarchies. Further, the chessworld builds on loosely coupled and diverse action scenes. After establishing the social character of chess, I argue that chess provides a *soft community*, an open and welcoming space in which those with a commitment to the game find a place, despite eccentricities that might make them outsiders elsewhere. Further, chess relies upon a *sticky culture*. By this I mean that identification with this world is explicitly linked to the acquisition of shared knowledge. The embrace of the cultural traditions of chess—its history, heroes, and styles of play—builds communal identity. Chess players comprise a community that accepts many and excludes some and a world with meaningful standards and traditions in which choosing to belong requires a commitment to learning histories, rules, behaviors, and expectations. While these features are particularly evident in chessworlds, they are found in many leisure activities and in other tight communities.

In the first chapter ("The Mind, the Body, and the Soul of Chess") I challenge the perspective that chess is essentially a game of the brain and the heart, claiming that it is a game of social relations. Mind, body, and soul are understood through behavior in response to the choices of others. While the person plays, the play is inevitably social. Chapter 2 ("Doing Chess") presents chess as enacted within social scenes. How is the game organized in light of the need for mutual adjustments? Tournaments, clubs, and friendly gatherings provide action environments. Rules and practices depend on the local cultures of the places in which chess is played.

The third chapter ("Temporal Tapestries") argues that chess, like all domains, is shaped by time and timing. The temporal organization of chess is found within large events such as tournaments, within the game in which two opponents must determine how to use the resource of time, and as a form of temporal pressure, shaping emotions. In chapter 4 ("Shared Pasts and Sticky Culture") I argue that as a cultural domain chess gains its communal power and the centrality of its identity by the shared knowledge and history of participants, permitting collective understandings. This communal knowledge builds on the long sweep of history, contemporary elites, and local settings. Chess is both a subculture, spread widely, and an idioculture—a shared culture found in tight-knit groups.

The fifth chapter ("The Worlds of Chess") examines the diversity of domains in which chess is played. Chess is not a single community but an interconnected network of communal nodes that overlap and separate but accept participation by those who share a "sticky culture." Perhaps chess attracts the socially ungainly as well as the clever and outgoing because of its specialized knowledge or hours of silence. Chapter 6 ("Status Games and Soft Community") addresses one of the most remarkable features of chess: the fact that serious players "know where they stand." Chess depends on a rating system (or several rating systems) that assigns each player a number that serves as a marker of ability. This rating serves as an identity sign, and it shapes patterns of social connections. Ability markers—statuses—organize the world of chess. As one's rating improves or declines, one's placement, options, and social relations shift. Chess is a "soft community" where talent on the board and commitment to the culture override personal defects and eccentricities. The seventh chapter ("Chess in the World") describes the politics of chess as a domain with institutional consequences. Over the years, chess has mattered for states and for social groups and has been shaped through technological innovation. Even though chess is play, play can under the right circumstances be serious work. Cold war chess battles demonstrate just how untrivial a trivial pastime can be.

1

THE MIND, THE BODY, AND THE SOUL OF CHESS

It will be cheering to know that many persons are skillful chessplayers,
though in many instances their brains, in a general way, compare
unfavorably with the cognitive facilities of a rabbit.

JAMES MORTIMER, 1906

Chess is a game of contemplation, of endurance, and of action. But thinking chess, living chess, and feeling chess, while they seem intensely personal, depend on community. While cognitive psychologists and psychiatrists can claim to understand chess, so can sociologists. I begin with the thoughtful mind, progress to the body in action, and conclude with the emotive heart; worlds may be biological, but they are also social.

Mind is often treated as simultaneously individual and universal. As people, we think as our hard-wired brains require, and as persons we think through our idiosyncratic life experiences, shaped by our genetic endowment. However, beliefs in cognitive universalism and cognitive individualism ignore the fact that thinking results from context, what Eviatar Zerubavel describes as the "sociology of thinking."[1] Nature and nurture depend on network, a basis of social relations that permit genetics and socialization to have consequences. While much has been written about how players conceive tactics and strategies and how they recall and judge positions on the board, the fact that these processes occur within an interactional order has been downplayed.

Chess is a mental game. Goethe remarked that "the game of chess is the touchstone of the intellect." Indeed, its popularity among ambitious parents stems from this belief. But what is a mental game? To succeed at chess one needs skills in calculation and evaluation. One must predict what is likely to happen and must judge which outcome will lead to a better result. According to psychologist Dennis Holding, this reflects a process of searching, evaluation, and knowing (what Holding terms SEEK).[2] Calculation develops tactics, whereas evaluation is tied to strategy—immediate choices and long-term plans. As my friend Jeremy explained, "You must calculate moves quickly and then interpret them coldly" (field notes). This suggests links between cognition and the social. First, assessments of current positions depend on assessments of future positions. Chess players claim to think several moves ahead. Although it is assumed that chess is about two competitors making tactical *moves*, the move is not the building block of competitive chess. Rather it is the *line*—a planned sequence of moves that establishes a strategy—that is critical. While strategies are fragile, dependent on the decisions of opponents, they force the examination of the future, much as philosopher George Herbert Mead suggests about baseball.[3] This emphasis on lines of play reflects the importance of planning. Chess players believe that "a bad plan is better than no plan."

Second, each player attempts to predict the behavior of his opponent. One operates through role taking—imagining the opponent's choices (assuming that they will be similar to one's own choices) and responding accordingly.[4] At the highest level of chess, players examine their own games as well as those of their opponent. As one strong player remarked of an opponent, "Obviously he's going to download my games and examine them one by one to assess my strengths and weaknesses and predict how I'm going to play against him. I'm trying to imagine what he is going to conclude."[5] As the eminent psychiatrist Karl Menninger pointed out, chess involves a "progressive interpenetration of minds."[6] Dialogue at the chessboard is internal, as top players assume the responses of their opponents. Often one is wrong. In most situations where moves are not forced, a player has numerous possible options. As a result, calculation is dynamic, and one often reconsiders an imagined future. Put simply, an imagined future depends on new realities set by the presence of two actively calculating players. The presence of one's opponent "can force you to look at the situation with his eyes."[7] In order to gain advantage, high-level tournament players examine computer databases to learn their opponents' stylistic preferences.[8] Often the best players "know what the others will play" (field notes). As Jeremy, an international master, explained as he arrived at the board a half hour late, "He's very predictable, but I don't trust myself to figure it out over the board. This punk only does one thing. . . . It also sends a message to your opponent that you are preparing by showing up late" (field notes). Not only does preparation involve awareness of the preferences of one's opponent, but it also upends those expectations. In important matches, players prepare lines of attack that are different from their usual preferences, leaving opponents unprepared. In crucial matches players wish to ensure that their past games are not good predictors of their strategy. A player who typically opens by moving the king's pawn might surprise an opponent by opening with the queen's pawn. Chessic selves can be altered in practice,[9] a shift equally evident among baseball pitchers, quarterbacks, and tennis pros.

Third, games can proceed in numerous directions, each dependent on choices of the competitors. Like many games, chess is structured through decision trees. The number of potential moves calls for comparative evaluations. In the introduction I refer to chess "brilliancies," surprising combinations that often rely upon the sacrifice of a piece, leading to triumph. However, as grandmaster David Bronstein points out, a brilliancy is a shared achievement: "The brilliancy prize is received by the winner alone, and no one ponders over the fact that the game is the product of the creativity of both players.... In chess you are left to your own resources, and at the same time you are strictly dependent on someone else.... Live chess, the game, is always 'thinking for two.'"[10]

Computer programs such as Fritz and Rybka are designed to evaluate a set of lines of play, providing a judgment of which has the greatest probability of success, although with each move evaluations shift. In over-the-board tournament games, reliance on chess programs is not permitted, and one reason that Internet games have short time controls is to discourage computer analysis.

The number of moves ahead that one can "see" is not identical with chess ability. The riposte to the question of how many moves one can see ahead is "one, the right one."[11] To analyze possibilities is valuable, but only given the responses of an opponent. When two strong players face off, each takes the role of the other, creating a hidden but real interaction. As one top player reported, "When you look at the games of modern grandmasters, so much of the fight is behind the stage. They are not happening on the board, because most players have already figured out the patterns" (interview). He explains that studying classic games is useful because the games have been so well analyzed by the chess community. As a result, these games are a part of a deep dialogue that is played out on a social plane. As the individual player accesses this collective wisdom, he is not thinking his own thoughts but those shared by the community.

Chess is a game of imagined futures, of role taking, and of contingencies and possibilities. A player strategizes but may change those designs in the face of auspicious possibilities, managing the intersection of plans and opportunities.[12] One of the most salient questions that a chess player is asked is how many moves ahead are planned. Seeing ahead gives chess players confidence, just as it does for the meteorologist or the pollster, but it carries potential danger.[13] Predictions can be wrong either because of misreading a past or not seeing what might affect a future. Thus one may not commit until that calculation produces a belief in a sure path to success,[14] just as meteorologists speak of the forecast of least regret, leading them to wiggle out of mangled predictions. Knowing the future results from extrapolating the past as much as from reading current facts. Kibitzers guess how games are progressing, and these guesses change as each move provides a new reality. As I listened to chess kibitzing, I heard claims that the same game was lost, drawish, or certain of victory. Onlookers suggested that a player resign a hopelessly lost position only to have that player triumph. Disagreement as to which move is best is common, as in this chat room discussion of an early move in a match between two grandmasters, where one player moved his white pawn to square c5 (the square on the fifth row forward from the white's side in front of the starting position of white's queenside bishop):

A kibitzes: they play like old men :-)
B kibitzes: ive never seen c5 so early
C kibitzes: c5 is horrible!!
D kibitzes: very common here
E kibitzes: it's played a lot by top players recently
F kibitzes: yes, c5 is horrible says the 1000 [low] rated player
G kibitzes: c5 is not horrible you fool
H kibitzes: but common now.
B kibitzes: c5 is the move any1 under 2000 never makes
C kibitzes: if the top GM play c5, they weak
I kibitzes: e5 for black solves all his problems puts an end to crap like c5. (Internet Chess Club website, May 22, 2010)

In the absence of context it is impossible for even the best player to judge whether c5 is horrible or impressive, but even with the context, it provoked vehement debate. In these chat rooms pungent disagreements occurred among those who took tournament chess seriously. But the value of c5 as a move can only be judged *after the fact*, by virtue of whether that line led to success or failure.

Part of the challenge of the evaluation of chess is that even though the game is inevitably forward looking, the interpretation of the game is read backward, tied to the intersecting choices of two players with different plans, each wishing to disrupt the plan of the other, leading to personal accounts of victory and defeat, as in this case of a player reflecting on a game that he felt that he should have won:

> [I said to a friend] "I lost to that Lee guy." He said, "I know. I was watching that game. Why did you play that crappy King's Indian again? How many times have I told you that opening is weak, man! People just look at that and they come in and crush you, man!" I said, "Well, actually the position wasn't all that bad for me, I didn't think. I should have beat him. It's just that I made a blunder. I thought I could win his piece and I couldn't, and then the position turned bad as a result of that blunder." (Antony Puddephatt field notes)

From this account we cannot judge whether this man or his friend was correct, but they attempt to evaluate lines of play, judging their goodness against the outcome. The assumption is that there is a truth visible in the position on the board—a right answer (part of the scientific logic of *chess as truth*). The challenge, as in many competitions, is to uncover truth: to answer the question "Where is the win?" This postmortem reflects the belief that by reviewing the past, the future can be determined. Each contest begins with either side capable of triumph, and it is the collaborative sequence of moves that produces the outcome.[15] As Paul Hoffman remarks, "Chess players live in an alternative world of what might have been."[16]

In chapter 3, I discuss how game history creates the chess community; here I emphasize that games are local worlds that are interpreted through shared or contending assessments, establishing communal thinking. Great play occurs only with the collaboration of talented opponents. As the chess grandmaster Savielly Tartakower pointed out, "Victory goes not to the one who plays well, but to the one who plays better."[17] Or as H. A. Kennedy observes, "A game of chess ... is an argument. Every move is a definite stage in the controversy."[18] The same might be said of other competitive activities, such as tennis or bridge. As agonistic contests, games are relational, however personal they might appear.

Chunks of Intuition

Perhaps no insect has mattered more for the understanding of genetics than the lowly fruit fly, *Drosophila*. With these bugs, geneticists have been able to test genetic changes. They serve as a model for science. And cognitive science has its *Drosophila*, chess. As Herbert Simon and William Chase write, "As genetics needs its model organisms ... so psychology needs standard task environments around which knowledge and understanding can cumulate. Chess has proved to be an excellent model environment for this purpose."[19] In addition chess neatly fits the brain-as-computer metaphor that has been at the heart of cognitive science. Because of its bounded world of full information, chess is a favorite model in artificial intelligence research to examine the dynamics of cognition.[20]

The vast number of possibilities in chess, even in a simple game, suggests that most individuals—even strong players—do not memorize games. Rather they recall chess positions as combinations or patterns. Put another way, games are narratives. For novices one of the most impressive feats of the grandmaster is "blindfold" chess (blindfolds are rarely actually used; the master simply faces away from the board). Even more impressive is when several games are played simultaneously.[21] How is this possible? The player does not memorize each square but remembers the relationship of pieces and how the pieces arrived at their location; the focus is on the most relevant clusters of pieces. Although I don't emphasize chess cognition, what is crucial is how information is lashed together, a contribution of scholars including the Nobel Prize recipient Herbert Simon and the Dutch scholar Adriaan de Groot. They claim that the cognitive focus in chess results from pattern recognition as opposed to precise memorization. De Groot discovered, not surprisingly, that the stronger the chess player, the more likely he is to recall positions. Elite players could reproduce 93 percent of the positions, whereas average players managed 51 percent.[22] Chase and Simon replicated de Groot's finding, but they also asked players to memorize random positions. In recalling unlikely positions, the masters were not superior to weaker players.[23] In other words, the superior memory of the grandmaster resulted from understanding the game context. Grandmasters operate within a community of practice. Their ability to reproduce meaningful patterns, impressive though it is, derives as much from interpreting the game as a competitive test against an opponent as it does from their neurons.[24]

The power of relational cognition—or chunking of information—is evident within the contest. In a tournament, players have limited time to select moves. They do not calculate the likely outcome of every option. Rather, they select a few candidate moves to compare—moves that appear to have the greatest likelihood of success based on chess theory and on experience. Players with less access to theory and experience are at a competitive disadvantage. They suffer from what one coach termed "board blindness." The competitors are faced with the same board, but because of their different mental maps, they do not see it equally. As one coach reported about a tournament game between two inexperienced high school players, "Neither player sees what they are seeing" (field notes). Players must come to see what is relevant. Experience—chess knowledge as a form of personal history—builds success in pattern recognition. As one coach emphasized, chess is like facial recognition: "You're going to be recognizing chess positions as your friends." To be learned, a move must be internalized. Jeremy gave the example of Boris Spassky, the Soviet world champion who was trumped by Bobby Fischer, claiming that he had received so much help from his Soviet colleagues that he had not recognized a critical move. Jeremy added, "Forgetting moves means that you didn't understand them. Fischer never forgot anything because he created it. I learned a whole body of theory in about six months, because I did it myself." Too much reliance on training in which one does not participate prevents the incorporation of knowledge.

Given the claim that chess represents an exemplary form of cognition—the mind at its most productive—the assertion that many decisions are intuitive and automatic is startling.[25] Players want to keep their "brain alert" or have it go at "warp speed" (field notes). At some points time-consuming calculation occurs, but often players simply "know" the right moves—a form of tacit knowledge found not only in chess but in many domains.[26] Even if cognitive scientists point to the production of chess knowledge through the chunking of information and pattern recognition, the rhetoric of sensing the right move is common. Paul Hoffman concludes, "In some 19 out of 20 positions on the board, [the strong player] ends up making the first move that pops into his head."[27] As the world champion José Raúl Capablanca allegedly informed a weaker player, "You figure it out, I know it."[28] In rejecting a move that others expected, Nigel Short, a strong grandmaster, commented, "It didn't smell right."[29] Whether aroma can be quantified, the idea of intuition is held dear by those whose expertise is inbuilt and cannot easily be shared. In numerous social worlds—from medicine to police work to chess—the claim of intuition is intimately connected to the idea of professionalism, separating the expert from the rule-based amateur.

The Strategic Nexus

In the child's game Candyland, no plan is needed. One rolls with the rolls. Even games like poker or bridge that incorporate strategic thinking in creating a style of play require less strategy within the hand itself. Too few moves exist to permit the weaving of tactics into a strategy. Not so chess. Many games involve sixty moves on each side stretched over six hours; the game can have an undulating rhythm, an unfolding story. This extended temporality permits immediate tactics to become embedded in a long-term strategy.[30] According to former world champion Garry Kasparov, "Every step, every reaction, every decision you make, must be done with a clear objective.... The strategist starts with a goal in the distant future and works backward to the present."[31] As grandmaster Boris tells his students, "You should be philosophers of chess." Kasparov noted that a great challenge is deciding what to do when there is nothing to do. In chess, unlike bridge or poker where one can pass, one must move. Moving is essential, so much so that chess players have a term for a move in which every option is worse than one's current situation. Chess players speak of *zugzwang*, or "compulsion to move," a term first used in 1858, although the concept may have arisen as early as the ninth century. Along with zugzwang is the stalemate. No matter how far ahead a player is in material, if his opponent has no legal move (and is not in check), the game is stalemated, essentially a draw. The two players are tied together in a sequence of moves that neither can escape. Short of checkmating him, a player must make sure that his opponent can move.

One way that a superior player gains advantage is to complicate the board. This means establishing many points of attack and defense that an opponent must consider in mapping out a strategy. Such complications provide an array of tactical options, confusing the opponent's strategic considerations. Tactics are immediate, whereas strategies depend on extended considerations. Younger and weaker players focus on tactics, and when playing peers this may be sufficient. As one chess teacher pointed out, "Tactics, tactics, tactics, threat, threat, threat. At the state [high school] tournament tactics are enough to win" (field notes). There is a trade-off between short-run responses and long-run plans. In many realms of action, tactics of the here and now are sufficient.

Futurework

Strategy is ultimately not about past or present, although it draws upon both. Rather, strategy involves an imagined and shared future.[32] Games, with their competitive structure, require envisioning the acts of others. The excellent chess player is not the one who can make the right move but the one who can imagine the right sequence of moves in anticipation of countermoves, creating a broad long-range plan. One finds this process in flirtation, in business negotiation, in ballroom dancing, and in muggings.[33] Each of these activities is a sociological waltz in which the participants must plan ahead to achieve their objectives, whether consensual or conflicting As one player commented about a loss to a titled player, "You can tell I didn't have a plan. I didn't know what to do" (field notes). The strong competitor develops a plan; the weak one simply plays.

MOVES AHEAD

The future is known by seeing ahead. How many moves can you see? The question assumes cognitive magic. There is a lot of joking about the matter; as one coach claims, "I'm currently thinking eighty-two moves in the future." More seriously it is said that Bobby Fischer could think thirty moves ahead, although Reuben Fine claimed that such vision is "pure fantasy."[34] Of course, players think ahead, even if an image of seeing dozens of moves ahead is misleading. Garry Kasparov points out: "Without a doubt, the question I am most often asked is 'How many moves ahead do you see?' As with most such questions, the honest answer is, 'It depends,' but that hasn't stopped people from asking or generations of chess players from concocting pithy replies. 'As far as needed' is one, or 'One move further than my opponent.' There is no concrete figure, no maximum or minimum. . . . It's more like figuring out a route on a map that keeps changing before your eyes."[35]

Kasparov's analogy of a journey emphasizes temporal structure. Seeing ahead depends on the stage of the game and on whether the moves are "forced," permitting an opponent only one plausible move, even if, when the other player's plan is correct, the sequence of moves will lead to disaster.[36] Forced moves and planned sequences are more common as players slide into the endgame, where there are few options and fewer pieces on the board. One collegiate player explained: "I would say on average [that I think] at least three or four [moves ahead], depending on what the position is. It could go up to fifteen. That is pretty rare, though. You need a position where you can obviously say he has to make this move. Before I make a move, I say to myself, 'When I make the move, what are the consequences?' Then you pretty much switch yourself over to their side, and say [to myself], 'Would I play this move in their position?'" (interview). In a forced move the position encourages a certain move, as is true in many behavioral routines when interaction is channeled by choices of others. Chess is but a more formal instance of how interaction is organized.

SACS

Discussions of sacrifices emphasize how the future affects the present. A sacrifice is, at first, counterintuitive. The player seems to become objectively worse off as the result of a move but makes the move on the assumption that he will eventually benefit. The goal, after all, is checkmate, not the hoarding of high-value pieces. In various domains one sacrifices to gain a desired end through a skein of events or perhaps to build one's reputational capital through altruism.

A successful sacrifice presumes that an opponent will choose a disadvantaged future. The "sac" appears to be a mistake or odd move that permits an opponent to capture a piece. But when the sac succeeds, the player eventually takes other, better pieces or gains a stronger position. Bobby Fischer's game of the century, which he played as a thirteen-year old, involved a queen sacrifice. At the time it happened, viewers felt that the sacrifice was a child's error, no matter Fischer's intention. Only later, once the outcome was known, was it seen as brilliance. An anecdote about another game addresses the heart of sacrifices and the uncertainty of the future: "In the course of a game, Sir George Thomas asked [chess writer George] Koltanowski, 'I see you are an exchange down. Did you lose it, or sacrifice it?' Koltanowski answered, 'How am I to know? I'll tell you when the game is over. If I win, it was a sacrifice. If I lose, then it was a mistake.'"[37] Koltanowski's bon mot reveals the importance of reading life backward. As in so many areas (electoral politics being a case in point), we know whether a choice was wise in light of subsequent events. Perhaps sacrifices are intended, but even mistakes can be called sacrifices if the outcome is positive (or vice versa if the result is negative). Whether we are certain of all of the contingencies that flow from our decisions, we act, and then, if necessary, provide justification. What makes sacrifices so beautiful and so dangerous is that they depend on an uncertain future.

The Embodied Player

The distinction between mind and body is so common that it has become clichéd. Certainly this dichotomy is meaningful in a limited way, as dichotomies often are. Thoughts seem to happen in a realm separate from physical reality, but this is misleading. Despite the fact that heads ache and ideas produce pleasure, the brain seems distant from the body. Yet concentration must be disciplined. Through the nexus of emotion, mind and body intersect, and both are shaped by the social. Mind and body are situated within communities and respond to those communities. The body is not entirely "owned" by the self, but it belongs to the interaction order. In the sections that follow, I address how emotion and body are implicated in chess, that seemingly most mindful of games, but this is an argument that applies to other social but thoughtful worlds (test taking, public prayer, or philosophizing). I start by examining the look of the body, the preparation of the body, and the body in (in)action.

THE BODY AS MANIKIN

A body is a tool of display. What one wears (or doesn't wear) conveys much about the self, the scene, and the community. Although tournaments were once formal domains with participants conveying their real or desired class location, today informality rules. At any large chess tournament one confronts a riot of styles. Dress often reflects the fact that most adult tournaments are held in hotel ballrooms (swimsuits and overcoats are rare). Clothing ranges from suits to slacks to jeans and from button-down shirts to T-shirts. Each is appropriate, although age, ethnicity, and gender shape how the body is draped. While top players are likely to wear more formal attire, much depends on personal preference and desired image. Some wear expensive suits. Others look "like bums." One of Bobby Fischer's early complaints was of the lack of sartorial concern of his colleagues. As a juvenile, he wore sneakers and jeans; he changed when he was sixteen, noting, "People just didn't seem to have enough respect for me, . . . and I didn't like that, so I decided I'd have to show them they weren't any better than me.... So I decided to dress up."[38] He complained, "When it was a game played by the aristocrats it had more like you know dignity to it. When they used to have the clubs ... everybody went in dressed in a suit, a tie, like gentlemen, you know. Now, kids come running in their sneakers."[39] Fischer believed passionately that dressing in bespoke outfits revealed respect for the activity. He argued that clothes make the scene. His later slovenly appearance was a sad irony. With the exception of high-level matches, players dress for comfort. Only when the status of the event outweighs a desire for comfort are ties and jackets worn. Of course, jeans as well as tweed or white linen or shorts convey messages and locate individuals in a social order, just as clothing defines professors and prostitutes.[40]

PREPARING THE BODY

In whatever activity one engages, one must ready oneself, not only mentally, but in light of physical demands. The boxer, the ballerina, the soprano, and the surgeon face different bodily challenges. Even sedentary activities such as long-distance driving may require a cushion or Preparation H. Because chess events are moments of focused attention, one's body can absorb the blows of lassitude. Yet as games can last over six hours, groundwork may be required. Players must have sufficient stamina. Alexandra Kosteniuk, a former women's world chess champion, explained:

It's ... a proven fact that thinking does use up calories, and many of them. For example, during the last world championship, which for me lasted 3 weeks from the start to winning the final, I lost over 5 kilos, only playing chess, not running or doing any other kinds of physical sports. I was able to hold on well thanks to the rigorous physical training program I had gone through the 6 months previous to the championship.... It's almost impossible to explain how physically demanding the game of chess is.[41]

Research suggests that blood pressure and breathing rates rise during competition. Nigel Short in his championship match with Garry Kasparov lost ten pounds in the first three games.[42] A respected chess teacher told me that his players will lose as many as ten to twelve pounds during a tournament. Like Kosteniuk, many chess champions incorporate an exercise regimen while preparing for important matches. Kasparov pumped iron, swam, and rowed. Fischer played tennis, noting, "Your body has to be in top condition. Your chess deteriorates as your body does. You can't separate mind from body."[43] A chess administrator told me, "I do consider chess more of a sport than anything else, partly because to be very good, you have to get yourself in very good physical shape" (interview). Admittedly, when one glances around a chess tournament hall filled with overweight endomorphs, one might wonder how true these claims are, but at the front of the hall many of the better players are buff, although it is unclear whether this results from physical preparation, mental acuity, or life cycle.

It is not only heads and hearts that matter, but stomachs and intestines as well. Players who face lengthy games eat ahead of time and bring food to the table. Like other athletes, they may "carbo-load." As one grandmaster joked, "The most important movement in chess is a bowel movement" (field notes). Being in time trouble and in intestinal discomfort is a deadly combination.

READY FOR INACTION

Those who describe chess as activity joke about its absence. Two men gaze across a table in silence, only occasionally pushing a small wooden or plastic object a few inches, notating a few numbers and letters, and touching a nearby clock. This represents the body in action, even while it ignores that body. Doing nothing is doing something. As those who must stay at rest for long periods can attest, such action is challenging. Perhaps the hardest feat of dramatic acting is to play a corpse. Freudian psychiatrists, enjoined to listen to their patients, face the same problem as does a security guard whose bodily presence is needed, even absent threats to public order. Fantasies control minds, and distracted minds leave bodies unguarded. One must be mindful in being inert.

Doing "nothing"—or perhaps thinking deeply—is enervating. A body can appear static, even as the mind roils. Realizing that one is about to lose a "won" game can produce turmoil. Grandmaster Pal Benko notes that "your body reacted exactly as though your life were being threatened: your heart pounded, your pulse raced, your stomach did flip-flops, your skin broke out in a sweat."[44] Successful players have higher levels of testosterone, and players reveal higher levels of testosterone before their matches.[45] However, bodily changes are seen behaviorally as well as chemically. Nervous energy is released through drumming fingers, fidgeting, or jiggling a leg. Former world champion Viswanathan Anand commented that he studies his opponent's bodily signs: "If the breathing is deep or shallow, fast or slow—that reveals a lot about the degree of his agitation. In a match that lasts a month even a clearing of the throat can be quite important."[46] At tournaments players can walk around, and at championship matches players may be provided a room offstage, where they can retreat when it is not their move, watch the game on closed-circuit television, and eat and drink.[47] These private spaces (called toilets) caused an uproar in the 2006 championship match between Vladimir Kramnik and Veselin Topalov. The latter became concerned when the former used his toilet too frequently, and Topalov's supporters charged that Kramnik was relying on a hidden computer. Even in events less exalted than the world championship, players wander the hall, even exchanging cautious words with friends, and use the public toilet. At the board players may arrange themselves as they wish so long as they do not make noise or enter the space of an opponent. No rules prohibit staring, rolling one's eyes, smiling or grimacing, coughing, or sighing. Players often sit quietly, holding their chin in their hand, resting elbows on the table, folding hands, or leaning back in the chair. In the game a player can move his pieces with a flourish—even symbolically screwing the piece into place—hit the clock with passion, or write the move with panache. (One can also touch pieces after announcing "J'adoube" or "Adjust.") These options permit the embodiment of thinking: performing through the body what is happening in the mind. One doesn't just think but acts out thinking.

The greatest physical threat to a chess player is exhaustion. It is not only the game itself, but tournament life is not conducive to sleep. At most tournaments games start in the late morning or early evening. Those that last six hours do not leave much time for recovery or relaxation. Some top tournaments schedule one game per day; other tournaments may have games in which each player has sixty or ninety minutes, permitting a tournament to have eight games in two or three days. Such schedules lead to exhaustion. Apocryphal stories are common: "One player was so tired that, as he nodded off in the opening, his head hit the board and scattered all the pieces. This woke him up."[48]

As a result of their exhaustion, players embrace a "politics of byes." Perhaps surprisingly, players are not required to play every round in a tournament. Tournaments permit players to skip rounds and receive a half point, ensuring that they will not lose the game. At most tournaments the last round must be played unless the player asks for a bye before the second round or unless he is willing to receive zero points for that final round, leaving early, often without a check or a trophy. These byes are a form of bodily preservation. Players attempt to determine what their bodies require and act accordingly. One coach suggests to his high school players that they should consider taking a bye during the middle of the tournament to prepare for the crucial final games. When one player won a long game after a bye the previous evening, he became convinced that the strategy was valid (field notes).

Contemporary chess champions (and high-level "super grandmasters") play more tournament or match games than they once did. The great chess champion Capablanca played twenty games each year; today an active grandmaster will play five times as many.[49] However, while the total may be wearing, each game, shorter and less formal, is easier. At the first international tournament in 1851 time controls were not in place, and a game could last ten hours. Time controls were introduced a decade later to facilitate competitive tournaments, and perhaps to protect the players. Of that first tournament, star player Adolf Anderssen wrote: "Chairs and tables are small and low; all free space next to the players was occupied by a [recording assistant]. In short there was not a single space where you could rest your weary head during the hard fight. For the English player, more comfort is not required. He sits straight as a poker on his chair, keeps his thumbs in his waistcoat pockets, and does not move until he for an hour has [surveyed] the chessboard. His opponent has sighed hundreds of times when the Englishman eventually moves his piece."[50]

Like so many regimes of action, chess demands that the body be displayed, prepared, and controlled. That the rules of tournaments (if not the game itself) have changed means that bodily control has shifted in line with a desire for shorter, focused bursts of energy. But even with these changes, a match strains and tests the body. These strains might not be quite as evident as in rugby or boxing, but because they are hidden by the belief that chess is all in the mind, they do not receive the attention that they deserve.

The Emotive Player

Just as cognition is located inside the head, the same is true of emotion. Famed chess teacher David MacEnulty extends Goethe's claim about chess as the touchstone of the human intellect to suggest that it is equally "the touchstone of the human emotions." Chess for MacEnulty and others "touches on all branches of our being."[51] Emotion and cognition appear internal, but they depend on sociality. They wrap the individual in a cocoon of involvement.

Before describing the emotions of adults and of children, I discuss the dynamics of engagement. This is what French sociologist Pierre Bourdieu describes as "illusio," the commitment to the game that "pulls agents out of their indifference … to distinguish what is *important* ('What matters to me,' is of *interest*, in contrast to 'what is all the same to me' or *in-different*)."[52] Bourdieu's perspective of illusio as self-investment builds on Dutch historian Johan Huizinga's concept of illusion and compares in its experiential quality to what psychologist Mihaly Csikszentmihalyi terms "flow." In his important book, *Beyond Boredom and Anxiety*, Csikszentmihalyi describes flow as "the holistic sensation that people feel when they act with total involvement.… Typically, a person can maintain a merged awareness with his or her actions for only short periods, which are broken by interludes when he adopts an outside perspective. These interruptions occur when questions flash through the actor's mind: 'Am I doing well?' 'What am I doing here?' 'Should I be doing this?' When one is in a flow episode ... these questions simply do not come to mind."[53] Csikszentmihalyi uses dancing, surgery, and rock climbing as core examples. And chess. He argues that these activities can separate us from our circumstances, particularly when we have the skills and motivation to perform at our highest level: the zone between being "on" and being overwhelmed. While each activity can generate attentional focus, each of them occurs within social space, as flow depends on the real or imagined presence of others as competitors or observers.[54] As Bourdieu puts it, "The *collusion* of the agents in the *illusio* is the root of the competition which pits them against each other and which makes the game itself."[55] Anthropologist Robert Desjarlais suggests that chess constitutes a "socialized trance."[56] While capturing the intensity of commitment to a world of action, flow has a romantic undertone. Csikszentmihalyi quotes two chess masters:

Concentration is like breathing—you never think of it. The roof could fall in and, if it missed you, you would be unaware of it.

When the game is exciting, I don't seem to hear nothing—the world seems to be cut off from me and all there is to think about is my game.[57]

These images are dramatic, but they do not describe action in practice. This is good talk, but not necessarily how people live their ludic lives. Roofs do not cave in often enough to test the first quote's claim. But few are so unaware of their world as these pithy comments assert. Participants do lose track of time.[58] At one high school tournament a young man urinated all over himself. His coach remarked, "He was so out of it. He was really into the game" (field notes).[59] Less dramatically, feet fall asleep as players remain awake. However, most players can distance themselves when they are not "on," as is true of surgeons. I describe the secondary involvement of players subsequently, but here I emphasize the embodied performance of the chess tournament where players stroll, eat, or observe other games. And distractions from other social domains (illness, family crises, or love) create barriers to flow, even when participants succeed.[60] The extended time controls of serious games prevent much chess from having the qualities that Csikszentmihalyi suggests. Flow exists, but as moments in a skein of routine. One can get lost in a game, but finding oneself is rapid.

A further aspect of flow is that players must be of relatively equal ability and that the game will reflect this balance, or "ratio of skills."[61] A game in which a champion plays a novice is unlikely to produce flow in either competitor. Thus flow builds from social relations. Still, one wonders whether both players must be in a state of flow simultaneously or, as in passion, whether one partner be tinglingly aroused, while the other merely goes through the motions.

EMOTIONAL BUBBLES

We speak of emotion as bubbling up from within. Yet as research on emotion has demonstrated, how we feel is closely linked to the circumstances in which that feeling is displayed. Emotion is shaped by the demands of a community and by the desire of the person to interact with that community.[62] Emotion work produces these adjustments between self and society, person and community, and is particularly salient in domains such as games that are entered voluntarily. A challenge for those who confront depression is that colleagues find that they look perfectly fit. The communication of emotions often occurs not through visual signs of affect, hidden in faces in repose, but in words that refer to internal feelings and are taken as definitive by audiences.

Beyond bodily experiences, such as exhaustion, chess emotions occur over the board: joy, dismay, and anger. The feelings are powerful, but we know them as performances. During a tournament, emotions oscillate from elation to frustration. Rarely does a competitor win or lose every game. As winners meet winners, and losers, losers, the sorting process produces mixed records and mixed emotions— peaks and valleys. The emotions of each game shape future games,[63] producing a knotted string of affect. Each contest produces a winner and loser, or perhaps two competitors who jointly decide to draw. Losers may not always be distressed, as some losses are satisfying, especially when a competitor can claim a "moral victory." A close defeat against a better player may be satisfying despite the outcome. Stories are often told about nearly beating a grandmaster, even if that near victory occurred in a simul in which the champion played dozens of opponents. Some victories—pyrrhic victories—have costs in energy spent on triumphs that audiences find unimpressive, questioning the victor's talent.

JOY AS JUICE

As an emotional realm, joy is fairly simple. It washes over one as a happy sign of a bright future. To be sure, joy grows from what has just happened, but central is the belief that the present signals what is to come. As Antony Puddephatt points out, "Appreciating improvement in one's level of play serves to inspire players to continue or intensify their careers.... 'Oh, it's amazing when you beat somebody who you could never beat before. It's the greatest high in the world ... like climbing a mountain.'"[64] One has been validated by having reached a new performance level, an achievement that later may be snatched away. Success has within it a scorpion's sting in that it can be undone by failure. In a competitive world, joy depends on ignoring the errors and limits of an opponent. But at the same time, joy validates performance. As one player explains: "I feel as if I couldn't do a wrong move.... I feel smarter, clever. Sadistic as it is, I can't stop a grin from breaking out on my face."[65] The display of joy outside of certain ritualized moments (such as a game's immediate aftermath) can have reputational costs. Joy must be transformed into modesty: one's triumph must be sheathed as fortuitous. In other words, elation must be contained by impression management so that it doesn't appear as though one thinks too highly of himself. An audience permits the victor momentary public satisfaction, but then he must retreat to humility. Muhammad Ali's claim that "I am the greatest!" provoked sharp criticism, even if it was eventually accepted as a performance. Like depression, joy must be tightly contained to prevent reputational damage.

THE DISTRESS OF DEFEAT

Most forms of emotional display are constrained by social convention and local norms. In a surprising defeat some acknowledgment of disappointment is expected, but players should suggest in their behavior that the outcome is transitory. Expected outcomes produce deference and grace, but surprise disappointments are more challenging, leading to internal despair or public anger.

Given the potential of emotion, it is striking how placid competitions seem when viewed from the outside. One coach suggests that most players maintain a "poker face." Only flashes of emotions shine through. As was said of a well-liked master-level player, "He's calm, but he's bubbling inside" (field notes). One player reports, "At the start of every game I feel sick. Before games I would be really nervous. I usually feel [nauseous] before my games" (interview). Another comments, "I lean forward and I get too crazy. My stomach starts going 'Mwooh.' I've got to play within the limitations of my health" (interview). These competitors feel the same anxieties as actors or university lecturers, but as the curtain rises, the emotional fog lifts.

Emotions oscillate during competitive events, but afterward the reality of defeat must be confronted, although the pain may last, particularly if the game is felt to matter. A loss is forever. Italian novelist Paolo Maurensig surely exaggerates when he remarks, "The players bear lifelong scars, neither body nor soul ever recovering fully. Anything that might reawaken memory of the mutilation is violently repulsed."[66] Yet active competitors appreciate his comment. Occasionally emotional turmoil rises to the surface, particularly when one feels that others are disdainful.

Much emotion is internal but may emerge as a public account, even for grandmasters. Despite his many triumphs, Nigel Short was quoted as saying, "If I lose badly, I will feel like committing suicide."[67] Vassily Ivanchuk finds that "defeat can affect him so deeply that he runs outside for solitude and howls like a wolf."[68] Josh Waitzkin reports in a similar vein, "When you lose, it is as if someone has torn out your heart and stepped on it."[69] One tournament organizer speaks of a "chess grieving process" (field notes). In extreme cases competitors consider quitting, feeling that the pain outweighs the satisfaction. Self-doubt consumes even the best players: after defeats, Garry Kasparov went into deep, inconsolable funks, the adolescent Bobby Fischer wept bitter tears, and Greg Shahade, the founder of the United States Chess League, proclaimed a loss to be "really just the worst thing that ever happened in my life."[70] Disgusted with his play, my friend Jeremy attributed his defeats to incapacitating headaches and considered withdrawing from a major tournament (field notes). One strong player, returning to play after years of inactivity, addressed the power of dismay:

I stopped after age seventeen. I retired. [He was winning the junior championship.] All I had to play was one more guy. I was a half point ahead of everybody else in the tournament.... He was older than me and a stronger player. I was beating him, and in the last few minutes of the game I'm in time trouble, and I just throw away a rook.... I was so disappointed by it, so psychologically traumatized [by] losing.... I was loving winning the game, like three feet above everyone ... and then it was suddenly taken away with a blunder. I don't think I have ever quite recovered from that. It hurt me emotionally and I remember just pushing the table away and got up and just walked out of the room.... I was never again committed to organized chess as a serious thing. (interview by Antony Puddephatt)

The defeat challenged his deep involvement. When fun leaves, justification melts. Why invest in the activity if the result is often painful? Fun is the guarantor of participation.[71]

THE ARROW OF ANGER

While despair is known through accounts, anger is performed. Of course, people can be angry internally, but anger is often acted out, despite constraints.[72] Players delight in recounting moments of anger, perhaps because drama suggests that the game, otherwise insignificant, really matters. Anger may be disruptive, but it validates the commitment of competitors.

The amount of displayed anger that is permissible is socially defined; over time boundaries have narrowed, as states and institutions have gained control over the display of aggression, what social theorist Norbert Elias describes as the *civilizing process*.[73] Dramatic instances are storied, transformed into communal narrative. On occasion players overturn their pieces in anger, destroying the physical trace of the loss. I heard several times about a player who was so upset after an unexpected defeat that he threw a piece at his opponent's forehead. I was told that on another occasion a mild-mannered player was so distressed at losing that although he "usually doesn't show his emotion, he was throwing his pieces at the board" (field notes). Of Garry Kasparov it was said that when losing "he'd start swearing and muttering to himself in Russian. [When a fan approached,] Garry shoved him up against the wall. A defeated Kasparov is a dangerous beast."[74] In his own words, Kasparov claims: "I hate myself at that moment."[75] But his response pales in comparison to acts of colleagues: World champion Alexander Alekhine destroyed the furniture in his hotel room. Aron Nimzowitsch climbed on a table, shouting, "Oh Lord, why did I have to lose to this idiot?" And William the Conqueror smashed a chessboard over the head of the crown prince of France.[76] One interviewee noted that a colleague "had just resigned [to a female master], and . . . he was just screaming at her, 'Fucking bitch, fucking bitch'" (interview by Puddephatt). Perhaps these narratives are apocryphal, but they suggest why some young women may make sure their boyfriends triumph in any competition, and it explains family tensions that arise as a once superior father now finds himself routinely trounced by his son. When victory does not correlate with status, emotions must be contained.

MODELS OF MODULATION

Given emotional heating, people desire some measure of control to permit life to proceed in a diplomatic fashion. A barrier must be in place to allow a smooth interaction order. Life may be emotional, but we pride ourselves on civility. Our norms venerate calm. The need for emotional dampening is found in all social domains, but particularly when uncertain outcomes affect one's equilibrium.

Players are able to control their emotions during matches because self-control is expected. This belief was stated nicely by Emanuel Lasker in 1913 in preparation for an important match: "During the course of the match, I expect that several times victory will smile joyfully on each of us, and several times defeat with its cold, evil eyes will stare us in the face, but neither of us, one must expect, will on account of this lose his self-control."[77] The ability to appear calm, limiting emotional expression, allows the social worlds that participants desire. While narratives add pungency to the breakdown of local routines, the activity requires the belief that outcomes do not matter enough to explode. We often learn of the need for an emotional front, not only by its own virtue, but for strategic purposes:

When you play chess, the important skill is perhaps to suppress an emotional reaction, because it can give your opponent an edge. [GAF: How do you suppress your emotions?] I think [suppressing emotion] is just the expression of your poker face. So if you are play-ing a match, and I have … completely screwed up, instead of going, "Gosh, why did I do that?" … pretending nothing is wrong can help because it doesn't give your opponent the "Oh, I got him now" edge. You know, it is a mental thing. (interview)

I teach my students, if I made a bad move, it is easy to give up. I lost the game. Instead you should be happy. From this point there is nothing to lose. Just enjoy the game…. Of course, it is easier to say than to do it. But you have to constantly search for positive emotions during the game. (interview)

These examples nicely encapsulate the dynamics of emotional con-trol. In the first instance, appearing to be in control serves strategic ends in directing attention away from failures on the board. As one player told me, "You can know when [an opponent] feels good about a position…. There are definitely little tells, like in poker" (inter-view). Facial distress is a cue that there is something for an opponent to notice. One can deceive through emotional display.[78] The second example, with its emphasis on disciplining oneself, is consistent with research on emotion work: draining emotion generates a revised be-havioral reality. The following discussion at a high school tournament is revealing:

Terry, a high school player, comments about a move that he missed, "I was so mad at myself. I was so bummed out." Boris, his coach, comments, "If you feel bad after the move, you have to know your emotions. You keep on thinking about your [current] move. Mis-takes never come alone. Games are lost on the second mistake [which results from thinking about the first mistake]." Donald, an-other coach, adds, "You have to play without emotion. You can go outside and scream afterward, but you want to scream because you won." (field notes)

By avoiding what provokes distress, one becomes a better player, whatever an opponent might notice on the board.

Emotional control is most evident in its absence. While chess em-phasizes the need for such control, other competitions permit acting out. Some, such as tennis, have moved from an emphasis on civility to a playing style in which emotion is part of the spectacle. One international master reported: "I threw a king once. I was upset. Throwing a king is like breaking a [tennis] racquet. 'Oh, no! You can't throw a king.' Chess would be better if you could. It would get more publicity. It would be more exciting. It's asking too much of players to bottle it up" (field notes)."

Emotional control modulates the game both through the player's internal gyroscope coping with a dynamic, pressured social scene and through maintaining a desirable definition of the game situation that hides cues that could expose the error. But in either case, the tamping of affect depends on social relations.

The Child at the Board

Given their frequent lack of emotional control, children provide an opportunity to understand the difficulties of public emotion. By examining those who find affective control a challenge and a developing process, improving over time, the self-control of adults becomes more apparent. By comparison, the violations of self-control that occur in scholastic chess demonstrate the impressive power of socialization.

Scholastic chess, like other settings in which children are on stage, can be emotionally brutal. Aside from Bobby Fischer, Josh Waitzkin was probably America's best-known child chess star. His father described his early years in the popular book (adapted as a movie) *Searching for Bobby Fischer*. Until he left competitive chess in his teens, his record of success was astonishing. For a time he appeared to be America's future. But his emotional life was not always placid: "The scholastic chess world is a deadly place. Every year, thousands of boys and girls put their hearts on the line, each child believing he or she may be the best. Glory is a powerful incentive. Inevitably dreams are dashed, hearts are broken, most fall short of their expectations because there is little room at the top."[79] These "failures" generate anger and despair.

Local communities are training grounds for emotion work. Children often compete in segregated spaces, organized by age. Sometimes these division are one-year cohorts (nine-year-olds, fourth graders), and sometimes they are based on the school players attend (elementary school, middle school). A few talented children have the skills to play lengthy games in the same tournament with adolescents and adults, but many children lack the cognitive discipline to remain focused while others are thinking. Often a child's cognition develops before emotional maturity. Perhaps many children who have won the kindergarten division at the elementary school national tournament quit within a few years for reasons of emotion rather than chess ability.[80] A survey I heard about (not strictly random and perhaps exaggerated) finds that one-third of the parents and coaches who bring children to scholastic tournaments claim that their charges cry at the tournament.

Emotion is particularly likely to break the surface of scholastic events, even in informal games between peers or between parents and children. Bobby Fischer was the poster child for emotional display. Fischer was not the first chess prodigy, and he is not the youngest person to become a grandmaster, but he demonstrated that a young teen could become an internationally competitive chess player. Fischer would cry after a defeat and would remain despondent for days.[81] His tears make him, despite his brilliance at the board, normal as a child competitor, although less so as an adolescent. The crying child cares little for his public front. No wall stands between internal dismay and outside display. For Fischer, and for many preteens, the game matters so much that a loss reveals a cataclysmic self-breach that cannot be tolerated. Some chess teachers, such as Alexander Shabalov, want their students to be intense. Chess must mean all. He comments, "When I'm assessing a young player, first I see how much of a killer he is. You can see it in his eyes.... If the guy doesn't look to kill his opponent, he's not going to be a good player."[82] Older players seeing the game trajectory are better able to steel themselves for defeat, but a sudden checkmate can be difficult to bear:

> [Willy] somehow squeezes out a win, and his [eighth-grade] opponent screws up his face and begins to cry. The boy lets out a series of thick, heaving sobs, and it seems as if he might never stop, and his wails begin to pierce the cone of silence within the cafeteria.[83]

> One prominent tournament director shares a situation in which a first grader doesn't want to lose, and when the close game is over "he began bawling" because he believes that his parents will be disappointed and won't purchase the toy sword that they had promised. She tells me that the scholastic tournament has a rule that for the youngest children that "if they are crying, they don't have to leave." (field notes)

Perhaps these episodes are quickly forgotten, but scholastic training often involves socialization to impulse control. One successful
coach with experience at both elite private schools and inner-city
public schools finds that each environment poses emotional challenges. At private schools, the children expect to get everything they
desire. They are sophisticated players who know the rules, but they
become upset when they lose. They have to become socialized to failure. As he points out,

> Everybody's been treating them like they were little princes and
> princesses.... But the impulse control is "I see something I want,
> and I try to get it." So I see, I move, I want to make it, not taking the
> time to say is this a good move? . . . So they grab the piece and they
> lose something of greater value, and then they get upset.... If you
> make a bad decision, you have to live with that decision. You have to
> take responsibility for what you have just done. But there is no anger
> overlay. It doesn't inspire them to want to leap across the table and
> grab their opponent's throat. (interview)

These pampered children must be persuaded that they will occasionally lose, but this is not a cause for distress. Life in an inner-city school
is quite different. These children do not have to be told that the rules
work against them. They go outside the rules to achieve, and winning
(and losing) really matter. Social control is more direct:

> Up there winning and losing carries a little extra weight. If you lose
> up there, then you are way down. So standing up for yourself, pro-
> tecting yourself, becomes a really big issue.... [For example] the kid
> who lost his knight simply reaches across the board and picks up
> the other person's king. What I had to overcome there was just the
> simple socialization of following rules. Impulse control becomes a
> huge issue. (interview)

All of these children attempt to survive in their world, but their
worlds are dissimilar, and strategies of self-control differ. The first
group of children has been cultivated by their parents, informed that
everything is possible within the rules; the second have grown in
rocky soil without hope.[84] In the former, children must be warned
against despair and encouraged to accept unplanned outcomes; in

the second, they must be warned about anger and taught to accept structure. In time most of them learn, but the remnants of earlier socialization remain.

While the emotional world of childhood seems quite distinct from that of adults, in both worlds emotions are set and judged in social spaces. They are never free-floating feelings but are embedded in cultural worlds. That adults have acquired skills that children have not allows us to award the label "mature" to adults and adultlike kids.

The Mind, Body, and Soul of Chess

I have begun the examination of chess as a social world—a cultural domain—by addressing three features that seem removed from sociality: thought, the body, and emotion. Chess is deeply thoughtful, a test of endurance, and wildly passionate. Yet these thoughts, embodiments, and feelings occur within a structure. They are shaped through the fact that chess depends upon a self, a competitive other, and an audience. If, as James Mortimer cynically suggested, chess players can be compared to rabbits, it is because both are sensitive to threats in their environment.

A complex game such as chess requires sophisticated planning, what players speak of as calculation and evaluation. But at its core this suggests that the future is judged in the present. What will the board look like in several moves? In this, they calculate the responses of their opponent, whose long-term interest is in direct conflict with their own. If a player self-consciously selects a strategy, such a strategy must respond flexibly to the changes caused by the tactics or strategy of another. In this fundamental way, cognition is lashed to the social character of the game, presuming a belief in a shared future. Planning and expectations depend on the rivalrous structure of the game, the competition that makes the game worth the effort.

But cognition is not the totality of one's internal world. Chess, like all activities, is embodied. A tournament is a congregation of bodies with each participant choosing how his body should appear: shaven, coiffed, and attired. While decisions are personal, they are also communal in that people appear in a way that they define as presentable. The standards differ according to how a player situates himself in light of the multiple fields of chess competition, but there is a linkage between the body and its public.

The body is always present for the contest.[85] Of course, some games are brief and strain body (and mind) minimally. The games of most of the forty million American chess players are casual (and an increasing number are online). However, the more intense the tournament, the more the body must be readied. While broken bones are unlikely, sitting and thinking affects legs, brains, and buttocks. The prepared player must cope with a startling body. Championship matches provide just such a test of neuron and muscle. The athletic challenge of chess is inactivity. High-level chess games may last six hours or more; half that time a player is not on. To be sure, during an opponent's turn, a player is planning his future lines, yet the stillness of players of chess is apparent. Silence is not personal but social. The players—and the audience, if present—are silent together. Silence is heard through sound—coughing, rumbling, tapping, scratching, and labored breathing—but these noises do not break the silence. A chess tournament is noisily silent. It is speech that is rare, perhaps a question to a tournament director, occasionally a whispered "check" or a request for a draw, but these are punctuations of a world in which speech has generally vanished. Every word edges toward impropriety.

Finally, there is emotion as social performance. Emotions in extremis produce stories, knitting a group together through narrated experiences. The distance that stories travel reflects communal boundaries. These accountings reveal the commitment of persons to the activity: joy, anger, and despair demonstrate that voluntary activity matters for participants.

But it is not only stories that are social; emotions are as well. Feelings demonstrate that people care about their shared activities. But here sociality takes another form in limiting emotional display, as social control creates a world in which placidity has priority. For children, not so well socialized to shading their feelings, control is more salient and harder to achieve and is tied to other features of their experiences, such as the desires or demands of nearby adults.

Those components of chess that appear to be fully individual are truly social, shaped by collective standards. The mind and the body and the heart are collective domains. And so, as the next chapter reveals, is action, the "doing" of chess within the context of an engaged community.

2

DOING CHESS

*I know of no spectacle on earth that can keep thousands of spectators
enthralled for five hours. Utterly immobile and deep in thought,
the players sit facing each other like the hieratic actors in a
Japanese Kabuki production.*

Spanish dramatist and chess writer
FERNANDO ARRABAL[1]

Social worlds depend on doing. Rules are established, negotiated, or disputed. Participants collaborate to permit events to flow smoothly, or they argue and battle. And people manage the impressions that others have of them with the hope of raising their own stature. In all social worlds, particularly in play worlds, selves are performed.[2] People perform, and often this performance is made possible through objects that serve to represent the player in the context of the game.

Voluntary activities such as Dungeons & Dragons or Second Life permit roles that are separate from the physical self, and that is part of their pleasure.[3] In chess the rivals, less elaborated, are termed white and black, and—as in our racial designations—this may mean, in the material form of these identities, tan and brown.[4] Typically the player does not fully identify with his king and is distressed not because the king has been "mated" or "killed" (as in the Persian *shah mat*: the king is dead) but because the player has lost the game. Even though chess depends on the material reality of the pieces and the game could not proceed without them (or their representation on computer screens), direct identification with the pieces is minimal, so that the loss of a knight only hurts because of how it affects the player, not because of how it affects the horse.

Still, chess action must be negotiated by the players, who find that their identities and their reputations are at stake. With their stilted and artificial rules, games seem to be set apart from the real doings of the world, but games (Candyland, Dungeons & Dragons, poker, and chess) have much in common.

The Rules and the Game

I own a 370-page paperback—no small pamphlet—entitled *U.S. Chess Federation's Official Rules of Chess*.[5] The book is in its fifth edition and has been published in various forms since 1956.[6] Not all 370 pages are rules, but the first 100 pages are. It was in 1929 that the World Chess Federation (the **Fédération Internationale des Échecs, or** FIDE) published rules referred to as "the laws of chess." The first printed rule book dates back to 1497.[7] While these rules are elaborate, chess shares with other games the need for rules that direct the choices of participants and invest their symbolic actions with meaning. In this, games are not so different from other rule-based, structured areas of life, such as investing, campaigning, and other contested domains. Social spheres depend upon mutually recognized conventions and procedures for judging novel proposals and resolving disputes.

Because chess is so evidently a rule-ordered game, I begin with the rules before examining how individuals act in concert. Later I consider "cheating," moments in which the moral consensus is upended and must be set right (see chapter 6). Along with the expectation of a defined outcome, the fact that rules are integral differentiates games from play. While rules in some games are negotiated in practice (such as handicaps or work-arounds), participants believe that rules are imperative. Although players vary in their proficiency, all operate under the same constraints. Each plays on sixty-four squares with pieces that move according to an established order. Rules permit games to be transported from community to community, constituting a universal system (recognizing the existence of local or house rules). As Antony Puddephatt noted: "Competitive chess regulates members' behavior in that all players abide by strictly enforced tournament rules, time controls, and etiquette. The rules of play are standardized internationally, such that seasoned players know how to behave and act in tournaments no matter where they are held geographically."[8] Tournaments are a highly structured form of ritual enactment.[9] Puddephatt posits that the organized constraints generate devotion. A similar argument is proposed by anthropologist Alan Aycock, who, following French philosopher Michel Foucault, speaks of a tournament as a "factory of thought."[10] Thought is regimented by the organization of the competition. When operating smoothly, ritual produces intrinsic satisfaction, even euphoria. The more constraint, the more ritual, the more security. This stands in sharp contrast to the insecurity and unpredictability of the game itself.

Beyond the rules of play, other rules involve the venues of action—tournaments and matches. If individual chess ratings are to be meaningful, there must be comparability or even universality in tournaments.[11] The knight moves the same everywhere, and even rules less linked to the game structure, such as having to move a piece that one deliberately touched, are found wherever serious chess is played. However, rule enforcement depends upon trust, as it is hard for a central organization, such as the United States Chess Federation, to monitor all events under its purview. Procedures must be strictly followed to permit the tournament results to count for ratings, but even here there is uncertainty.[12] These rules channel behavior within the leisure community, not activity within the game frame.[13] A game can continue even if the tournament deviates from the procedures of other tournaments, such as the length of games or penalties for a ringing cell phone. The USCF rule book also specifies proper forms of chess notation, standards for equipment, procedures for submitting ratings, rules for correspondence chess (chess through "snail mail"), Internet chess rules, and rules of blitz chess. This is a lot of structure. While there are more rules than could easily be memorized, many are acquired in learning the game: to play is to know the rules, such as "the pawn may only move forward" or "white makes the first move. The players then alternate moves until the game is over."[14] They are part of the structure of the game. As in most complex games and sports, other rules are esoteric. For instance, under some conditions players may ask to see the score sheets of their opponents; under other conditions they may not.[15]

Rules are tied to philosophies of how the game should be *fairly* played, even if they seem obscure. Rule 16C1 announces that "each player must operate the clock with the same hand that moves the pieces." One cannot move a piece with the right hand and hit the clock (stopping one's time and starting one's opponent's time) with the left. Such a rule may seem odd, but it recognizes that even small slices of time matter. Using both hands provides, the rules imply, an unfair advantage. As one tournament director explained, "The rules are made to help ... the sportsmanship aspect of the game. It is unsportsmanlike to play too fast. If you are hitting the clock too fast, you are not being sportsmanlike" (field notes). So a chess player, in effect, plays with one hand tied behind his back. While some rules, such as the requirement for writing moves at adult tournaments, are waived when a player has fewer than five minutes left on his clock, this is not one: there are rules and five-minute rules. Another rule states that when castling, the king should be moved before the rook; however, in this case the rule book states there is no penalty for moving the rook first, as long as the castling is legal.[16] As one coach told me, "It's a rule, but no one ever complains." The violation goes unseen.[17]

Because I do not focus on the mechanics of chess, I pass over the microscopic complexity of the rules, except to note that seventeen pages are devoted to the conditions under which games can be drawn, and another eleven pages are devoted to rules about the clock. Most actions, however voluntary, have a substantial body of rules, backed by "case law." Few know all of the regulations, a fact that leads to disputes by one player focusing on one section of the rules and an opponent emphasizing another. Like the Bible and the United States Constitution, rules are believed to have inerrancy, even when multiple interpretations exist.

But no matter how much groups specify their rules, a blurry zone will exist. Gaps must be filled. This is what sociologist Harold Garfinkel terms the "et cetera principle."[18] He recognized that no set of rules, however detailed, could regulate every contingency of interaction. Institutional power sets constraints on action, even if in tournaments, as elsewhere, negotiation and local adjustments are needed.

When games are informal, players must determine house rules. In a tournament or a match, some person or group must have authority to set requirements at variance with standard operating procedure, adjudicate which rules are applicable, and decide particular cases. The rule book is filled with what the authors label "TD [Tournament Director] Tips." Tournaments, particularly those that attract novices, distribute fliers with the procedures that the director has established.

In the lived reality of tournament life, many unexpected judgments are needed, whether about technology (e.g., broken clocks) or accusations of cheating. The tournament director and his floor staff have the authority to decide, sometimes with the help of an appeals committee. Few tournaments are without disagreements and challenges. Aycock, in describing a Canadian championship, notes twenty minor disputes and a few major conflicts.[19] In one dramatic instance a tournament director was punched by a coach who refused to move from a table at which his students were playing (field notes). Even rule-governed scenes can become anarchic.

While rule challenges do not occur often, their presence justifies the certification of tournament directors; the formality of certification depends on the stature of the event. Two types of challenges to rules exist, both in chess and in other systems in which rules (or laws) are prominent. The first I label *exceptions*, which recognize that contingencies exist that designated rules were not designed to cover. The second are *disputes* in which the players have different perspectives on whether particular rules apply. Social systems hope to achieve communal satisfaction and smooth interaction, however defined, and a system of adjudication is intended to provide "justice." This *interactional pleasure principle*, found in all rule-based systems, suggests that rules promote interaction without real consequence. In a diverse community individuals bring their personal interests to a world that should operate through general principles. Take the case of an Orthodox Jew on the Sabbath, unable to use a digital clock, now nearly universal among chess players. An analog clock did not pose such a problem, not being electronic. The player with the black pieces should bring the clock, but suppose the Jew has the white pieces. Further suppose that his opponent refuses to use an analog clock. Should he be forced to? Is this within the zone of rules that can be altered? In one tournament a player received word that his child was hospitalized. He started the game waiting for news. When that call came, he asked for the clock to be stopped, which the tournament director allowed until the call ended. The tournament director recognized the exigencies of his situation and "violated" the rules. The ideal of the reasonable man triumphed over the formal stricture.

But reasonable men differ. A tournament director explained that some colleagues, pointing to a friend, are "conservative," while others, and he pointed to himself, are "liberal," more flexible in interpreting rules. The conservative responded, "What is the point of having rules if you don't follow them?" My liberal friend placed his contextual judgment over the rule book, stressing that satisfaction should be maximized. They differ in the degree of discretion to be assigned to an authority—the loan manager, test proctor, police officer, or tournament director. Such debates, common in bureaucratic settings with rules that are designed to be enforced identically, often arise in regard to individuals with special needs. Can competitors without sight play with assistants or with different equipment? These exceptions are often settled amicably if the authority is flexible and the opponent is generous. But ultimately rules have different moral stature. Some rules can be violated, while others are sacred.

Occasionally officials must settle rivalrous claims. The same action is evaluated differently, either because of dissimilar interests or because of divergent frameworks of interpretation. Consider *j'adoube*. Players are permitted to adjust their pieces (or their opponent's pieces), typically moving the piece to the center of the square and sometimes changing the direction that the knight faces.[20] It is preferred that the player announce this adjustment by saying "j'adoube" or "I adjust," but this is not absolutely required (rule 10F). This potentially conflicts with one of the sacred practices of competitive chess, the "touch-move" rule. If a player touches a piece, he must move it if there is a legal move, no matter how disadvantageous. At times a player believes he is adjusting a piece, and his opponent believes that he is touching it; the physical act is identical. The rule book recognizes the sociality and morality of the chessworld: "Without a neutral witness Rule 10 depends on the reliability of both the claimant and the opponent. If they disagree then the TD should strongly consider denying the claim [that the touch-move rule was violated]. In most cases, by denying the claim the TD shuts the door to all false claims. Upholding a false claim usually does more harm to more players than denying an accurate claim."[21] The advice considers reputation ("reliability") and suggests the chessic equivalent of the presumption of innocence. Perhaps one day cameras will watch, but even then, motive will be uncertain. Judges must determine which claim makes more interactional sense. Even if resentment remains, the game can continue.

Rules appear eternal, but they are only valid until they have been revised or repealed, either officially or through "house rules," revealing the power of local settings. Over time, chess rules have altered significantly.[22] Most widely discussed is the change of the movement of the vizier, now termed the queen, to make her a more powerful figure. The queen is no longer limited to moving one square diagonally but is now able to move as far as possible vertically, horizontally, or diagonally.[23] But other changes have also occurred. In the thirteenth century pawns were first permitted to move two squares for their opening move. The move termed *en passant*, which gives an opponent's pawn the right to capture a pawn that moves two squares if it lands next to an opposing pawn, was first suggested in the fifteenth century and fully accepted in 1880.[24] More recently rules permit either player to force a draw if, after fifty moves, no piece has been captured and no pawn has moved. Sudden death games (often blitz games) are now used to determine the winner of a tournament, adjourned games have been eliminated, and time delays and increments have been instituted to avoid having players "lose on time." While a social domain may appear stable, it changes in light of player preferences and perceived dissatisfactions.

Bloody Play

Like any contest, chess depends on clash. Whether or not we should describe chess as a "war game," it requires engaged competition between two opponents. Games generate winners and losers or sometimes a result—a draw—that suggests the need to fight another day. Except in the few moments of public emotion described in chapter 1, aggression is hidden at the board, but fulsome in chess literature. Competitors relish voicing how the contest is red in tooth and claw. Josh Waitzkin, the central figure of *Searching for Bobby Fischer*, learned the game at the open tables of Manhattan's Washington Square Park, where banter and hustles are common. Waitzkin remarks, echoing the great chess champion Emanuel Lasker, "If you want to be a good player, you've got to be a fighter."[25] A French proverb claims, "You cannot play at chess if you are kindhearted," which a helpful author corrects as "You cannot *win* at chess if you are kindhearted."[26] Violent metaphors reappear, including Bobby Fischer's claim, "I like the moment when I break a man's ego."[27] Other grandmasters share Fischer's sentiment: "I remember standing beside Nigel [Short] and Yasser Seirawan ... as they analysed their game from the 1987 Barcelona world chess cup tournament. Nigel, who had won the game, described his winning process as 'TDF.' ... I asked what it stood for. Almost in unison the two grandmasters chanted, 'Trap. Dominate. Fuck.'"[28]

While these attempts at humor might be distinct from internal states, the expression of such feelings is legitimate at the highest levels of competitive chess and may even be found at the scholastic level, where one chess teacher explains that he attempts to teach students the "warrior mentality" (interview). The theme is part of the culture, so much that a seventh grader explained, following Bobby Fischer, that his goal is "to make my opponent cry." If chess is sublimated war, as some claim, the sublimation is not very deep. The metaphor of violence in chess is evident in the psychoanalytic literature. Many psychoanalysts play chess, and they bring their theories into the game, seeing chess as a means of containing (their own?) sadistic and aggressive impulses.[29] As one master put it, "Chess is pure id" (field notes). But such aggression must be sheathed. One high school player, bothered by a weaker opponent, decided on a tactic of interpersonal humiliation. He avoided checkmating his opponent until he had promoted three pawns so that he triumphed with four queens. His coach insisted that he write a letter of apology. As one player noted sympathetically, "When you feel like you are winning, you feel that you have to rub it in" (field notes). Another player explained, "I get a tyrannical sense of power. I feel ... as though I have the fate of another human in my grasp. I want to kill!"[30] Perhaps such attitudes are not shared by all, but the claims are treated as legitimate.

The desire to humiliate is found not only among adolescents but among world champions as well. Consider Garry Kasparov at one of his simuls, challenged by dozens:

> After nearly two hours, Kasparov had disposed of everyone except Nelson Farber, an attorney in his late thirties. . . . Farber sat there stoically, only to subsequently blunder in a position that looked dead even; when he finally acknowledged defeat, Kasparov broke into a wide grin and pumped his hand. . . . Kasparov [remarked] . . . , "For a moment before he blundered, I thought of offering him a draw. But I didn't like the way he looked. He was too smug and self-confident. I wanted to crush him."[31]

An adult master was reported as saying, "You must be ruthless and have the killer instinct. No matter how bad you are, there is always someone worse. If you lose to a 10-year-old, then try a 9-year-old and go down the line until you find someone slightly worse than yourself."[32] Cruising for a child to crush seems extreme, but the competitive urge makes this form of talk acceptable. Read literally, these claims seem sadistic. However, in a competitive world such metaphors are privileged and not treated as character faults.

How are opponents perceived? People differ in their responses and in what they admit. Some players deny that they dislike their opponents. They see chess as a game—like Candyland—that doesn't affect their self-image. There is no room for hatred in such a casual world. Others make competition personal. One longtime player speaks of "the contempt factor" (interview). A grandmaster claims that he has no chess friends, feeling that to fully engage on the board—to be motivated—social distance is essential.[33] Mikhail, an older player I came to know, explained one evening: "I can't find that anger—almost hatred—that chess players need to win.... You find something that you dislike about that person. You find an excuse, and that starts the heat. It helps you play. You need to find something to stimulate your fighting spirit" (field notes). In grasping for animosities, he is not alone. Chess coach Michael Aigner reports, "In order to really keep your edge at chess you have to hate your opponent. That doesn't mean you can't be his friend or his teacher but you have to hate him during the game itself."[34] Like Mikhail, Aigner finds it difficult to reach this level, but success depends on this spur. Perhaps it will be a previous game, a (real or imagined) insult, or an ethnic or racial stereotype.

Rivalries provide a rich stew of hatreds: familiarity breeds contempt, particularly when fighting over indivisible resources, such as electoral victory or job placement. The most striking instance of an *institutionalized hatred* in the chessworld was between Garry Kasparov and Anatoly Karpov, who played a series of world championship matches in the 1980s and in 1990:[35]

> It seemed to Kasparov that he had spent half of his twenty-seven years and sacrificed much of his life's joy trying to rid himself of this sallow, physically frail man who stuck to him like a shadow. Half a lifetime sitting across from Karpov, whom he loathed, toes practically touching, conceiving his finest ideas ... while smelling Karpov's smells, listening to his digesting ... the quivering of Karpov's stretched, nerve-wracked face when he was losing, or his preening, apple-cheeked self-admiration when he was winning.[36]

Granted, this account is overly dramatic, but the intense matches between these two men defined the best chess for a generation.

Occasionally players recognize that competition becomes moral evaluation, a disturbing proposition as in this anecdote from esteemed chess instructor Bruce Pandolfini about his exit from tournament play:

"We were playing speed chess …" Pandolfini said. "I won the first two games, but I didn't deserve to…. I won through cheap tricks and gross blunders on his part. He was getting angrier and angrier. In the third game, he was outplaying me again, and once more he let his advantage slip. I began to feel terrible. Then I lost on time. He looked at me and said 'Justice triumphs.' And I thought Justice triumphs? He wasn't just making a statement. He really meant it—that he was the Just and I was the Unjust. It became very philosophical for me. I started to question whether I thought the same. Was I there just to beat him? … After that I gave up competitive chess."[37]

Players must feel that their performances lead to "just" outcomes. One strong player remarked, "I can't talk to someone who beats me" (field notes). A weak player explained that his friend could not bear losing to him: "[My friend] got very angry when I beat him the second time. He took off and I couldn't find him for three hours" (interview). If the "wrong person" triumphs, the game can lose its attractiveness, as in this case of a young girl and her older brother:

I learned to play from my father. I kept playing it because it was an activity I could do with my brother. That ended one day when, unbeknownst to me, I made what was the start of a complicated opening. At this point, I didn't even know what openings were. And he accused me of getting lessons on the side from my dad…. I was probably six and a half, maybe seven. He would have been ten or eleven. So he basically declared that his baby sister was not going to be able to beat him in chess, and he wasn't going to play me anymore. And we didn't play again. (interview)

Competition may be handled in various ways, embraced or mistrusted, but a game in which participants do not desire to win is a thin activity. Competition provides the motivation that permits social worlds to continue.

Games as Action

Eric Leifer, a sociological theorist, distinguishes between the skills necessary for *solving* games and the skills necessary for *playing* games. When one first sits at a chessboard, a fully formed strategy is impossible. Too much depends on one's opponent's choices. Only later can one trace a path to victory. As Leifer puts it, "The object of skill is how to play the game until a favorable solution becomes apparent. Players must use actions that bring the beginning of the game toward its end."[38] One aspect of skill is the ability to keep a game going until it can be brought to a desired conclusion. While games do divide players into winners and losers and those who draw, all must learn to find satisfaction in the act of play, even if unsatisfied by the outcome.

My interest is the playing of games. How is chess performed at various levels? What are the conventions that stabilize the activity? What creates commitment? Here Erving Goffman's point about games in his provocative essay "Fun in Games" is apt: "Games can be fun to play, and fun alone is the approved reason for playing them. The individual, in contrast to his treatment of 'serious' activity, claims a right to complain about a game that does not pay its way in immediate pleasure."[39] Of course, players make commitments, and escape is not as easy as Goffman imagines. Some games, particularly those cemented in social relationships or in tournaments, have high exit costs.

It is odd that talking at the chessboard is frowned upon or even punished at tournaments and in "serious" games (informal or club games can be raucous). Players are not expected to communicate, except (perhaps) for greetings, announcing check, asking for a draw, and a few other ritual occasions. Why should this be? A friend involved in the chessworld attempted to dissuade me from watching the games and only watch before and after. He warned, "Watching chess games is more or less like watching paint dry, and the value of observing the tournament will be exhausted in about fifteen minutes once the round starts and everyone is focused on just managing the mechanics." What happens on the board might be engaging, but what happens beside the board is not. One can watch players perform thinking in their facial responses, but interest fades.

We assume that to play seriously is to concentrate. Internal discipline makes cognition active. Mental focus is never pure, as distractions do occur, but it is the goal. One player remarked, "Concentration is like breathing: you never think of it."[40] Instructors extol the virtues of concentration, warning about attention deficits (as one put it, ADHLAB, "Attention Deficit, Hey Look, a Butterfly").

However, minds are not easily tamed, and the issue in practice is, in the words of a leading female player, "balancing intense concentration with relaxation ... to save energy for critical moments." She notes, "Many players get up between moves to pace, eat an energy bar, or glance at friends' games."[41] Concentration oscillates. Minds and bodies demand secondary involvements. Wandering around is one approach, but real food and imagined sex disrupt concentration as well. At most tournaments players are permitted to eat and drink; food is often found on tables. One club president describes a colleague's game supplies: "He has all of that whole variety store at his table with the milk, pop, medication, chocolate bar, potato chips, five or six various snacks" (interview by Antony Puddephatt). Tournament directors have discretion in controlling repasts, as when one player brought a plate of lasagna and another brought a beer. In the past, air was filled with smoke, and nonsmoking players had to steel themselves for opponents who exhaled. Banning smoking advantaged some players and disadvantaged those who relaxed with a cigarette. Some younger players hope to gain an edge by medicating themselves. One international master told me, "Some of these kids take Adderall. It gets you in the zone and allows you to concentrate" (field notes). Others gobble amphetamines or slurp caffeine. Still others listen to music while playing. The concern that earphones are used to provide advice—not music—is such that many tournaments prohibit their use by players who are contending for prizes. The Atlantic City International Chess Tournament posted the following rule: "Players, and their opponents, after round 3 with a score [winning percentage] of 80% or over may not use headphones, earphones, cell phones, or leave the playing area without TD/Organizer permission." The rule permits discretion, but it emphasizes that communities can limit secondary involvements. Players with a winning percentage of 75 percent are not restricted.

In most social worlds private imaginings are common. Focused concentration can turn to other matters. Among men, sexual fantasies are never far from the surface; blue movies are spooled in players' minds while the clock ticks. One grandmaster joked, "In most games I am thinking about girls for about fifty to seventy-five percent of the time, another fifteen percent goes to time management, and with what's left over I am calculating."[42] A second player notes, "I would be a grandmaster if only I could stop thinking about sex during the game for more than fifteen minutes."[43] This underlines the distinction between the rhetorical commitment to focused cognition and the reality that other domains impinge, while still permitting effective performance. If fantasies and multiple involvements destroy concentration, it is hard to imagine that any adolescent could complete biology or any pilot fly a plane.

I distinguish between secondary involvements and external distractions. In tournament play distractions are violations. Rule 12.5 of the World Chess Federation rules reads: "It is forbidden to distract the opponent in any manner whatsoever."[44] This sounds definitive, but what is a distraction?

In practice, players must cope with small distractions that surround them. Mere copresence implies distraction. People crack their knuckles, tap their pens, sigh, cough, shift heavily, move their chairs, stare, or eat. One father of an expert player explained: "You get the coughers. People rock back and forth. You think that you are at the Wailing Wall." Players breathe, sometimes loudly. Which constitutes a distraction? One hopes that opponents realize that they belong to an interdependent dyad and that courtesy to a playing partner will produce courtesy in return. This is implied in the tournament ritual that players shake hands both before and after a game, providing brackets on the competition. Those moments in which players do not show respect are the exception.

Personal courtesy norms vary, and players may struggle to create a dyadic culture. As a result, a small chess community has advantages, whether a high school team or a network of elite grandmasters. By virtue of cordial surveillance they enforce expectations of propriety.

The belief that chess is silent is central to ideas about distraction. An "absolute prescription of silence during competition"[45] is established, even if violated. Aycock reports:

> Noise-makers are glared at, hushed, rebuked, or even penalized by the loss of their game or by ejection from the tournament hall. The very posture and demeanor of players emphasizes, indeed sometimes parodies, this strict rule of silence: some will sit motionless at their boards, hands cupped around their faces to blot out all external stimuli, while some wear rifle shooter's earmuffs.... Even those who pace during play do so with an exaggerated soft step, circumscribed gestures, and blank facial expression that almost caricatures silence by its cautionary restriction of the civilities.[46]

There is nothing inherent in chess that demands this silence, as other activities that require concentration can be quite loud. Even Bobby Fischer was not John McEnroe over the board. Outside the hall was another matter. Further, the rule of silence is situated within social relations and within a particular form of chess. Chess consists of intersecting social worlds whose practices can differ greatly. As a result, players can treat talk as a pleasant addition, just as talk in informal poker contributes to its popularity. Two serious chess players explain the situated quality of silence:

> While I totally adhere to the rules, I am the one guy who might once in a while make an offhand comment to someone. And it depends on the player. If I am playing Harvey Deutsch, I know I can have a good time at the board, and we could joke and say a few words or comment on the position or kid around a little bit. But if I am playing some ... player with a serious disposition, then I am more than content to be quiet. (interview)

> [GAF: Is it against the rules to talk during a game or just against the norms?]
> It's against the norms, but it is all situational. You can banter if you know someone. An occasional banter might be completely appropriate.... It is common to talk to friends. (interview)

In contrast, speed chess is often accompanied by raucous trash talk. Since these games do not depend on calculation so much as intuition, expectations differ. Varied scenes create their own allowances, not only because of what is possible, but because of what fits the self-image of the actors. Whether we consider operating rooms, cockpits, courtrooms, or library archives, the rules for silence are based on subcultural values, are locally monitored, and are sanctioned—or not—by systems of authority.

Chess as Theater

Fernando Arrabal, the Spanish playwright and chess journalist, emphasized that chess can be enthralling despite the limits of action. For grandmaster David Bronstein chess is a form of theater, featuring "actors on the chess stage."[47] But what do these comments mean when faced with the game's world of stillness? How do small and short movements produce enthrallment? How are little nothings performances? And how can chess be made dramatic for a public that may understand little of the subtlety on the board? Scholars argue persuasively that games constitute theatrical performances.[48] For performance theorist Richard Schechner, games are inherently performances: creating and enacting stories, under conditions of temporal ordering, valuation of objects, and a shared commitment to rules.[49] As a realm of performance, games simplify the world. Chess is solidified play in which rival thought processes are staged in dynamic tension. There is the action on the board, and there is the action over the board. What happens on the chessboard is a distillation of the world of the players, a play within a play. Add to these performances a third performance of the social world around the board that incorporates the tournament or match as a spectacle with its own drama and subtexts.

Chess is played on an action space, a miniature stage: a checkered board of sixty-four squares, half filled with thirty-two pieces, sixteen white, sixteen black. The majority of these figures—knights, bishops, queens—stand for human actors (castles, or rooks, are the exception, even though human habitat is involved). They dart about, intersecting with each other in captures, jumps, traps, and pins.

In its original formulation chess pieces reflected a military order, but by the Middle Ages, this was transformed into a social order, a manageable stage on which life could be simulated without carnage.[50] The characters (pieces) who live on the board and whose lives are animated by their handlers (the players) encounter one another in battle. Although the possibility exists for pawns, the most disenfranchised in this chessworld, to elevate their social status, a more common fate for them is death. In the mid-nineteenth century, the sport began to appear at international exhibitions and world fairs with both the players and their pieces serving as the embodiments of their respective nations and the outcome of their matches suggesting a new world order. Over the subsequent century, throughout the Cold War, important chess matches symbolized international conflict. Throughout its long history, chess has always been more than a game. Like the great works of literature, these games are metaphors that stand above and beyond themselves.

At first glance such claims may seem baffling, particularly for those who are not intensely engaged. Despite the fact that games have much in common with theater, chess as an action arena seems especially dry.[51] The event is constituted by slight hand movements of a duo seated silently on opposite sides of a table. Pieces do not move by their own free will but are animated by players. As Arrabal notes, there is much thought that stands behind the action on the chessboard stage. Through their moves players are performers. The movement of pieces is the extension of the flickerings of fingers. Cognition is precipitated into action.

The oppositional quality of the game generates conflict, but the conflict must be read into the movements. Perhaps the minute actions are sufficient, but movements in themselves do not enact an argument. Still, chess has a following, a lively and articulate one. As one of the oldest systems of symbolic action (some fifteen hundred years old), chess drips with tradition and is laminated with meaning. The game permits involvement as action understood through the changing location of pieces (interpreting chess from the inside out, available to those committed to the activity) and as metaphor through seeing the game as representing a larger social order (interpreting chess from the outside in, available to external publics).

Championship matches are structured as theatrical events. To some degree this was always the case, but it became more evident as the result of the highly publicized "war" between Bobby Fischer and Boris Spassky in their 1972 match in Reykjavik. World championships are now produced to be attractive to the serious chess community, even if little attention is paid by the public at large. The matches are designed for an audience, even as they remain subcultural.

Producing a major match is big business, closely resembling a theatrical production (the 1993 match between Kasparov and Short was held at the Savoy in London)[52] or even championship boxing., The pugilistic metaphor became explicit when the challenger Bobby Fischer and world champion Boris Spassky met in Iceland to draw for colors in preparation for their first match: "After shaking hands, Spassky humorously tested Fischer's biceps as if they were two boxers 'weighing in.'"[53] Expensive tickets are sold to fans with the hope of recouping part of the promoters' multimillion-dollar investment.[54] Matches, which once could last indefinitely, now have limits on the number of games, although they can end earlier if a player reaches a set number of victories.

In most championship matches, the top competitors are seated on a stage, separate from the audience. The set design can be a matter of dispute. Bobby Fischer and Boris Spassky sat on a stage in Reykjavik's Laugardalshöll, a large sports hall, but how that was to be laid out proved contentious, particularly given Fischer's demands. As Frank Brady reported, "After an eighty-minute inspection, [Fischer] had a number of complaints. He thought the lighting should be brighter; the pieces of the chess set were too small for the squares of the custom-built board; the board itself was not quite right—it was made of stone, and he believed wood was preferable. Finally, he thought that the two cameras hidden in burlap-covered towers might be distracting when he began to play, and the towers themselves, looming over the stage like medieval battering rams, were disconcerting."[55] Fischer recognized, consistent with Bruno Latour's subsequent argument from the discipline of science studies, that material objects are *actants*.[56] That is, objects have the power to shape the form of interaction of human participants. Pieces can move players, not just the reverse. To be sure, Fischer had an exquisite sensitivity to his surroundings, but a chess championship is a space that often requires considerable negotiation. In Fischer's case the complaints continued after the match began. Despite the carpeting and sound baffles on the ceiling, Fischer complained bitterly about the whirring of the cameras and the noise of candy wrappers. The material world keep impinging on his internal world and therefore with his competition with Spassky. Fischer demanded that the games be played in a small, private room; he eventually relented but still insisted that cameras be removed and that the first several rows of seats be emptied.[57]

Despite the theatrical trimmings, the audience must embrace the game. Julian Barnes, a prominent British novelist, referred to chess as "a most curious form of theatre: austere, minimalist, post-Beckettian."[58] It is, in short, subcultural theater: thrilling for those who can read the text with its historical references to distant games and can see the emotion in the performance of two men sitting silently in comfortable chairs. Anthropologist Victor Turner writes that experiences only become meaningful when "communicated in terms intelligible to others."[59] As a result, until chess strategy—and not merely chess moves—is known by a large public, chess is likely to have a limited audience. If chess is to become a spectator sport, the rituals must be married to the staging of a recognizable thought process to create theatrical intelligibility. For instance, the global conflict evident in the representation of Bobby Fischer and Boris Spassky as representations of West and East, surely much of the match's appeal, built on a compelling view of global strategy.[60] Something similar—a rendition of the battle between man and machine—might be said of the 1990s matches between Garry Kasparov and the IBM computer Deep Blue.[61] The macroenvironment of the match as performance must be linked to the dyadic environment of players. For a successful performance both levels must convey meaning. In the Fischer-Spassky and Kasparov–Deep Blue cases, the chess match illuminates itself and something beyond. As Turner noted, through performances a community can "portray characteristic conflicts and suggest remedies for them, and generally take stock of its current situation in the known 'world.'"[62] That these tournaments were staged before live audiences who purchased tickets suggests a powerful desire to be in the presence of action.

The Actor on the Board

Just as chess is a performance, the player is an actor, presenting himself through dramaturgical techniques, relying on the arts of impression management to smooth the course of interaction. To some extent players shape the impressions that others gain, but because chess games have a definitive outcome, a strong front only takes one so far.[63] Still, in those scenes that surround the board considerable self-presentation occurs.

DEFERENCE AND PRESENTATION

If players treat defeat (and victory) as too closely linked to self, the continuation of the activity is undercut. As a result, participants must treat competition as a form of play with temporary outcomes. The game must be set apart from what is "serious." Games are framed as inconsequential, draining the outcome of lasting significance. This is evident at the opening and the closing of the game. These are moments of transition and require joint involvement of both persons, as with a handshake. Given that the game is symbolically bellicose, these handshakes serve as the kind of frames discussed by anthropologist Gregory Bateson that communicate to all involved that even though the actions might appear aggressive, they are coded as play or at least as not descending to violence.[64] Before the game the participants are friends, and this friendly relation is reestablished after the game. The tradition that the defeated person can request the victor to review the game, revealing the turning points in the game, has a similar component of politesse, coupled with deference. Before and after, players may collaborate and commiserate, but not during. Often the winner asserts that the loser played a good game and points to a few crucial moments, pretending that the two are equal and that the game could have gone either way. The loser will understand—for the moment at least—his opponent is superior. Each player salves the other's ego:

> I ran into the guy that beat me. He approached very politely with a humble demeanor and a friendly face, and he said, "That was a tough game" and he smiled. I said, "Yeah, it was close. I kind of opened badly and once you had your pawn stabilizing your knight in the middle, it was basically over. That was a very strong move." And he said, "Yeah, by then for sure it was over. Oh, but I'll tell you, I've had some really bad losses over the past couple of weeks. I'm glad I could finally get one." (Smiling). And I said, "Well, you played very well tonight for sure." (Antony Puddephatt field notes)

Since chess is treated as a test of mental prowess, defeat is threatening to the ego. Accounts, excuses, and alibis are necessary to preserve one's vulnerable identity. Henry Bird and Savielly Tartakower are each attributed the bon mot that they had never beaten a healthy player. Heat, noise, exhaustion, and smoke all explain defeat, even though such claims are often viewed skeptically. Thus I was surprised to hear my adolescent friend David explain candidly, "I blocked one piece with one of the pieces I was covering. I moved it and blocked the second piece so he could mate me, and then everyone on the team laughed at me. I just kind of missed it. [GAF: How did you feel?] Stupid" (interview). Players with enough "board cred" may admit error, but the stronger one's reputation, the more potentially threatening are claims of incompetence.

DARK PRESENTATIONS

Impression management, linked to rituals of deference and respect, situates participants in a community of caring acquaintances. In competitive activities, however, victory ennobles the self, and defeat corrodes it. In chapter 6 I discuss cheating, but here I focus on actions that, while not illegal, provide advantage. This strategic interaction is a form of "gamesmanship," the attempt to gain status through techniques that are not quite against the rules but jostle them.[65] A game of the mind becomes a mind game. Such attempts were remarked on early in the history of European chess. In 1497 Luis Ramírez de Lucena published a book that included a set of tricks. He suggested that in day games seat your opponent so that the sun shines in his eyes; during the evening place the candle by your opponent's right hand so when he moves with his right hand the shadow will distract him; and encourage your opponent to dine well, while eating lightly and avoiding wine yourself.[66] When smoking was permitted, some players selected strong cigars or chain-smoked to discomfort their opponents.[67] Before world champion Mikhail Botvinnik was to play American grandmaster Samuel Reshevsky, he hired an assistant to blow smoke as they practiced, inoculating himself against Reshevsky's cigarettes.[68]

Players may attempt to misdirect their opponents, particularly those they do not respect, through their facial movements. Sometimes this is as simple as staring at a part of the board or appearing happy (or sad) to mislead an opponent, tricks that are well-established techniques of bluffing. One hides useful cues through facial feints—a "poker face."[69] As one high school student explained, "Sometimes if I am trying to get them to do something stupid so that I can get a really good move, I won't look at that section of the board. Sometimes if you notice someone is looking at the section of the board, that is what they are thinking about.... So usually if I am trying to plan something there and it isn't my turn, I just look at the other side of the board" (interview). Another claimed, "I do bluff as needed. If I lose a pawn or go for a counterattack that doesn't quite work but could, depending on how I play it [I look confident]." (interview). A classic instance occurred in 1959, when fifteen-year-old Bobby Fischer played Mikhail Tal for the right to compete for the world championship:

> Fischer first wrote down the move 22 Ra1-e1, without doubt the strongest.... And not very deftly he pushed the scoresheet towards me. "He's asking me for an endorsement," I thought to myself, "but how was I to react? To frown was impossible, if I smiled he would suspect trickery, and so I did the natural thing. I got up and began to walk calmly up and down the stage. I met Petrosian, made some

joke with him and he replied. But the 15-year-old Fischer ... sat with a confused expression on his face.[70]

Fischer changed his move and lost. Few today would show their planned moves to their opponent, and Fischer's naïveté did not last long, as his drive to win at all costs led to dread that came to be called "Fischer fear ... an aura of a killer."[71] Tal behaved properly, but his response misdirected young Fischer.

Strategic interaction may include symbolic violence: refusing to shake hands, staring, slamming pieces, leaning over the board, making faces, or laughing at an opponent's move.[72] One strong high school player explained how he protected a younger teammate:

> Several opponents had tried to intimidate one of our best players, a freshman. At the start of the match, a physically domineering senior shot my freshman teammate a dirty look in an attempt to unnerve him. In life, I'm generally a kind-hearted person, but when my team is in the battlefield, I mean business. I stared right back, unleashing such a scathing look when the senior caught my eye he knew to back down. Right after that, I made a move in my game and slammed my piece down so hard the entire table shook, and everyone looked over. This is a very psychological tactic in chess, and my teammates took this as a sign to play confidently and to play hard. We went on to win the match and with it the state championships.[73]

Impression management trumped impression management.

Early versions of these strategies occur at elementary school tournaments. One tournament director explained, "I've seen kids fake crying in order to get a draw [from a sympathetic opponent] and then saying 'Ha-ha, I fooled you'" (field notes). My informant suggested that the lack of ethics of adults had infected scholastic chess, adding, "I've been amazed when you do see players treating each other nicely and with compassion" (field notes). In his view, strategic interaction is the norm and decency the exception.

The Board and the Couch

Standing behind impression management is the ability—claimed or real—to predict how others will react. This is the phenomenon of role taking, found throughout group life. Is there a single, "correct" strategy, or are strategies a result of those who surround us? Should we make our decisions based on what is best through an objective strategy, or should we recognize that action is embedded within a set of social relations. This involves recognizing that attention depends on how one sees the social setting, as argued by cognitive sociologist Eviatar Zerubavel.[74] Should competitors play the board or play the opponent? Is the location of the pieces all that matters, or should one imagine the plans and goals of the person sitting opposite? While the position of pieces is crucial, the self of the opponent might matter as well, as observing closely permits a reading of what poker players speak of as "tells."[75] In Erving Goffman's terms, these signals are not deliberately *given*, but *given off*.[76] They are unintended communication, and this makes them salient. These "tells" are a direct line to the brain, separate from how the person wishes to appear: "Peter Svidler, for example, sways his head from left to right when he doesn't like his position. Garry Kasparov grimaced when he saw something bad. Lev Polugayevsky turned pale when he was in time trouble—but Mikhail Tal turned pale when he was going for the kill. And as for Magnus Carlsen ... he curled up slightly in his chair, slipping his left leg under the other and propping up his head with a hand. Veteran Magnus-watchers said this indicated he was in trouble."[77] Even if we assume that these claims are correct, once a player can fake these "unintended" cues, he has the power to mislead.

Both chess stars and less-esteemed players differ on whether to rely on information gathered from observing an opponent. Bobby Fischer claimed that "I believe in good moves."[78] Akiba Rubinstein didn't care about his opponent, saying, "Today I play against the black pieces."[79] Others emphasize the centrality of psychology. Michael Stean, an aide to top grandmaster Viktor Korchnoi, felt that at the grandmaster level chess is 30 percent psychology, but at the level of the world championship, it is 90 percent psychology.[80] These guesses suggest the power of the psyche. The world champions Emanuel Lasker and Alexander Alekhine claimed that psychology matters:

> Emanuel Lasker was the first to realize that behind the moves of the chess pieces there is concealed a human being with his own character. Lasker understood that it is impossible to learn the secrets of a chess contest without the human element, without the player's psy-

chology, his experiences during the clash, his idiosyncrasies and his preferences. To Lasker chess was, above all, a struggle between two personalities, two intellects. He maintained that "It is two human beings who fight on the chess board, not the wooden pieces." ... Often he tried to play moves that were not, objectively, the best, but which were the most unpleasant ones for a particular opponent.[81]

"Psychology," Alekhine wrote ... "is the most important factor in chess. My success was due solely to my superiority in the sense of psychology. Capablanca played almost entirely by a marvelous gift of intuition, but he lacked the psychological sense."[82]

It is not that these champions psychoanalyze opponents or trick them but that they are aware of their opponent's preferences and weakness. The same position may require alternate strategies. Some prefer complicated, closed games with many potential combinations, while others reduce the number of pieces, simplifying the board and reaching the endgame more quickly. Playing the board, one's response would be identical, but if one focuses on a specific opponent, different lines of attack are possible. The *psychology* of chess is really the *sociology* of chess in that beliefs about the opponent's preferences as an actor shape choices over the board. In this, chess, like life, is a minuet.

The Politics of Defeat

When I started my research I was naïve. I believed that chess games end when one player checkmates the other. Every elementary rule book explains this. After a novice learns how the pieces move, this is the first thing he is taught. The rule is true in principle but false in practice. Throughout social life many things are not carried through to their bloody end; outcomes can be seen through the fog. With the exception of lower-level scholastic tournaments and rare special occasions, players do not checkmate their opponents. As the end becomes clear, the defeated resigns. As one writer explains, "I have never been checkmated; we all resign first."[83] Defeat is a communal recognition.

Eric Leifer, examining game theory, suggests that higher-skilled players are most willing to terminate the game when the outcome becomes apparent, as involvement then drains from the game.[84] They can see ahead but also have the interactional requirement to demonstrate this foresight through deference. As a player who has made huge blunders, this puzzled me. Why exchange a certain loss for a probable loss? I came to understand why a player might resign with the same pieces as his opponent. The resignation involves "the shared view of the inevitability of defeat" (field notes). But resigning, an outcome not found in basketball, tennis, or gymnastics, must be learned. Even "folding" in poker is not identical to resigning in chess, as it is a recognition not that one will lose but only that it is not worth investing further resources in the face of a likely outcome. The resignation is a ritual act in which the performance of the act itself conveys meaning, communicated through a handshake, tipping one's king over, stopping one's clock, or announcing, "I resign" or the equivalent (*aufgegeben, abbandona*).[85] The ritual is so firmly in place that when Boris Spassky resigned the final game of his match with Bobby Fischer by phone, Fischer still showed up at the board at the appointed hour because he feared a trick.[86] Endings are as formalized as beginnings.

DEFERENCE AND DEFEAT

In life there are good losers and good winners and others not so sportsmanlike. Not to resign at the proper moment may be taken as an insult, a lack of respect. Of course, this assumes that a player will understand when he is likely to be defeated, being able to see into the future. For a player like me, along with many third graders, such foresight might be a move or two ahead. Others might see a dozen moves ahead. Clues abound. Being down a queen or having an exposed king suggests weakness. These features of the board guide one's beliefs about the future. However, because of the possibility of an opponent's blunder or a stalemate, some scholastic coaches emphasize to their charges that they should never resign, even if they are humiliated in slogging on the long path to defeat. The goal is, at least rhetorically, "If they are going to win it, let them win it. Don't just give it to them" (interview). This is a remark by a high school player, but even at that age it is understood that often resignation is proper.

In practice, resignation preserves the egos of winners and losers. Why make the status gap explicit? For the loser, resignation avoids the claim that one cannot understand what everyone else sees. As one college student explained, "Resignation is more like losing with dignity, because to be checkmated means that you missed the checkmate, and if you miss an obvious checkmate, that is embarrassing. . . . At the higher level [of the grandmaster] if you are checkmated, you lose a certain amount of respect from your peers. . . . You admit that the other person played better than you, and you admit that in the end they were decisively winning" (interview).

The act of resignation shows deference to one's opponent. As one player suggested, "It is the gentlemanly thing to do" (interview). If a tournament player does not resign when appropriate, it may be taken as an insult, suggesting a belief that one's opponent will blunder. It is like refusing to give a "gimme" on the putting green.[87] Perhaps one cannot win by resigning, but one can preserve esteem. In one instance an older player complained about a child who did not resign. The man announced, "That kid should know better than that. You should just tip your king. If it is a lost game, it is a lost game for God's sake." A friend added, "You gotta resign with honor" (Puddephatt field notes). Another player notes, "People detest you if you don't resign. They don't want to waste their time on a game [that is already won]. If they won the game theoretically already, they don't want you to play it out. And they hate you" (interview). In practice, delicacy is evident in symbolic social relations. As a weaker player explained, "I played a game against a master where I sacrificed a little bit of material and it didn't pan out, but there was a little bit of a chance of making a complication, so I ended up playing about ten moves down the row, and I apologized to him after the game, and he said, 'No, no, you know it was complicated.' But I felt that really I should probably have resigned" (interview). He believed that the apology was necessary so that his higher-status opponent would not think ill of him. Over the board as well as in board meetings, one must not push a losing position too far. Proper closure is a means by which the world's status system is upheld.

THE CHECKMATE OF RESPECT

At some moments potential insults can be transformed into compliments when their meanings shift. Local circumstance matters greatly in interpretation. As a result, sometimes permitting a checkmate is not an insult but an honor. A game that ends in checkmate is a game in full. One leading grandmaster explained: "A lot of players resign one move before they are checkmated. But David once allowed me to checkmate him on the board. [He said,] 'You played such a great game, so I thought it would be nice if you won the game'" (interview). On another occasion a coach explained that sometimes opponents will permit checkmates after a particularly good game, saying, "He wants to crown the game. He wants to see the checkmate." (field notes). I was told that on one occasion grandmaster Vassily Ivanchuk applauded his opponent Anatoly Karpov before resigning a championship game. He resigned, but the applause was a symbolic recognition of checkmate. Sometimes players who are not allowed to checkmate their opponents after a show of brilliancy are frustrated. Bobby Fischer explained that an opponent's resignation after a dazzling game was "a bitter disappointment."[88] Like Fischer, a high school player explained that he was upset when an opponent resigned two moves before the end, commenting, "I was hoping he would let me checkmate him" (field notes).

Ultimately the meaning of a resignation depends on the imagined personal relationship and the action on the board. Refusing to resign is insulting, but permitting the opponent to checkmate is respectful. Both assume that the parties understand the meaning of the act.

The Draw Disease

Games are designed to generate winners and losers. How can a social system exist without such differentiation? Organized outcomes, the distribution of rewards and the establishment of hierarchy, are central, particularly in those artificial orders that games represent. But imagine a world in which more than one-third of all contests end without a winner. Such is chess. Some 37 percent of high-level chess matches are won by neither white nor black but are drawn. In the aborted world championship match between Anatoly Karpov and Garry Kasparov in 1984, the outcome was 5–3, Karpov, with forty draws when the match was stopped. But the politics of draws are not eternal. Beginning in the 1860s each player received half a point for a draw; previously tournament games had to be replayed until there was an outcome, leading to lengthy events. The definitive draw resulted from organizational needs to have a predictable and closed-ended tournament.

Perhaps in discussing draws the term *irresolution* is not correct, since today draws in chess are common, occurring even at elementary school tournaments, although the proportion of drawn games increases with the ability of the players.[89] The better the players, the less likely one of them will win. In fact, at the highest level, examining games that are included in databases, there are more draws than black victories and almost as many as white triumphs. Black often hopes for a draw, while white wants to win. One player explained that the great player Mikhail Tal commented that "to play for a draw with white is a disgrace" (field notes). Not to win with white in a tournament in which half the games are played as black is to "waste a color" (field notes). As a result, some players consider draw offers from black as insulting, while draw offers from white are treated as more sincere (field notes).

However, while draws are fully institutionalized in tournaments, they pose a problem in that they do not produce a hierarchy. Many players believe that there are too many draws,[90] and some tournament directors feel that quick draws threaten the integrity of the event. The world champion Capablanca noted almost a century ago that the game was suffering from what he described as "draw death" and what others speak of as the "draw disease." Chess players joke about certain grandmasters, too prone to take easy draws, who have authored texts such as "How to Draw like a Grandmaster," "The Art of the Draw," "My 60 Easy Draws," and "How to Bore Your Opponent to Death."[91] One strong player was known for not "fighting enough," and as a result he was given the nickname "the Drawing Master."[92] The strong grandmaster Loek van Wely competed at a Dutch championship against a weaker player who played for a draw, much to van Wely's disgust. The game finally ended on a rule-based draw based on the repetition of position. Van Wely had previously rejected two offered draws: "I didn't want the draw, and I didn't want to give the impression that I was happy with a draw. I wasn't.... Why didn't he play something sharp? . . . I got very angry when I realized he was going for a draw right from the start.... Instead of getting some experience here, this idiot just goes for a draw."[93] Van Wely subsequently explained, "Why isn't he taking his chances?" (field notes). Is this an insult, or is it simply smart chess against one of the world's best players? Van Wely surely wanted to win, but he was also viscerally offended by an opponent who felt that playing for a draw would be better than chancing defeat.

If chess is to become a spectator sport, draws are not desirable. Audiences need conclusions. A 0–0 soccer match might be beautiful for experts, but most viewers hope for the thrill of sudden death. As American grandmaster Joel Benjamin points out, referring to draws that end too early, while either player could triumph, "A draw without a fight always disappoints the crowd."[94]

Two types of draws exist. Some draws emerge through the rules of the game, based on the placement of pieces on the board; the *U.S. Chess Federation's Official Rules of Chess* devotes sixteen pages to draws, with references in other sections.[95] The best known of these is the *stalemate*, in which a player is not in check but has no legal move that would not place the king in check. Even if the opponent had all of his pieces and pawns and the player had only a king, the game would still be a draw. This reality permits players to continue to play even when they are behind in "material" (pawns and pieces) and constrains the decision to resign. Other forced draws include the lack of sufficient material on both sides to checkmate. For instance, a player cannot win with only a king and a bishop if the opponent has only a king and bishop (on the same color square). Draws are also required if an identical position has occurred three times during a game, if players have moved fifty times without a capture or a pawn move, and if one player will be in perpetual check, but without a checkmate. The draw is built into the structure of the game.

Other cases—which are sociologically more interesting—involve voluntary acceptance by both players. One player offers a draw and the other player, typically through a handshake, accepts. If the draw is rejected, the other player can offer a draw later. A player can offer a draw again, but only if the position has changed substantially, a matter of the judge's discretion, although rarely enforced. In theory draw offers and acceptances should occur because both players are convinced that the game will eventually end in a draw if they play it out. These are termed "book draws" or "theoretical draws" to indicate that the draw follows from the best play.

But the game itself is not the only basis of a draw. Competitors sometimes find it advantageous to agree to a draw without fully playing the game. These are sometimes referred to as "grandmaster draws," an indication that they tend to occur at the higher level of play when games are exhausting and when players compete for monetary prizes. As one writer claims, "The game in front of you is part of [a] larger game. Whether to draw or push for a win is often decided not by the position on the chess board, but rather the standings on the wall charts."[96]

A draw can be strategic, as grandmaster David Bronstein points out, "The whole organization of chess events is dictated by competitive, rather than entertainment, interests. This is possibly one of the reasons why modern masters do not feel any pangs of conscience when playing for a quick draw."[97] For instance, entering the final round, a strong player might be a point ahead of all rivals. An additional half-point would ensure first place, and a draw is tempting.[98] In turn, a weaker player might gain rating points from the draw.[99] So rather than playing out the game to its conclusion, both players may prefer a strategic draw, achieving their ends in a way that is legal, though not dramatic. Prearranged draws are considered unethical, but penalties are rarely assessed. Many games in the final round of a tournament end in quick draws. For instance, in the final round of the Chess Olympiad, each game between Armenia and Hungary was drawn in less than fifteen minutes, assuring the Armenians the gold and Hungary a good finish. Such an outcome in basketball, boxing, or skating would be shocking. To avoid this, some tournaments insist that before a draw is offered there must be a minimum of twenty or thirty moves by each player or they must play at least an hour, but this does not eliminate private agreements, only delays them. The existence of strategic draws is widely known, even if regretted as unsportsmanlike:

> The U.S. chessworld, in its spiritual and material misery, has spawned its own sad compromises. It is so difficult for strong masters here to make a living from the game today that, frequently, in the final round of a tournament, the two players vying for first place will agree in advance to draw the game in order to share the first and second place prize monies.... Agreeing in advance to draw key games is so widespread in U.S. chess that strong players, as well as organizers, take it for granted.... "What's wrong with sharing the top prizes?" said one of them outraged by the suggestion that prearranging games ripped the sporting heart out of tournament chess.[100]

Not every player will agree to a draw.[101] Bobby Fischer was famed for his desire to win at all costs.[102] However, practices in games and sports may violate imagined notions of fairness, such as the expectation in cycling that some members of a team might ride slightly behind their teammates to gain the benefits of lowered wind resistance. Rules of fairness are locally constructed, despite what outsiders believe. As American grandmaster Joel Benjamin emphasized, "A lot of excellent games end in draws. Draws are part of our established endgame theory."[103] Draws are woven into the social fabric.

Playing the Game

In contrast to the previous chapter which focused on the mind, the body, and emotions, here I focus on the social relations between two rivals, sometimes under the gaze of judges or audiences. Chess is a performance of actors as players or competitors. The doing is as social as thinking and feeling. Impression management and the social psychology that comes with it is part of how a community organizes itself.

However, while chess is my site, it is only one example of how voluntary fields of action are regulated through rules, norms, and expectations. Games are useful examples in that they are explicitly rule governed, if imperfectly so. Rule books make the claim for universality, erasing local differences. Yet informal games have house rules, and tournament directors may alter important features of the game, such as time controls or penalties for disruptions. Rules are in some ways equivalent to laws (and are referred to as such by the World Chess Federation), and so they are institutionally embedded.

The voluntaristic aspect of participation means that people vote with their feet. Exit costs are small, other than the loss of benefits that come from communal belonging. Loyalty and exit (and "voicing" a complaint) affect allegiance, as those who are dissatisfied have little compulsion to remain.[104] The illusion—and often the reality—is that, despite the hot competition, participants see themselves as a cool community.

Now that I have examined chess in three dimensions, the next chapter examines the fourth dimension, time. Activities unfold as part of a temporal structure, and this chronology gives a dynamic reality to any sphere of action.

3

TEMPORAL TAPESTRIES

*If you take too much time for one move, you have
that much less for the rest of your life.*

LAWRENCE FERLINGHETTI, "Deep Chess"

The influential German sociologist Norbert Elias argues that, while people feel time as personal, it is organized as a communal reality, developed in concert with others.[1] Technologies of time force us to adjust our social engagements through the demands of institutions.[2] In effect, chronological experience is a form of temporal capital, used for strategic ends.

Time as resource is evident at home and at work but is particularly salient in voluntary worlds, such as games and sports that are artificial and voluntary by design. In these realms, participants use time to create equal participation and provide common opportunity. Shared understandings of time connect to what sociologists speak of as "mnemonic communities," social worlds based on shared memory.[3] Turn and time are not personal choices but part of a tradition or an agreed-upon understanding.[4]

Competition requires rules that order activity so that an unequal outcome results from an equitable process. Fair access to the use of time is critical. Time can be used in several ways, directly or implicitly (the latter through turn taking, where turns may be of variable length). Examining the organization of competition, I refer to five competitive structures, each of which presents a model of fairness, although the form of time measurement varies: segmental structures, completion measures, temporal comparison, shared time, and time as resource.

First, turn-taking competitions can be organized so that success depends upon independent achievement within *segmental structures* with rotating ownership of the segment. Time is not measured directly, but a sequential shifting of control occurs, even if the segments are of variable length. Examples are "inning" games, such as baseball or bowling, or match games such as tennis or Ping-Pong, in which one participant has an active role, such as serving the ball. A variant of the segmental form is when the segments are timed, and participants compete to achieve goals in that time period. This is evident in word games like Taboo or the television show *Password*, in which competitors must guess words hinted at by partners in a fixed time period.

A second organizational form is based on the comparison of *completion measures* of a set of tasks that participants compete to achieve in parallel without the measurement of time being directly tied to the criterion of judgment. While there is often a turn-taking sequence (as in golf, when the player who is farthest from the hole has priority), players perform the same activities together (forms of croquet are similar in that one gains a point by "running a hoop"). Success is judged on numbers that define the efficiency of task completion. Golf, with its number of strokes per hole, is a primary example, although with eighteen holes, golf also constitutes a set of segments.

These forms of organization involve sequence, but not timing as such. In contrast, the most direct use of time involves *temporal comparison*: activities in which the duration to complete an activity is measured and compared with other participants, such as track or swimming events. The person with the shortest time to completion wins. Time is explicitly the gauge of success. A fourth organizational form involves *shared time*, in which opponents compete to use a period of time with the more successful declared the winner, such as in a soccer match.

Finally, domains exist in which time is treated as a *resource*, common in competitive two-person games, and the focus of my analysis. Each player is allowed a set amount of time to spend as desired. Competitive checkers and go have the same structure as competitive chess. This assumes a period of active calculation prior to each move. Time can be used by each of the players, even if one player owns the time. This structure permits a player to use his opponent's time for calculation and evaluation. The total amount of time in a contest is an additive result of the separate temporal choices of the competitors. While this reflects a particular form of leisure organization, it constitutes a more general example of how time is apportioned in competition. The assumption is that each player "owns" a certain amount of time, which can be utilized as a tactical weapon to support one's calculations or limit those of an opponent. While it appears that each participant has control of his temporal resources, this masks the fact that personal time is used in light of what is happening in the contest.

Temporal Collaboration

Chess is a game of mind, a game of heart, and a game of space, but when played competitively, it is also a game of the clock. Outside of tournament activity, chess may have a timeless quality, but even without explicit limits, social pressures impel players not to spend too long considering their next move.

At tournaments players can lose a game in two ways. The first is widely recognized and is essential to chess. One's king must be in a position where it cannot move out of check (checkmate) or is recognized as likely to be so eventually (leading to resignation). In informal play this is the fundamental outcome: time is not measured. However, tournaments operate with a second form of closure. Players can lose "on the board" or they can lose "on the clock." While players determine how much time to use for each move, they have a time limit for all their moves. If they exceed this, they lose.

Time is so central to tournament chess that its use has a formal name, "clock management." As one player explained, "If people are ahead on material [pawns and pieces] they shouldn't lose, but clock management is part of the game" (field notes). A player who forgets about the clock has a lot to answer for.[5] Time matters even if there is no clock; there are unstated understandings as to how long a move and a game should take. If a player chooses to move rapidly, his opponent may feel pressured; if too slow, bored. Neither provides the fulfillment that encourages voluntary activity, leading to an unwillingness to continue.[6]

Significantly, a key sanction in a tournament is to subtract time or to give the opponent extra time. For instance, if a cell phone rings in a tournament room, the offending player will lose time. In the professional United States Chess League, if a team switches players after a deadline, the opposing team is given a time advantage (field notes). Time and material have different standing; the punishment *never* consists of removing a pawn or awarding an extra move. That time is used as the sanction suggests that time has a negotiable quality, whereas the moves or pieces are treated as sacred, not to be altered by a rule violation.

Throughout the domain of chess, time matters. It can be conceptualized in macro terms (the structured temporality of the tournament), meso terms (the strategic temporality of the game), or micro terms (the experienced temporality of the player). Time shapes the event, the relationship between players, and the players' lived experience. It is essential to fair competition. These dimensions overlap so that a tournament is organized in light of desired schedules; within the event, games have temporal structures, and within the game, strategies and emotions are shaped by the experience of passing and pressing time. These dimensions create a *temporal tapestry* of action; they are not independent, but each shapes the others.

Macrotemporality: Games Just in Time

Events have an expected temporal structure, essential for organizing collective action.[7] These expectations are crucial for both organizers and participants. In practice, actors have personal preferences, and decisions advantage some participants and disadvantage others. In scheduling an event the organizer must establish boundaries. The length of a tournament is a choice that affects the number and types of players who participate.

Many assert that the experience of time has sped up in modernity.[8] Chunks of time are sliced ever more thinly. Prior to the 1860s, games had no formal limits and could last a day or more, constrained only by implicit norms. That timeless time has passed. Currently the United States Open, a nine-round tournament, lasts nine days, with one game each day from a Saturday to the following Sunday. Until 1967 the tournament comprised thirteen rounds over nearly two weeks. Relatively few players now want such a lengthy commitment, and organizers permit players to choose a shorter time period, such as four days, with more games each day. In 2011 more players selected a shorter time frame, with most preferring a six-day schedule, followed in popularity by a four-day schedule; the nine-day schedule was the least popular. During the final days the schedules merge, so that a single winner of the Open emerges. Alternative schedules are common in large tournaments.

When a single game is slated, it often starts in the late afternoon or early evening. A two-game schedule is played in late morning and late afternoon, permitting late-night socializing. Moreover, games vary in the time allotted to players. One form of chess (bullet chess) provides each player a minute to make all his moves; blitz chess allows five minutes; action chess allows thirty minutes per player. Long-form ("traditional") tournaments may be game/60 (sixty minutes per person), game/75, game/90, or game/120. The choice determines the number of games that can be arranged. As the length of a game affects the temporal contour of the tournament, it shapes the commitment necessary to participate.[9] This dedication is affected by competing obligations, age, skill, and engagement with the chess subculture, and in turn it affects how tournaments are arranged.

Two time limits are common at high-level chess tournaments. The "classical" format has each player receiving two hours (or two and a half hours) for the first forty moves, one additional hour for the next twenty moves, and then thirty minutes for the rest of the game. In this format (excluding the possibility of time increments, discussed below), games are completed in seven or eight hours, a good day's work. A second format, used by the World Chess Federation, allows ninety minutes per player and awards an additional 30 seconds after each move. This alternative structure is derided by some as too brief for the adequate evaluation of moves.[10]

To understand how time is perceived in chess is to appreciate changes in modern society.[11] The clock colonizes social life, permitting certain forms of activity and discouraging others. Norbert Elias emphasizes that clocks are an institution that represents time but are not time itself.[12] In this they build the intensity found in many places. As J. C. Hallman notes, "The history of chess is a history of acceleration. Nearly every significant change to the game has seen it become faster."[13] A long-standing belief exists—whether among medieval players with the "faster" movement of pieces across the board, nineteenth-century players institutionalizing a chess clock, or contemporary players with shortened time controls—that the younger generation wishes the game and the world faster. The same desire is seen among those not so committed: "[It] will be much easier for spectators to follow, with a lively rhythm like every other sport.... Chess is for *fast exchange* of ideas.... Chess should be like tennis—risky ideas, inventions, for the pleasure of the opponent and the audience."[14]

Compressed time is said to be moral, creating more "humane," shorter games. One organizer remarks, "Can you tell me how they can play ... and still eat and bathe?" (field notes). As time is telescoped, tournaments must be shortened and the games abbreviated. This changes how one thinks and how one plays. Deliberation is replaced by instinct, treasuring efficiency, which reflects the control of modernity and an emphasis on rationality. Lacking this, the event becomes esoteric. With the exception of a dramatic event such as the televised Fischer-Spassky match, only a change in format is likely to attract corporate sponsors. Tennis, boxing, and poker re-created themselves as rapid events. Pool has moved from "straight pool" to "nine-ball" in order to produce this same excitement (interview). Some argue that this is necessary in chess,[15] although it assumes that audiences have the knowledge that would create sufficient interest. One prominent grandmaster explained: "It's the twenty-first century. Life is changing.... The only way we get chess on television is if you speed it [up]. And we have to have lively commentary and exciting personalities and develop a show out of it. Just like poker did and golf did and billiards and pool. All these different activities, honestly speaking, don't seem visually so exciting either" (interview). Novelist Julian Barnes comments: "When all is said and done, the basic and constant visuals in television chess are of two seated players pushing wood. Or, too often for comfort, not pushing it."[16] Just as theatrical performances and concerts have been compressed to fit schedules and budgets, so has chess. Recently time controls at the Denker Tournament for High School Champions were halved from three hours per player to ninety minutes. As in much of modern life, more things mean shorter things.[17] Immediacy trumps deliberation in the politics of time.

THE TECHNOLOGIES OF TIME

Although the rules governing how pieces move have been stable since the Middle Ages, the temporal rules of chess have evolved. Tournament time controls are regularly readjusted. Once it was common for chess games to adjourn overnight, typically after forty moves, when players could review their moves and use as much time as desired for preparation. With the development of extensive databases and strong computer programs (discussed in chapter 7), adjournments were eliminated after 1993. Adjournments recognized a temporal order, but they also reflected the idea that the "proper" length of a chess game would be between forty and sixty moves. Shorter games are distinguished from full games by being labeled "miniatures." Play and work depend on collective understandings of temporal propriety and technological consequences. Still, such changes, despite real effects, are treated as not affecting the game itself.

It is one thing to believe that chess games should be shortened but another to organize the activity to make that happen. This requires a marriage of chess and technology. It wasn't until the last half of the nineteen century that time controls were established, first with hour-glasses, then with chronometers, and finally with analog and digital chess clocks.[18] The 1851 tournament in London, the first major interna-tional competition, was played without time controls. Several games lasted twelve hours, and one lasted twenty.[19] Temporal limits were a function of implicit expectations. Chess players spoke of the skill of *Sitzfleisch* ("sitting flesh")—the ability to sit at the table for extended periods. An apocryphal tale claimed that in an 1858 match between Paul Morphy and Louis Paulsen, the two waited in silence for eleven hours. When Morphy finally stared at Paulsen, his competitor re-sponded, "Oh, is it my move?"[20] Chess champion David Bronstein asserts, "Multi-hour games are monstrous, like dinosaurs from past ages. They kill lively thought, spread out in time the creative energy of the players."[21] As chess became institutionalized with tournament schedules, time had to be tamed through rules and procedures. But as with all systems, the choice creates what Paul Hoffman terms a "tyranny of time," as the amount of time available influences styles of thought and of play.[22] In 1852 players were given a limit of twenty-nine minutes per move, and in 1862 each player had an hourglass to make twenty-four moves in two hours. The first double chess clock was used in tournament play in 1883, giving players an hour for fifteen moves.[23] In the early years the penalty of having one's time run out was a fine, but subsequently the penalty became game forfeiture. Given that time could only be judged through its mechanical inscription, it is no sur-prise that players charged opponents with fixing their clocks to gain an advantage.[24] As noted above, the advent of computer programs and databases eliminated overnight adjournments, as the availability of cached knowledge would have shaped the outcome. Technology changed the temporal organization of the game, as in many domains (such as surgery, secretarial work, and airplane scheduling).

Shortening the game made time more valuable, and players increasingly "lost on time." This required the development of alternative systems of controlling time. The invention of digital and electronic clocks, such as those produced by Chronos, proved crucial, as these clocks could be programmed. One solution was to have clocks delay for five seconds before starting to count down. With this technology each player gains a few seconds "outside of time" for quick thought, and the game can continue until one player blunders. Another solution was to add an increment to the time available, typically thirty seconds after each move, permitting more extended thought and building the extra time into the game structure. Time can be stopped or gained. Bobby Fischer argued that a chess game should not be lost because a player ran out of time. As a result, he invented (and patented) a clock that could be programmed to add time. As a result, following actor-network theory, the clock became, in effect, a central agent in the game, with the ability to shape interaction.[25] A two-hour game was transformed into a 115-minute game with added dollops of seconds. Today both time delays and time increments are used in tournaments, although increments have become more popular at larger and more formal tournaments. This system requires that players learn to program their clocks, emphasizing the linkage between technological competence and game competence. The consequence of these changes, particularly the addition of thirty seconds, means that players less frequently lose on time. The choices of the tournament organizers affect outcomes through the experience of a temporal order. As one top player remarked, "In several games [without an increment] I was just completely shocked because my time was moving really fast."[26] In his experience chess time with its artificial increment came to feel "natural," and the absence of the increment made judging time challenging.

Along with increments, a second rule was instituted at many tournaments that when the clock of one player reached five minutes, the players did not have to note their moves. Moves are written in case of a challenge or should a player knock over the board. In the last few minutes, hands are surging, errors more common, and the need for written moves may be more salient. However, technology may come to the rescue. Boards are becoming electronic, permitting moves to be recorded automatically. Again, the intersection of technology and temporality affects how games are played.[27]

Meso Temporality: Time as a Resource

Time shapes encounters as well as gatherings. While tournaments are temporally ordered, encounters are structured as well. Participants must manage the duration they have been allotted, and in this they collaborate and compete with each other. As one coach emphasized, "The clock is a weapon" (field notes). But what are the skills of this weaponry? While the experience of time results from institutional demands, it also results from strategic choices of actors, emphasizing temporal agency.[28] In examining restaurant kitchens, I wrote of the complex and interlinked behaviors that affected behavioral coordination and shared commitment.[29] Chess is no different. Two players, forced to wait on each other's choices, rely on enforced sequence as they coordinate their actions. Without rotating turns the game cannot continue, and in this chess is similar to most conversations. No player can move twice without a response, and no player can refuse to move, even when a move weakens his position (*zugzwang*). If no legal move exists and the player is not in check, the game is a draw, a *stalemate*, because it prevents the alternation of moves.

Because the clock is visible, the relative temporal positions are known by all. As the balance of minutes change, cognitive and stylistic opportunities shift. Having more time available, particularly in the endgame, allows a resource-rich player deep calculation. With many minutes, a player can move more deliberatively, while the player with few seconds plays intuitively. As a result, a player rich in time may "complicate" the board, forcing his opponent to spend time calculating or to make a quick error because of a poor evaluation. However, a competitor with much more time may choose to move rapidly to deny the other the luxury of consideration while waiting. In other words, a player can use an opponent's time to calculate future moves.

Beyond this to-and-fro, quality chess involves a set of moves that, as unfurled, represent the game itself. Moves cannot be taken back, institutionalized by the touch-move rule. The alternation of moves between black and white reveals the chronology of each game. Action oscillates like a metronome. Significantly, a move is termed a *tempo*, suggesting the centrality of the temporal. The tempo is the point of action, the moment in which thought becomes behavior. As Benjamin DiCicco-Bloom and David Gibson explain,

A turn is a coveted resource in chess ... and it is a cardinal sin to squander one. One can do this, for example, by taking two turns to move a piece to a location that could have been reached in one. In such an instance, Nimzowitsch would say that one has "lost a tempo." One can also lose a tempo, or several tempi, when one is forced to retreat a piece, especially if that means reversing a previous move, or when one loses a piece that took several turns to develop when there is nothing else to show for the effort.[30]

Losing a tempo is a retreat, a circling back. Using a tempo wisely forces a response.

As a result, the intensity of concentration or the breaking of that intensity creates a complex temporal tapestry,[31] tied to skill and experience. In large tournaments, called Swiss tournaments, discussed in chapter 7, players are matched on their success in previous rounds. I imagined that weaker players might need more time to evaluate moves, but I was surprised that the playing hall emptied from the rear. The games of the weakest players end quickly, even if they play the same number of moves as stronger players. They lack the knowledge, history, and commitment to think deeply. This is true at scholastic tournaments in which games between first graders end before games between fourth graders, which end before games between seventh graders. For less adept players the excitement of chess is the moves, not the thinking. Thought does not fill the time allotted.

Players face the practical matter of how to use time. Given that time evaporates, one may be pressured to act quickly, but time is a resource that should be used to the fullest. An anecdote is told of the grandmaster Viktor Korchnoi. It was said that he sat at the board for an hour before his first move, trying to see the possibilities in a game that had not begun.[32] Surely the story is apocryphal, but it captures a belief that time is to be used to figure out the best move.[33] As one strong chess player advised, "Use your time to think. If you have to sit there and use forty-five minutes on your clock to figure out the right move, use it, because it pays dividends later. Even when it is only ninety minutes, use the time. Because not only do you survive that move, you also come to understand the position so much better.... If you rush or move when you haven't fully analyzed a situation, that is when you're going to lose" (Antony Puddephatt field notes). A key time management challenge for coaches of children and mediocre players is to have them embrace deliberation. One coach explained:

> The main thing we try to teach kids in chess is to slow down. That is job one for any scholastic coach. I have begun to teach patience more explicitly than I used to. I try to talk to kids about the feeling they have right before they make a move—to pause for a second and ask themselves are they just out of patience. Is that why they are making the move, or are they really settled on the move in their hearts, or do they just want to keep it going because they don't want to think anymore? (interview)

Another noted, "If you find a good move and you have got time, it is not going away, so you can find a better one. If you can't, you can always fall back on that one good move you had" (interview). The coach of a third-grade chess club emphasized, "You must play slowly. Grandmasters can play fast. The rest of us must play slow. You've got to be more disciplined and move more slowly and think before you act.... I want you guys to really take your time here. The way to avoid trouble is to be very deliberate in your actions" (field notes). Some coaches have their young players sit on their hands, slowing the impulses of fingers.

Deliberation is essential, but players must know when there is no more thinking to be done, when more calculation produces diminishing returns, just as when graduate students spend decades writing dissertations that becomes no better, only more dated. One of America's top grandmasters confessed that the amount of time he spends in the opening prevents him from being a stronger player. He says, "I waste a lot of time in the beginning, and I am often in time trouble. It would be nicer if I was better prepared in the beginning" (interview). David Bronstein agrees, suggesting that "the best players in the world ... are noted for their rapid play, perhaps instinctively sensing the importance of utilizing the very rich resources inherent in rapid intuitive thinking."[34] A balance exists between instinct and deliberation, a dual-process cognition. Moving a piece is rewarding (for the moment, at least), and as a result, a quick move may feel better than a slow one; further, if one has not been trained to calculate, there may be nothing to think about but only time to waste, especially as one's opponent is simultaneously considering his strategy.

No one right way exists to utilize time in chess, in studying for exams, in seduction, or in public speaking. (Some strategies, of course, are more effective than others in context.) Time is praxis. One must gather oneself and, as pragmatist philosophers assert, prepare to perform.[35] Games do not have a *natural* length, but their preferred length emerges through communal desire and institutional need.

While *duration* may be easily manipulated, simply changing the time limit has complex effects, as duration is also a social reality: the clock is read in context. With two competitors phenomenology is doubled and becomes intersubjective. Do I experience my two hours the same as you experience your two hours? Do I experience my two hours the same as I experience your two hours? I watch you think, as you watch me. I judge you thinking, while you judge me. Thus players rely on temporal impression management. At the World Open, the strongest players often arrived after the games start, checking an opponent's history or simply to convey their own confidence. One star player confessed that he liked to be "fashionably late." Less talented players strive to start precisely on time, treasuring every second.

Watching the clock is part of being a professional, and being in time trouble is "a sign of bad form" (field notes). This stigma was evident in one match that I observed in the United States Chess League; a coach was angered that a player used eighty minutes for the first five moves (each player has ninety minutes for each game). This player was seen as being too cautious against a higher-rated player. He found himself in permanent time trouble in a difficult game and made it worse by choosing a style of play that complicated the relations among pieces, requiring additional thought. His teammate groused, "If you don't have time, why do you go into complications? If there's a simple way to win, you do it" (field notes).

Chess is competitive not only on the board but on the clock. As the game goes on, one player may have an hour, while his opponent has only minutes. One of the greatest chess players—one known for his psychological strategies—was Mikhail Tal, called the "Wizard of Riga." Tal was explicit about using time as a weapon: "After [the world championship match in 1960 between Tal and Botvinnik], some commentators tried to tarnish Tal's achievement by suggesting that the decisive factor was not his tactical brilliance but rather his psychological cunning. In his book on the match.... Tal answered his critics with a terse pragmatic defense of the psychological method: 'I know I made what appeared to be bad moves at times, but they served the purpose of making my opponent use up time, figuring why I made such a move.'"[36] Tal was skilled at playing the clock, transforming time into temporal capital. I heard high school players suggesting, as did Tal, "He was almost out of time. I wanted to complicate [the board position] for him" (field notes). Tal understood that the use of time was a strategy.

With time controls comes the challenge of clock management. Chess is a rhythmical game, whether it be fast and planned, slow and thoughtful, and rushed and intuitive. Given that competitors have different amounts of time available, one player might think deliberately, while his opponent is rushed and stressed. Here the rule that in formal games one receives an extra hour after forty moves changes the player's rhythm; a player can permit his time to be exhausted, rushing into move forty, and then slow down once again. The rhythm of the game shifts through its temporal organization.

Beyond this, segments of the game have different rhythms. One must have enough time to calculate strategies in the middle game but leave enough time for the endgame so that one does not select moves thoughtlessly. Both players rely on the same temporal playbook. In high-level tournaments, early moves occur rapidly. Players typically select well-researched opening lines (discussed in chapter 4). Often the first dozen moves are played quickly. But at a certain point, players reach the complex middle game, when most pieces have been moved from the back row. It is here that the most calculation occurs. As novelist Julian Barnes commented about the Kasparov-Short world championship match, carried on British television,

> The players would in the first few minutes rattle out a familiar open-ing, until one produced a prepared variation from the known line. The player who had been varied against would then settle down for a long and slumberous ponder while the innovator went off and made himself a cup of tea.... After the first eleven moves had been flicked out in couple of minutes, Kasparov varied. Short thought. And thought. Commercial break. And thought. And thought. Second commercial break. And thought. Finally, after using up forty-five minutes of live television time, he castled.[37]

No wonder so few games are telecast and few are likely to be until the temporal structure game is compressed, although not so much that—as in blitz—it becomes a blur. Time as a resource over the board came into sharp conflict with time as a resource on the screen.

The endgame involves fewer pieces, and strong players are aware of effective strategies, such as two rooks versus one rook and a knight or two pawns versus a bishop. Some endgames last more than a hundred moves, but under traditional time control players must use the time available. As a result, at this stage, players may rush, playing intuitively. As one grandmaster put it, "You just don't calculate. You just guess the moves. You play lottery instead of chess. You just throw the piece on some square. It's an uncomfortable feeling" (interview). One writer comments about rushed endings, "Players still move chess pieces, but now they're playing not chess, but something more like table tennis. Clocks bang, pieces hang, pawns race.... At this critical stage of each game, manual dexterity rules."[38] The game is no longer to be won by the most thoughtful competitor, but by the most dexterous. At the conclusion of the 2008 US Women's Championship, the final, sudden death "Armageddon game" came down to a wild time scramble when one player had twelve seconds and the other eight seconds. Classical chess had become a blur, requiring different skills. The rules were identical, but the game was different. The final outcome was a time forfeiture in which the winner had a second left. Controversy erupted when video indicated that one player moved before the other pressed her clock.[39] In their urgency the sequencing of moves was violated. The ending was not satisfactory, and procedures have changed, but *some* ending was necessary to resolve the championship in the time allotted. These wild endings remind us that chess has a temporal cycle: steady moves that become slow and then become rushed. If the first segment is routine, the second may become stagnant, and the third thoughtless (interview).

In the chessworld players distinguish between games won on the board and those won on the clock, with the former being *real* victories. This belief is so powerful that some players choose to lose on time to preserve self-esteem. In the competition between rivals time is strategy.

Micro Temporality: The Rush

In chess, as in other intermittently hurried activities, a moment comes in which pressure ratchets up; restaurant workers, air traffic controllers, and emergency medical technicians experience a similar pressure. To be professional—to be skilled in a communal domain—one must react instinctively when time is scarce. One set of skills helps us to think calmly and another to react intuitively. The clock ticks down, but demands continue. As minutes ebb, time's passage makes itself felt. A high school player explained:

> When you are time-pressured, it's surprising how you can't think quickly when you need to.... This year I think I got used to time pressure more, and once you get used to playing under time pressure, it's easier to control your emotions.... When you play with under two minutes on your clock in scholastic tournaments, it's like there is a nervous feeling you get, and you don't know what to do. But once you are used to the nervous feeling, you sort of know how this is going to go. You sort of just get over that and are able to think more clearly once you are used to it. But if you are not used to it, it can be pretty difficult. (interview)

This player may have had as little time as before, but it had a different meaning. Time pressure is managed through experience, often through the subjective allocation of attention.[40] But there are also individual differences. Certain players rarely need the time allocated, calculating with ease, while others gobble their time and must cope with the belief that they are "time pressure players."[41] Some savor the game as it progresses; in a subjective sense they have "more" time available.[42] Grandmaster Hans Ree proposed a fanciful parallel between time trouble and drug use: "Time trouble is an addiction, perhaps even a physical addiction to the opium-like substances secreted by a chess player's brain during the time trouble phase."[43] Whatever the adequacy of the analogy to getting high, the claim explains the embodied enjoyment of rapid play. Those skilled at rapid response are primed for intuition.

The structure of time can alter the meaning of a social act, as well as how information is processed.[44] When action speeds up, sexual intercourse becomes a "quickie." A dinner becomes "fast food." A test becomes a "quiz." Chess, too, has temporal boundaries. Is a chess contest of ninety minutes the same game as a contest of three hours? Each affects chess ratings identically, but this is not the case when the limit drops to five minutes. Together competitors can play a game of "correspondence chess" in two years or a game of "bullet chess" in two minutes.

What is the temporal boundary at which chess stops being "chess"? Temporal structures create "different" games with different experiences. Game/120 (two hours per player) is recognizably similar to game/90, and some tournaments include games of both lengths. Game/75 and game/60 are still "real" chess. In practice, one finds a change in meaning around game/30, half an hour for each player. Participants clarify the distinction through naming. Game/30 is labeled "action chess," evident in the National Youth Action tournament sponsored by the United States Chess Federation. Each game lasts an hour at most.

Shrinking the amount of calculation creates a game distinguished from "traditional" chess, the longer game being the standard by which variants are judged. As one player said, "There's chess and then there's blitz" (field notes). The salience of the thirty-minute boundary is evident in Garry Kasparov's comment that he played the first "serious" match of "rapid chess" against Nigel Short on the stage of the London Hippodrome; each player had twenty-five minutes. Kasparov felt that "it was still possible to play deep concepts despite the difficulty of calculating deeply on each move. Instead of a profound study of a position we had to rely more on instinct."[45] As one strong blitz player explained about a friend, "People used to say that he wasn't a good chess player, but just a blitz player" (field notes). For one contributor to an online discussion: "1 min chess aint chess. That's panic game!!" Should every chess game count toward one's rating? When does chess end and something else—judged differently—begin? The boundary between traditional chess and speed chess is seen in different categories of ratings. For a game to be included in the standard USCF rating system, each player must be allocated at least thirty minutes. As a result of the popularity of speed chess, a separate rating system has also been established, preserving the moral sanctity of the ratings of the long form of the game (a third rating system, between the two, for quick chess also exists). As of March 2013 the USCF instituted a blitz rating, for games in which each player has between five and ten minutes.[46]

As time controls contract, distinctions increase. Excitement is institutionalized through the organization of the activity.[47] Intuition grows, calculation shrinks. Players flex their tactical muscles. A formal, deliberative game becomes informal and spontaneous; silence is replaced by trash talk as informality shapes the game.[48] Before the introduction of digital clocks in the 1990s, accommodating increments of seconds, chess clubs sponsored "rapid transit chess." An organizer rang a gong or called out "Move!" every ten seconds, and a player had to move immediately.[49] Time was ladled out in small spoonfuls. Digital clocks provided the technology necessary to create a swift game, as time could be measured in small increments. Games shrank: fifteen minutes, ten minutes, less. How far can time shrink? How little can minds and hands accept? Marc Esserman, an American international master, claims to have created bullet (one-minute) chess.[50] He and his friends began playing one-minute games on the website of the Internet Chess Club. He gained a high rating, beating many strong players. Soon the website prevented these games but within a week gave in and began rating these one-minute games. Esserman reports that through bullet chess, "young people were treating chess as a video game" (field notes). The image of chess as a board game, tied to slow cognitive processing, had been upended by intuition, even if, as often the case with intuition, it is based upon deeply internalized, tacit knowledge.[51]

In an 1858 essay in *Chess Monthly*, "Chess in Hades," the American chess editor Willard Fiske wrote of "those demented wretches who exhibit a morbid fondness for ... five-second games."[52] He wrote with cutting disdain of players who moved too quickly, suggesting that they deserved to bake in the ovens of hell. These were not gentlemen, but damnable scoundrels. As one book sardonically noted about an early version of blitz, "There is ... a move-on-move insanity, Blitz, which requires no clock, for no time at all is allowed the players. Blitz is a 'relaxing' sport to topnotch players, each of whom must counter at the very instant a move is made by the opponent. Blitz is not recommended to persons afflicted with hypertension or cardiac disturbances. Nor is it recommended to persons who are not so afflicted."[53] A mature player comments scornfully about one-minute chess: "It gives you a big advantage in playing with your nerves, but at the same time it causes you to move too quickly without thinking. I think it is a total waste. I hate one-minute chess. I just don't like it because the quality is so bad. We have an instant gratification society" (field notes). Recognizing that speed chess is popular among younger players, one writer, referring to "steroid chess," fears that "many of today's young (under-20) players are being bred *without knowing what serious chess is all about.*"[54] Yet, in a world of short segments and rushed culture, speed chess has an enthusiastic following.

Today speed chess has cachet, being played by the strongest players as well as by the marginal patzer. Grandmasters, tournament-level players, collegians, adolescents, and street players relish the energy of a fast game. The World Blitz Championship was established in 2006 and has since been won by some of the strongest grandmasters of long-form chess. The hierarchy of "real" chess and "speed" chess is being erased.

Temporal boundaries demonstrate that activities are differentiated both through the feel of the activity and its social placement. Perhaps they are covered by the same canopy: the mile run, the javelin, and the hundred-yard hurdles are labeled "track and field," although each requires different skills. Because of distinct phenomenology, special rules are created for speed chess: rules about touch move, illegal moves, and hitting the clock. These result from the rushed physicality of blitz. Bodies err, but how should those blunders affect the outcome of the game? One answer is to assert that there are fundamental differences that permit each type of play to coexist, but separately. A prominent grandmaster remarked: "I think chess should have all these different elements.... You look at running: they have marathon runners and they have one-hundred-meter dash, and they have in-between. All three formats in chess: regular (slow), rapid, and then the blitz (the real fast), I think they should all have their own right and their own champions, and they should live in nice harmony because you want to have the slow games for the real quality games" (interview).

Perhaps blitz is "sloppy" or "sacrifices quality," but it is energizing. In creating boundaries, a new object or form of interaction is justified through experience, and in turn the new form shapes how chess is learned and how it is viewed, building an appreciative public. Each activity demands legitimacy in the face of marginalization. For David Bronstein "intuition, fantasy, and daring" are revealed in rapid play: "Corresponding to the rapidity of intuitive thinking and the creative potential concealed in it must be the rhythm, the tempo of play. It is in rapid play that the intuitive mind triumphs.... Practically all the top players possess a rapid, intuitive positional grasp.... A strong chess player requires only a few minutes of thought to get to the heart of the conflict.... In blitz, all shallow, banal and uninteresting situations 'gallop past' the mental glance."[55] One international master explained that watching a blitz game allows you to "get inside [the player's] head and see how he thinks" (field notes). Books don't matter; phenomenology does.

Rather than playing one game in an evening, opponents play dozens.[56] Losses and victories pass quickly. An evening with thirty games has a different texture than an evening with three, limiting deliberation and the emotional economy. Each game slides into insignificance. Psychiatrist Charles Krauthammer suggests that blitz has a therapeutic value in a hypercompetitive world:

> At our club, when you lose with a blunder that instantly illuminates the virtues of assisted suicide, we have a cure. Rack 'em up again. Like pool. A new game, right away. We play fast, very fast, so that memories can be erased and defeats immediately avenged.... We do not sit in overstuffed chairs smoking pipes in five-hour games. We play like the vagrants in the park—at high speed with clocks ticking so that thinking more than 10 or 20 seconds can be a fatal extravagance ... No time to recriminate, let alone ruminate.[57]

Krauthammer contrasts the pipe smoker (wealthy, old) to the vagrant (poor, young), distinguishing between the unhurried, thoughtful player and the active, intuitive one. Both belong to the world of chess, but with different experienced realities.

Chess builds on the phenomenology of time, affecting the experience of participants, drawing them in or pushing them away. All temporal structures have a phenomenology, but in arenas in which action is intense, the insistent reality of time is especially powerful in altering the balance between thought and deliberation in contrast to emotion and intuition. From the tournament to the game to the moves (and movers), temporal capital creates a complex, layered social world.

Watch-Ing the Game

Competition can be organized in various ways through choices of sequence and duration. Although examining the politics of time as situated in local scenes has been rare, such scenes deserve more attention. While every social world has unique characteristics, competitive chess, so tied to its temporality, is dramatic in this regard.

Research on competition addresses how games are framed in light of constraints, how rules are strategically deployed, and how experience affects involvement.[58]

Time is a fundamental building block of social order, but in contemporary society it has been telescoped and increasingly managed by institutions. We have ceded control of the clock to those with authority. This is especially true in the realm of voluntary activities. The chess clock, now refined as a digital clock, has transformed free and flexible time into measured and mastered time. The minutes barely evident on older analog chess clocks have been replaced by technology that places seconds front and center. Chess, once a game of days, became a game of hours, and then a game of minutes, and now is a game of seconds. This change is evident in the structuring of the tournament, the game, and the experience of the move.

Part of the challenge that chess faces in becoming a public spectacle is to make the event—which is so compelling for the participants—enthralling for an audience. In this, it has not succeeded, but the hope of brokers is that with more action the public will not have to snooze through empty moments. Whether fast chess will have public appeal remains to be seen, but this is the fantasy upon which chess entrepreneurs operate. Perhaps chess will be the new poker, perhaps the old bowling.

The organization of time influences social activity on multiple levels: macro, meso, and micro; these may be distinct, but they are intertwined, as is evident at tournaments in which the event, the game, and the experience meld in a temporal tapestry. For these organized gatherings promoters create time structures that appeal to potential audiences, and this depends on how much time participants have available and choose to spend. To create an event requires sensitivity to external temporal orders. Within the tournament is the game, and here players strategize the use of available time. They consider when and how to use the hours and minutes that they have been allocated, and they do this in light of their opponents' temporal resources in a realm of double phenomenology. Finally, there is the experience of the game, shaped by the pressure that time limits produce. Rushed or contemplative, competition involves emotion that is shaped by the reality of duration. For organizers, for competitors face to face, and for the individual listening to his internal conversation, time matters.

Ultimately time is a resource in competition, used by participants and organizers. If long chess is a bore and blitz chess is a blur, they are so because those invested find pleasures in thought and in action. Whether we consider traffic patterns, factory lines, food service, or musical events, we see time's cultural power. Just as we have social capital, cultural capital, and material capital, we have *temporal capital*: time hoarded or strategically deployed. This resource, found in chess and beyond, makes activities salient for those who engage and for those who observe.

Time directs our attention to how chess is organized as a community. In the next chapter, I continue this analysis by examining how participants embed themselves in this community by means of their shared knowledge and common history, treating chess as a repository of *sticky culture*.

4

SHARED PASTS AND
STICKY CULTURE

Chess gives not only contemporary fame, but lasting remembrance.
To be a great chess player is to be surer of immortality than a great
statesman or popular author.... The chess player's fame once
gained is secure and stable. What one of all the countless chivalry
of Spain is so familiar a name as Ruy Lopez? What American
(except Washington) is so widely known as Paul Morphy? Chess,
in fact has lasted so long that we are sure it will last forever.
Institutions decay, empires fall to pieces, but the game goes on.

ROBERT SHINDLER, "In Praise of Chess," 1889

Chess players, frustrated by the absence of public regard, will surely
find Shindler's proclamation about the power of shared memory
amusing. While the empirical warrant for Robert Shindler's 1889
quotation is doubtful, he captures something fundamental about local
communities. Communities create heroes and recall crucial events.
As leisure theorist Robert Stebbins emphasizes, communities with a
common focus develop means of keeping their history alive, cement-
ing their ties through shared awareness.[1] People want their favored
activities to matter; a robust culture has this effect. History creates
allegiance by creating a *sticky culture*.

Excluding national cultures and expansive subcultures, bolstered
by institutionalized systems of power and control, most collective
memory is embedded in local communities based on the recognition
of common interests and shared resources, supported by ongoing
interaction. As sociologist Tamotsu Shibutani suggested, "Culture areas are coterminous with communication channels."[2] Affiliation and
contact create the emotional basis for remembrance, and remembrance is a means through which identity is situated. Community
members are linked because they firmly believe in the value of their
shared concerns. We establish memory through joint activities, organized through churches, social movements, artistic domains, and leisure groups. These domains constitute social worlds: scenes in which

participants recognize that they hold meanings, emotions, and commitments in common.[3] Collective memory operates not only through communal knowledge but through the recognition that knowledge is shared. Representations are collective.[4] Meaning is established and solidified through networked realms of action.

Shared meaning, when growing out of routine interaction, builds affiliation. This constitutes *sticky culture*, a body of understandings that glues participants to their community. It is not memory itself but rather a common culture that demonstrates that community can generate group consciousness. Shared awareness supports active participation.[5] Culture is more than mental representations but is displayed in spaces where groups of people gather. Unfortunately, much research on collective memory has ignored these bounded publics, despite their prevalence.[6] Social memory studies define memory rather than defining the group to which memory belongs.[7]

I build on the concept of *tiny publics*, small communities and focused networks, whether explicitly political or not, that constitute the basis of civil society.[8] Participation in these publics allows individuals to feel a part of a larger scene: they *belong to* a community and share communal knowledge. Some groupings are instrumental (work domains, political fields), while others are based on a shared commitment to forms of leisure culture, but in each case memory links the individual to the community.

Memories are not separate from communities but integral to them. People are pressured to reveal commitment by displaying awareness of what matters to others. Put another way, a public requires collective memory but cannot be reduced to it. Publics, such as chessworlds, are more than cognitive domains: they are interaction orders. People are linked through what they know, and this facilitates what they do together.

Chess as a Bounded Public

Students of collective memory emphasize the placement of memory: what French historian Pierre Nora calls *lieux de mémoire*.[9] History is preserved in solidarity. But what does it mean that a community uses the past to build commitment?

Many social worlds demonstrate the power of sticky cultures to connect individuals and groups. Any group that distinguishes itself from others by its history could suffice: Quakers, surfers, libertines, librarians, or libertarians. But not every activity is equally regarded, and chess has a longer history and more public recognition than many voluntary activities. (Shindler contrasts chess favorably to whist. Whist?) The forty million American chess players or even the eighty thousand members of the USCF provide a large public from which to build groups. Chess, like baseball or film, has a strong sense of history, including heavy volumes on its development, with particular attention to changes over time.[10] "Chess historian" is an honored title in the chessworld.

As a social world, chess is not unique in the desire of members to create a shared history, but its depth and longevity make it an ideal case for examining the dynamics of collective memory. To cement affiliation, participants establish a radiant past. Memory reveals that one is the kind of person that belongs. These worlds draw boundaries, critical to identity.

In emphasizing that the chess community creates remembrance, Shindler was correct. People are devoted to chess and to chessworlds, just as they are in other voluntary domains. As Pierre Bourdieu posits, some activities are characterized as fields, linking person and action in networks of power.[11] These fields are built on shared knowledge, recognized and elaborated by participants. Just as society can be treated as a game,[12] games are societies.

Of the world's games, perhaps only go has an equally robust history. Certainly checkers or Candyland cannot match chess. The chess community is inordinately proud of its past, and the recognition of a chess *community* indicates this fact. Chess depends on readers as well as players. The number of books published on chess is extraordinary. The chess bookshelf is surpassed only by those of religion and health. The Library of Congress lists 4,767 books under the keyword "chess" (compared to 452 for checkers). Amazon.com has 15,707 titles that are listed in response to the request "chess" (2,342 for checkers).[13] One author claims that there are more how-to books written on chess than on all leisure and sports combined.[14] These are imperfect measures, but they indicate that even if other voluntary activities have histories, the extensiveness of the chess literature is notable. The John G. White Collection at the Cleveland Public Library has the most extensive collection of chess books in the United States, with more than thirty-two thousand volumes. During my research I was shown personal libraries with hundreds of volumes on floor-to-ceiling bookcases. Chessic literature includes instruction manuals, biographies, accounts of tournaments, and novels. Blogs, discussion forums, Facebook pages, and websites provide a field of discourse. Further, chess champions, grandmasters, and chess teachers often author books consisting of analysis of particular games, part of the knowledge infrastructure of chess. With its extensive literature, chess is an extreme example of what is found in many voluntary social worlds.

Within self-referential communities history operates through dual paths: the heroic and the eventful. Champions and particular games provide connection with the activity's past, demonstrating the lasting authenticity of the community.[15] Chess theory—what Puddephatt calls "esoteric knowledge"—creates shared perspectives.[16] One can examine a chess game and figure out from the moves when the game might have been played—early queen checks and capturing pawns suggest that the game was played before 1900.[17] Finally, there are individual histories that link the person to the activity, what psychologist David Pillemer refers to as "personal event memories."[18] As a result, players use their experiences to shape heroic stories, tragedies, and comic anecdotes.[19]

The Hero at the Board

One of the most consequential features of a social field is a pantheon of recognized heroes, often enshrined in the material architecture of halls of fame, establishments that in their bricks and mortar demonstrate a concrete history. Not every community has physical sites of memory, but many create ceremonial or literary remembrances. I use Candyland as an example of a game that exists in its own local moment. No list of Candyland champions exists, perhaps not surprising, since the target audience is three- to seven-year-olds and the game is based on chance.[20] Historical memory is a function of audience as well as of commitment. Games such as bridge or checkers or Scrabble[21] do have histories and heroes although not as broadly elaborated as that of chess. A list of heroes would certainly include Morphy, Steinitz, Lasker, Capablanca, Alekhine, Fischer, and Kasparov.[22] In Russia, Botvinnik, Karpov, and Tal might be added.[23]

Reuben Fine suggests that the veneration of heroes results from a player's need for worship and idolatry, but perhaps to claim that they are role models would be more accurate. Referring to Bobby Fischer, Fine avows, "There is a deep need on the part of many people to project their own grandiose ambitions onto him."[24] What Fine misses is that this regard needs to be tied to a tight-knit community in which admiration is collective. It is not individuals who admire these chess greats, but groups. That is, individuals, because of their participation in groups, know to admire greats. As a result, players debate with great fervor who is the greatest player of all time, a problematic assessment because of the growth in chess knowledge. How good would the ancients be if they knew contemporary chess theory? The World Chess Hall of Fame, now located in Saint Louis, provides an institutional site for collective memory. Each year American chess players are inducted, modeled on the Baseball Hall of Fame and similar *lieux de mémoire*.[25] These are places in which memory is set in stone.

A heroic past is central to affiliation. Fred Reinfeld writes: "Whenever I had come to the Manhattan Chess Club to play in interscholastic tournaments, I had always found myself drawn to the portrait of Paul Morphy. He was a glamorous figure.... My first glimpses of Lasker, Capablanca, and Alekhine at once established them as beings from another world.... Ever since those early days I have been a hero-worshiper of the World Champions.... For thirty years I have reflected on their lives, their destinies, their triumphs, and their failures."[26] A middle-aged chess player explains: "When I was young, chess was about hero worship; now that I'm old, it's ancestor worship. You have an obligation to the game. It's like Buddhist philosophy. I feel that I am in the middle of the great tradition" (field notes). Garry Kasparov, writing a "comprehensive history of chess," published a five-volume series entitled *My Great Predecessors*, on the successes, failures, and discoveries of the heroes of the game. For Kasparov and for many others, this is the "great man" theory of chess. In this regard Jeremy, an international master, tells me that "I take my notation in Russian.... I take it so I can summon the Russian school" (field notes). He too wants to be part of the great tradition.

Hero worship is particularly evident at simuls. At these events people hope the master's fame will rub off, particularly at simuls with world champions such as Karpov and Kasparov. Participants are "playing against history." At one event at which former world champion Karpov was the guest, he shook hands with each of his thirty opponents, had his picture taken, and signed the chessboards. On those rare occasions in which a player draws—or wins—the amateur will repeat the story endlessly, creating an imagined relation that does not otherwise exist.

Bobby Fischer: A Sticky Hero

Many communities have touchstone figures, canonical icons to whom all respond. Fame makes personal connections enduring.[27] The awareness of heroes transforms an activity into a family (or in male-dominated chess, a brotherhood). Shared admiration generates emotional energy, binding people together.[28]

For chess players, no more consequential figure exists than Robert James "Bobby" Fischer (1943–2008). Bobby Fischer is central to chessic memory. He is like the weather that all can discuss. Whether Fischer was the greatest player ever, he is surely the most widely debated. He is idealized as a fighter in an activity that is often considered the preserve of nerds. Fischer was the dominant player of his era (1962–1972), he shaped Cold War politics by defeating the Soviet world champion Boris Spassky, he inspired parents to teach children chess (producing the "Fischer Boom"), he wrote two influential and best-selling chess books (*My Sixty Memorable Games* and *Bobby Fischer Teaches Chess*), and his demands, outrageous at the time, led to multimillion-dollar prize funds. Even after he left competitive chess, Fischer represented chess for good and ill. He had magic.[29] Later in life Fischer continued to capture public attention. He was known for anti-Semitic rants, and in a radio interview on September 11, 2001, he reveled in the attacks, suggesting, "It's time that the ... U.S. got their heads kicked in.... Death to the U.S. This is a wonderful day!"[30] Whether or not he had a "paranoid mental derangement,"[31] Fischer was central to how chess players defined their game: as a world of creativity and edginess, a domain in which eccentricity was often taken as a mark of brilliance.

Fischer's charisma generated a shelfful of books. An early one was by Frank Brady, a longtime acquaintance, who in 1965 published *Profile of a Prodigy: The Life and Games of Bobby Fischer*.[32] A recent one, published in 2011, was by the same Frank Brady, entitled *Endgame: Bobby Fischer's Remarkable Rise and Fall—from America's Brightest Prodigy to the Edge of Madness*.[33] From Fischer's victory over Boris Spassky, the Fischer literature flowed in books such as *Bobby Fischer*

vs. the Rest of the World and *Bobby Fischer Goes to War*. One count
found more than thirty books about the match.[34] As with connections
to other celebrities,[35] many recount a Fischer story. Observing at the
Marshall Chess Club in Greenwich Village, I was struck by the number
of older members who eagerly shared their Fischer story—winning a
game against him, sharing a meal, refereeing in a tournament that he
attended, or watching him analyze a match. The fluency of the stories suggested that they were regularly performed and that the ability to share a story revealed status. Fischer's interpersonal network
was such that one player commented, "You've heard of six degrees of
Kevin Bacon. This is six degrees of Bobby Fischer" (field notes). The
popular book (and movie) *Searching for Bobby Fischer*,[36] even though
not about Bobby himself, captures the fascination with the man. The
community searches for the next Fischer and often anoints a young
player as successor.

At first, Fischer was the great hope of American chess. Noting the
increase in prize money that resulted from his intransigence, Boris
Spassky labeled him "the honorary chairman of our trade union."[37]
But over time his reputation became tarnished. The trouble with
Bobby Fischer as a touchstone is that players must apologize for him
or distance themselves from his deviance, suggesting that although
they love him as a chess icon, they dislike or pity him as a man. One
player mused, "Fischer should have died young."[38]

Fischer's brilliance was recognized early. By 1956, at age thirteen,
he was a significant presence in American chess after defeating Donald Byrne at the Rosenwald Memorial Tournament in the "Game
of the Century" (a century then only half over), a game so labeled
by the tournament arbiter Hans Kmoch to publicize the event.[39] By
1965, aside from Paul Morphy, Fischer was considered the "greatest
American chess genius."[40] World champion Mikhail Tal called Fischer
"the greatest genius to have descended from the chessic sky," and
grandmaster Raymond Keene described him as an "angry chess god
incarnate."[41]

But Fischer's difficult reputation, particularly after 9/11, made him
toxic as well as beloved. The United States Chess Federation, which
never examines the political positions of its members, revoked Fischer's membership in 2002, a decision that provoked controversy.[42]
(American grandmasters are automatically members of the organization.) The decision was overturned in 2006. After his death in 2008,

comments referencing "triumph and tragedy," "hope and disappointment," "rise and fall," and "pride and sorrow" were common.[43]

The relationship of community and hero is shaped by publicity and built through celebrity. The hero's presence defines the field. Celebrities make attractive all they touch. In chess we speak of the "Fischer boom," but a century before, there was the "Paul Morphy boom," coincident with Morphy's grand tour of European chess capitals: "The New York *Chess Monthly*, to which Morphy himself had been contributing games as co-editor since early in 1858, reported in 1859 that 'Hundreds of people now play chess who, a half-year ago, were utterly ignorant of the moves.'"[44] When Morphy withdrew from active play, "chess-mania" evaporated.

A century later it returned as another heroic and flawed figure demonstrated that America could hold its own against the world. Now the competition was the Soviets, and the moment was the Cold War. The enormous attention to the Fischer-Spassky world championship in the summer of 1972 contributed to the Fischer boom. The game of chess became a well-publicized space for childhood education: chess was treated as a training ground for science and mathematics. Membership in the USCF doubled from 1972 to 1973. By 1980 half of those new members had been lost. Perhaps if Fischer remained in the public eye, chess would have thrived, but the moment passed, and Fischer the hero was left to those committed to the game and to those who were willing to forgive his now-tarnished persona. Borrowing Isaac Newton's refrain, communities stand on the shoulders of giants. The hero provides the sticky culture that justifies an arena of action.

The Sparkle of Dusty Games

It is not heroes alone who create communal remembrance but events as well: elections, battles, marriages, or civic commemorations. When chess players consider indelible moments, they typically think of games. In examining the community of chess, Cary Utterberg argues that games provide shared intuition; he labels this *existential understanding*.[45] Others suggest that games from different periods "fit together like links in a chain," revealing a knowledge sequence on which chess depends.[46] Although most games are quickly forgotten, chess continually builds on its past. Chess games lay down roots, treated as part of the infrastructure of memory. Publications such as the World Chess Federation's *Chess Informant* make major tournament games available (over three hundred games are annotated every four months). Online databases provide millions of games. As a result, the past never dies but is illuminated and extended through replaying and referencing games. The commitment is such that for many players studying past moments is the heart of the activity. As Harry, a well-regarded chess teacher, explained, "[The game] is the chess equivalent to ... art masterpieces. Each game is like a painting of Renoir or a Cezanne or *The Brothers Karamazov* by Dostoyevsky, or *The Magnificent Ambersons*, or *Citizen Kane*. Each one of those is where the form takes on its highest expression of beauty and where it delivers the most" (interview).

One player remarked, "I was fascinated by the fact that here I was. I was playing out a game, and this game had actually taken place like a century before. To me that was a romantic feeling" (interview by Antony Puddephatt). The Game of the Century (Bobby Fischer vs. Donald Byrne, 1956) and the Immortal Game (Adolf Anderssen vs. Lionel Kieseritzky, 1851) have been studied by generations of aspiring players, both for technique and for inspiration. While we may participate without reference to the activity's past, we only become committed through collective memories. As J. C. Hallman notes, "The end of a good chess game is more like a birth than a death—it's a beginning. Once completed, games become public fact and property that are scrutinized, appreciated, distributed, and retold. They may achieve a fame of their own, wriggle into databases both figurative and literal, and eventually constitute lore."[47] The games studied typically involve a victor and a loser (some games are draws), and the goal is to learn how the hero triumphed in pitched battle. I have watched a dozen Fischer games replayed, but in the five years of my research I never watched one of his defeats analyzed. The games chosen are not just good but are symbolic, ratifying the moral order. They are Fischer triumphs, even though, for the game to be significant, his opponent needs to be a player of note (such as Reuben Fine). The fame of the opponent ratifies Fischer's genius. Great games depend on the participation of two experts.

Recognition is not just momentary but contributes to memory. The more intense one's commitment, the greater the awareness of communal events. World champion Garry Kasparov observed, "A grandmaster needs to retain thousands of games in his head, for games are to him what the words of their mother tongue are to ordinary people, or notes or scores to musicians."[48] As one chess teacher emphasized, "Intuition is the historical knowledge from your brain that you can't quite recall, but that you think is right" (field notes). Intuition links the player to a skein of history.

That a grandmaster can reel off the moves in numerous games is astonishing for those with less training. Bobby Fischer was known for his prodigious feats of memory; he was a walking encyclopedia of chess history: "When Bobby Fischer was preparing to play Spassky in 1972, he studied Spassky's games.... Fischer was lucky that this book containing 353 of Spassky's games existed and was in his possession. A friend of Fischer's told me that you could give Bobby any number between 1 and 353, and he could tell you all the moves to that game."[49] Fischer was in this and in so many ways unusual, but he was only an extreme example of a more general phenomenon. Andy Soltis, for instance, describes a game between two young grandmasters, in which black, losing, moved his rook to square e5; white quickly agreed to a draw. Looking at the position, white remarked, "The ghost of Lasker," referring to an identical position taken by Lasker in the 1908 world championship.[50] The century-old game was known to both players, suggesting a common bond.

For some teachers, such as Boris, this ability to teach "the history and geography of chess" and relate this to the play before them is crucial (interview). In the words of anthropologist Alan Aycock, these "stem games"—such as Fischer's widely studied Game of the Century—provide the basis for further innovation.[51] But just because a game is old and famous doesn't mean that one can simply borrow techniques blindly. As computer databases become more extensive, young players are tempted to rely upon the perfection of the past without understanding the interior logic that created genius. World champion Garry Kasparov explained that he once was analyzing a game with a talented twelve-year-old, who had been asked to provide a game he had lost:

> I stopped him and asked why he had played a certain pawn push in the sharp opening variation. His answer didn't surprise me: "That's what Vallejo played!" Of course I also knew that the Spanish

Grandmaster had employed this move in a recent game, but I also knew that if this youngster didn't understand the motive behind the move, he was already headed for trouble. This boy's response took me back to my own sessions with Botvinnik thirty years earlier. On more than one occasion he chided me for committing the same sin of blind emulation. The great teacher insisted that his students recognize the rationale behind every move.[52]

The past can be either a shackle or a lamp, depending on whether one merely repeats moves or learns from them, a challenge shared by chess with studies such as art history or architecture, in which one is instructed in past glories but must transcend by rejecting them.

Given their concern with history, it is significant that some players archive their own games. This is feasible in that, unlike in most other games (baseball being a partial exception), moves are recorded in chess. Unlike, soccer, say, chess does not flow; it is punctuated, and each punctuation point has potential meaning. At a tournament each player receives a score sheet that is to be filled out and then signed by both players. The player who sees himself as having a leisure *career* can keep a duplicate for study or for memory. Coaches often insist on reviewing these records. In time, electronic devices such as MonRoi will make these notations automatic. Each player records not only his own moves but those of his opponent. Through these documents, players curate an archive of their life in chess. While one might expect that grandmasters would keep these records, I was startled that less talented players (including a few whom I beat) retained these documents. A friend claimed that he was doing this for "posterity." Another player took notation for even the most informal of his games, and insisted that I do the same. Leather-bound books filled with score sheets are available for purchase.

Given the belief that score sheets are sacred, it is worth noting that players frequently err in the rush of the game. This happens with grandmasters, although less frequently. In my observations most games recorded by players with ratings under the expert level of 2000 will have some error. So in replaying the game, participants have to adjust their score sheet based on their memory; otherwise they will find impossible moves. Still, the salience of the past as an organizing principle makes both collective recall of classic games and personal recall of locally treasured games so valuable.

Tactics and Memory

I have on my desk a weighty paperback. The 734-page book is entitled *Modern Chess Openings* (*MCO*), currently edited by three-time American chess champion Nick de Firmian. It is called the "chess player's bible."[53] I purchased the 14th edition. The 1st edition was published in 1911. Reuben Fine helped to revise the 6th edition. The 15th edition was published in 2008. Each edition asserts that the standard opening moves from which chess players choose have evolved, reflecting communal progress. The *MCO* is the equivalent of the psychiatrist's *Diagnostic and Statistical Manual* (*DSM*). Every new volume adds new lines and deletes those deemed outdated, providing a space between the latest innovations of grandmasters, not yet in the *MCO*, and those that amateurs can access.[54] Along with the *MCO* is the *ECO*, a five-volume *Encyclopedia of Chess Openings*, first published in 1966. These volumes contain five hundred openings arranged in five broad categories. Their purchase constitutes a serious commitment. Openings tie players to the community. Like other domains, chess has core knowledge that has been awarded the honorific title "theory." This justifies the claim that top players are "professionals," whatever their income. They have specialized knowledge, not easily accessible to those not dedicated.

Openings are the theoretical heart of chess, predetermined beginnings that have stood time's test. Each has a style, described alternately as quiet, sharp, boring, classical, formal, crazy, or murky. Some prefer airy combinations that permit movement over the board; others like tight ("cramped") play that depends on precision. Anthropologist Robert Desjarlais suggests that "different motifs and auras apply to different openings. . . . The French Defense resembles a labyrinth of forking paths, while the Najdorf Sicilian is a brutal street fight, with a swirl of knives slashing about."[55] Desjarlais suggests that chess players fall in love with particular openings and make them central to their identity. He suggests of his own opening play, "In playing the Sveshnikov, I felt I was participating in its history, however minutely. The more I played and studied the opening, the more Sveshnikovesque my thoughts became."[56] Numerous books purport to explain openings in more exhaustive (and sometimes numbing) detail than the *MCO* or *ECO*: *Easy Guide to the Bb5 Sicilian*, *The Chigorin Queen's Gambit*, *Nimzo-Indian Defense*, *Play the Benko Gambit*, *Play the Caro-Kann*.

The names sound exotic and enigmatic, linking a participant to present and past.[57] One chooses an opening and builds a library.

Nothing similar exists for middle games, too complex and diverse for a single book, or even endgames, which, unlike openings, lack names. Endgames have tactics, and a considerable literature has been written on strategies, but pieces do not start at the same point and depend on the detailed and precise analysis of each position.[58] Each segment of the game requires a different approach. It is almost as if chess is three games in one. As Rudolf Spielmann advised, "Play the opening like a book, the middle game like a magician, and the end like a machine."[59] Middle games are for the attacking and dynamic player, endgames for the cautious and calculating one. Some players find the middle game a confusing muddle, while others describe endgames as sterile, technical, boring, or like eating spinach.[60] Endgames are not swashbuckling.[61]

All players know how a chess game begins. White moves a pawn (one square or two) or a knight, and then black moves a pawn or a knight. There are no other possibilities. Twenty options for each player, even if most are not effective strategy. By black's first move the players are in conversation. Each move is a response and a provocation. These moves became codified into named "openings." Accomplished players use the term "book" to refer to opening theory: "Is this book?," being "booked up," "playing book," "getting off book," using "book knowledge." Some players are known as "theory players," if their moves follow standard openings. These openings are also termed "lines" or "main lines." This commitment to book, lines, and theory reveal an attachment to the community, constituting what one chess grandmaster termed "opening theory addiction."[62] When Reuben Fine wrote of Bobby Fischer's world championship victory, he expressed the widespread belief that "the codification of the openings does not have far to go before it is complete."[63] This claim justified the creation of increasingly popular Fischer Random Chess (or Chess 960), where back row pieces are shuffled to disrupt opening theory. One newly minted grandmaster explained, "I get more frustrated that more and more games are determined by opening theory. In other words, there is not enough creativity. Ideas are not coming up by themselves, but through the analysis of the computer. I don't dislike opening theory. I just dislike that computers came up with it" (field notes).

New openings potentially create new culture. As Garry Kasparov notes, the shaping of opening lines represents the heart of chess: "By the time a player becomes a Grandmaster, almost all of his training time is dedicated to work on this first phase. The opening is the only phase that holds out the potential for true creativity and doing something entirely new. For finding something that no one else has found."[64] Opening theory reflects the triumph of collective memory, revealing both the hardened stability of the game and the possibility of change.

Over centuries many opening lines have developed, each with their own reputation. The *Encyclopedia of Chess Openings* lists five hundred, although some are quite esoteric (or just plain bad, such as the Sokolsky Opening or the Grob). Some named openings have a dozen moves. As anthropologist Thierry Wendling points out, openings developed with the professionalization of chess.[65] In 1749 the French chess commentator François-André Danican Philidor (1726–1795) named only five or six openings, and not until the first half of the nineteenth century were openings such as the "French Defense" or the "Sicilian" or the "English" named. As chess became a historicized, self-referential activity, openings were codified.

The naming of openings depends on the characteristic elements of the position (the King's Gambit Declined, the Queen's Pawn Game), geographical areas that locate the development of the opening (the Dutch, the Vienna), or a player associated with the opening (Bird's Opening or the Ruy Lopez). A few refer to the style of play (the Giuoco Piano, or quiet game). Players in their local cultures create names for openings, such as "the cheesecake," because it is "smooth and easy" (field notes).

In general, games can be open (getting pieces out early), semi-open, or closed (a slow development of pieces). Attacking players prefer open games, defensive players closed games. Learning openings involves a slow process of acculturation. Casual players do not make the effort, so they stand outside communal culture. Openings are so important that some chess instructors, including at least one elementary school teacher, begin with basic openings, such as the Two Knights Opening or the Caro-Kann, feeling that even if students do not recall opening moves, they learn that openings are important and perhaps allow them to avoid opening traps, such as the Fool's Mate or Scholar's Mate (field notes). As Bryce, a high school player, remarked of his youthful training: "In elementary school we toyed with the idea of knowing openings, but we didn't really know them.... I know I thought I played the French. What I was playing is not what it really is, and it was actually quite different" (interview). But for young players, just like sex talk, talking about openings suggests maturity and brings status. In time, based on experience, local cultures, and personality, players become committed to a set of opening lines to use as white and a set of preferred responses as black.[66] As one international master reported, "You want to choose an opening that matches your style of play" (field notes).

But beyond personal taste, openings are faddish within chess communities. The Scotch Game was unfashionable until Kasparov used it. One player remarked ruefully: "I find it hardly fair that, for example, the Alapin Opening or the Nimzowitsch Defense, among others, are described as 'relics' or having only 'surprise value.' Then, suddenly, because an official source has made such pronouncements, players start learning what they believe are winning opening lines by rote."[67] Donald, a chess teacher, explained, "Openings come and go. Openings that are not currently in will be in again.... The Colle might come back. You never know what the next thing is to be brought back to life" (interview). These choices may be esoteric, but they establish chess culture.

On the Lakeside High School team, players enjoyed using the Fried Liver Attack, also known as the Fegatello Attack ("dead as a piece of liver," a variation of the Two Knights Defense) when playing as white. It was central to the team's culture. Perhaps these teens liked the colorful name, but the opening has a history that can be traced back to Rome in 1610 and is a reputable attacking strategy.[68] Students recognized that the Fried Liver Attack was not as effective as others, but it was beloved:

[GAF: When did you start to learn openings?]
DAVID: Probably fourth or fifth grade when I started playing what is called the Fried Liver. If the opponent doesn't know what he is doing, you can get a knight and basically a rook for free. But it doesn't work nowadays as well. (interview)

If I am playing someone I don't think is very good, then I will try to play Fried Liver. It sort of freaks my opponent out when I sac [sacrifice] a knight. They have to bring their king up to the center of the board in order to keep pieces.... I think most new players or people who haven't seen that will not know what to do and how to defend it properly. (interview)

A teammate concurred: "I want to learn the c4 opening [the English Opening] for when I play good players, but I want the option of Fried Liver as a backup" (field notes). Like the Scholar's Mate, the Fried Liver can trick those not skilled. These teens, socialized to the opinion of their community, realize that the success of the opening depends on the opponent's skill. While players have preferences, they select an opening based on judging their competitor. At the higher levels of chess, this decision results from examining databases to see with which openings one's foe has had success. My friend Jeremy discovered his opponent preferred the French Defense, which he factored into his own plans. The choice of an opening is linked to social relations—a game against *another*—and so action results from an evaluation of that other. Jeremy explained that his selection of an opening depended on "age, rating, my reading of [my opponent's face], and how I'm feeling. I don't want to play something too crazy because that takes up too much energy if I'm tired" (field notes). One's choice may shift with mood as well as reading one's opponent. Further, this choice might shift with each move, as there are many lines within standard openings.

Openings are not just effective or not—they may be admired or disdained, evaluated within knowledge communities. As Boris explained, "An opening cannot be good or bad.... There are bad openings, and everything else is playable. You study and you say, 'Oh, if I like it, I should be able to play it for both sides.' It's a style question, of course" (interview). On the high school team, Tristan joked with his coach, "Would you hold it against me if I play the Latvian in a tournament? . . . It's like the black King's Gambit, but it's crap," and Cameron remarks, "The Sicilian, basically that's the one that everyone learns first, but it sucks. It gets all your pieces stuck" (field notes). Evaluations of openings are common at all levels of chess, although the sophistication of the remarks differs widely.

Opening theory is both historical and interactive, making up a large part of what it means to be a serious chess player. There is too much for anyone to know, but by limiting one's scope one demonstrates expertise. Opening theory is historical, reflecting the history of the group and the history of the game.

Chess Style

As Nina Eliasoph and Paul Lichterman argue, style characterizes groups and cements participants to their local idioculture.[69] One selects routines of interaction, working within an emotional register. But style can be more or less explicit. In some settings one merely acts in a predetermined way to achieve a desired end, and in others possibilities abound. When one regularly selects an approach over time and across settings, this becomes a style.

This is true in leisure worlds where style can be found in the action of the game or in the approach to the game. Sometimes, as in Candyland, there is play, but no style. The more moves rely on tactical, strategic, or aesthetic choices and the less they rely on chance, the more the game develops a recognizable quality. One doesn't just play but reveals one's allegiance in play.

Few other game worlds involve so much choice as does chess. That is its glory and its complexity. Over time how chess has been played has changed. I am not referring to rule changes but to shifts in the style of play. This leads some to suggest that chess is like science—physics, geology, evolution—with distinct paradigms, ideologies, and experimental tests within the game itself.[70] This history of ideas is well described in Anthony Saidy's *The Battle for Chess Ideas*.[71] Saidy and others speak of the Romantic school, the Scientific or Classical school, the Hypermodern school, and the New Dynamic Approach. His chapters focus on the perspectives of leading players. Reuben Fine does not receive a chapter, but he is described as "the man who best epitomized the 1930s." Perhaps because he was a synthesizer of the Classical and Hypermodern ideas, he is treated as pragmatic rather than theoretical.[72]

While writers divide the history of chess ideas in various ways, four periods of chess knowledge are typical. For the sociology of knowledge, the examination of such histories is valuable, even if one must be careful to remember that the history of ideas, as is true for so much history, is written by the proponents of currently dominant approaches—the winners in the battle of ideas. This is what is described as "Whig history."[73] Like other examples of esoteric knowledge, the development of chess as a "science" or theoretical enterprise has a contingent historical development that assumes progress.[74] Analogous to scientific theory, chess theory has evolved in fits and starts as certain strategies were declared better and became more widely adopted. Perhaps it was only the players who were better, but the theories were given the credit as well. Innovation is necessary for a new generation to dethrone its predecessors. Effective tactics and strategies gain moral and intellectual virtue. As games are won and lost, the community venerates "objective" approaches.

It is widely accepted in science studies and the sociology of knowledge that an uncritical model of cumulative scientific progress is insufficient. Knowledge advances through changes in practices that are treated as legitimate as a result of being embedded in social relations. Thomas Kuhn's influential analysis of scientific advances as well as contemporary studies of scientific practice demonstrate that knowledge is always linked to cultural contexts, politics, career trajectories, and reputations.[75] In chess, as in science, players claim allegiance to one paradigmatic approach over another: they might focus on positional, defensive strategy or aggressive tactics, the two broad principles that distinguish styles.

The model of scientific revolutions developed by Thomas Kuhn rejects disciplinary knowledge as a steady and linear accumulation of neutral facts. Instead, Kuhn argues that knowledge advances in dramatic shifts and spurts.[76] The solidification of beliefs within a community is crucial to the development of forms of practice. When past beliefs are felt to have failed, new perspectives—or paradigms—arise in response. This view is no longer startling in science, but it is striking that paradigms are found within leisure.

To understand game culture as a knowledge regime, I briefly summarize here the stylistic history of chess.[77] While chess is distinctive, a close analysis of bridge, go, poker, and other widely played games reveals similar themes. I draw heavily on *The Development of Chess Style* by the grandmasters Max Euwe and John Nunn.[78] When one examines the development of chess theory, heroes or exemplars mark changes in perspective. We associate knowledge with revered persons. As Euwe and Nunn emphasize, "Succeeding generations of experts have contributed to the development of chess play, but it was the style of some outstanding individual which moulded the thinking and style of play of his time."[79] The reputation of these chess heroes justified change, even if the reputation was based on that change. This perspective trickles down to tournament players and even novices.[80]

In the early recorded games of chess under modern rules, little coherent theory was in place. People didn't rely upon models of play. Games must be seen as capable of being recalled in order to be systematized. We do not have a theory of Candyland. A systematic account of chess principles was absent for centuries.

Philidor was the first chess master to approach the game in a way that outlined basic principles in his classic 1749 publication *L'Analyse des Échecs*. Philidor argued famously that "pawns are the soul of chess." Chess players distinguish between pawns and pieces, and pieces had been given greater weight, but Philidor recognized the importance of pawns for providing structure, allowing pieces to attack and defend. Presaging Carl von Clausewitz's theory of war as built on defensive structures, Philidor recommended a slow, methodical approach, delaying until a dominant pawn structure is established.[81] Today Philidor's belief in the power of pawns is less central, but the importance of pawn structure remains. Philidor presented the first principled contribution to a coherent paradigm.

Philidor's preference for a slow, positional approach to pawn development was challenged by opponents who found success using other strategies. In time a new focus on combinations of pieces, gambits, and strong attempts to checkmate without worrying about pieces being captured became the dominant principle of chess in what is labeled the Romantic approach: "Everything turned on attack and counterattack. Passive play, defence, refusal of sacrifices ... the setting up of a pawn phalanx—these and all such ideas were right outside the mentality of the chess player of the first half of the 19th Century."[82] The leading proponent of this approach was Adolf Anderssen. Anderssen emphasized the sacrificing of pieces to achieve tactical attacks that lead to checkmate. Pal Benko and Burt Hochberg capture the swagger of the Romantic style: "A typical chess game of a hundred years ago was like a medieval jousting contest: brutal and direct. Both sides, intent on straightforward attack against the enemy king, generally galloped toward each other with lances bent.... Manly pride played an important role in this philosophy.... When a player attacked, he attacked the king; he would no sooner pick up a loose pawn than he would joust with a child."[83] Following the success of Anderssen and subsequently Paul Morphy (1837–1884), the preferred style of chess for most of the nineteenth century was filled with tactical assaults without explicit consideration of pieces or position. In time this Romantic tactical style was supplanted by a more "scientific," positional approach.

By the end of the nineteenth century, world champion Wilhelm Steinitz (1836–1900), founder of the "Modern School," led chess into yet another paradigmatic model in which long-term positional thinking dominated the immediacy of raw tactics. Many contemporary chess players revere Steinitz for his focus on fundamental principles of positional play and the "accumulation of small advantages," a form of "scientific" analysis. "Prudence and pragmatism began to supplant bravado.... One was not being a sissy to decline a sacrifice, he declared, if concrete analysis showed that accepting it would be dangerous."[84] Put another way, a sacrifice is not a move that one player makes but a move that must be accepted by his opponent, capturing the piece that was made available.[85]

As the best player and most prolific chess writer of his time, Steinitz had the reputation and the forum to disseminate and popularize his beliefs. Eventually his theories coalesced into a body of systematic knowledge still taught to young players today. Steinitz believed that all chess positions could be objectively evaluated, as each side has advantages as well as weaknesses.[86] Today players often refer to squares as "strong" or "weak" and pieces as "good" or "bad." Equilibrium is the point at which the advantages and weaknesses of each side, based on the positions of their pieces, cancel each other out, and this led to the increased likelihood of draws. Some suggest that the institutional structure of the tournament system penalizing the loss of any one game contributed to this cautious approach.[87] After Steinitz, successful players developed hybrid versions of both positional and tactical play.

In time, a new approach developed that challenged the model of the previous era, now defined as stagnant. This is often referred to as the "Hypermodern" approach, associated with Aron Nimzowitsch and Richard Réti, the former the author of the influential *My System*. The Hypermodern system favored controlling the center squares through active pieces on the edge of the board.[88]

Chess knowledge continues to evolve, as the Soviet chess school, or the New Dynamic Approach, emerged as dominant in the 1940s and 1950s, generating a string of Soviet world champions, such as the electrical engineer Mikhail Botvinnik, extending the scientific, positional approach of Steinitz. The dominant metaphor was that chess was organic. Reuben Fine noted that "whatever happens, flows naturally out of the position."[89] Nothing was assumed; everything was tested. For the past half century, perhaps because of the dominance of computer analysis, we have been in a stage of pragmatic synthesis. Neither Fischer nor Kasparov created a "new" style. Fischer was known for "stunningly simple moves" (interview), designed to counter the complications in which the Soviets delighted. Kasparov claimed, somewhat fancifully, that he and Fischer fit their historical moment: "I fitted the period of revolutions, like Fischer fitted the period of hippies and individualism."[90] The *New Yorker*'s David Remnick saw in the different styles of Anatoly Karpov and Garry Kasparov different moments of Soviet history: "Karpov, the world champion, was an exemplar of the Brezhnev-Andropov-Chernenko "era of stagnation," an obedient member of the *nomenklatura*. As a player, he was a defensive artist, whose style ... was to absorb and smother attacks and then destroy his confounded opposition.... Kasparov represented a new generation. At twenty-one, he was ironic, full of barely disguised disdain for the regime.... His chess style was swift, imaginative, daring—sometimes to the point of recklessness."[91] Perhaps this assessment reflects the seepage of politics and popular culture into theory. Today technique, skill, calculation, and knowledge have become overshadowed by detailed research and preparation and memorization of deep opening repertoires.

Through the development of chess as systematic knowledge, each paradigm is a response to that which came before. Chess knowledge did not develop steadily and cumulatively but advanced in dramatic shifts that were treated as a response to previous orthodoxy, evaluated in light of the models and metaphors of the community. These perspectives oscillated between Philidor's emphasis on cautious, positional play and Anderssen's dramatic, active play: two distinct models, one emphasizing caution and deliberation, the other focusing on risk and contest. Players had to judge how much risk to embrace. A Romantic objects to the banal, the positional player to the eccentric;[92] each treats a chosen style as the ideal.

Style and the Self

Cultural fields have styles that not only characterize historical periods but define participants. Reminiscing, Richard Nixon's secretary of state Henry Kissinger revealed that Anatoly Dobrynin, the Soviet ambassador to Washington, once challenged him to a friendly game of chess. Kissinger refused. As he reported, "The KGB doubtless thought that they could deduce from my play the characteristics of my personality. The collection of games of a chess player is a powerful indicator of his character."[93] Perhaps the KGB, like American citizens, understood Kissinger's personality from his academic writings, his press interviews, or the bombing of Cambodia, but Kissinger felt that playing chess might provide rich insights. As far back as 1862 a commentator asserted, "The chess-board is a mirror in which the broad features and no less the minuter traits, that make up individual character, are distinctly and visibly shown."[94] The psychiatrist Karl Menninger concurred: "All authorities agree that chess is a miniature war in which the aggressive patterns characteristic of different personalities are clearly discernible in the nature or style of play adopted. As every chess player knows, there are strong attackers, the strong defenders, the provocative players, the cautious players, the attack-from-behind players, the so-called classical and romantic styles of play, etc."[95] Within a community of evaluation, style may be judged harshly. Emphasizing the aesthetic components of chess, some styles are judged "ugly" and others in this masculine world are considered "girly."[96] Some criticism is generational, as when one rising star, judged too cautious, is said to play "like an old man."[97]

The force of style is linked to the identity of community members. This approach links self and style, as personality and temperament—shaped by childhood experience—are evident in action.[98] The problem, as Boris explained, is that "from a psychological point, it can be seen from two sides. One of them is [that style is] compensation of one's character, and the other is that it is the reflection of one's character.... People can be calm in real life and sometimes do crazy things on the board.... [Mikhail Tal] in his real life he never cared about what is going to happen tomorrow and on the board it was the same" (interview). If one is timid in life, one might be timid on the board or aggressive. The theory can explain anything. Such explanations do little to recognize that stylistic choices are part of socialization and situation. One player, a talented African, was admired for a distinctive approach. A friend remarks: "He plays a little crazy, a little unstable.... It is jungle style. Very chaotic and original" (field notes). A chaotic (unpredictable) style attempts to gain advantage from "civilized" lines as quickly as possible, evoking stereotypes about the "Dark Continent." The chess grandmaster Peter Leko determined to change his style because of criticism from his peers: "I used to play cautiously. Now I no longer believe that I should play quietly.... Now I have started to play much more aggressively.... Korchnoi had said in an interview that I play like a coward. I found this a bit harsh, but I also knew that it was the truth."[99]

Players often assert a personal style and refer to some historical role model, a form of hero worship.[100] One player feels that he plays like the nineteenth-century champion Paul Morphy and is flattered when this is recognized by others. Others name Tal, Fischer, or Kasparov as their models. Style connects with collective memory in producing a sticky culture that develops identity and commitment.

Writing Chess

As noted above, the literature on chess is massive. Instruction manuals, biographies, histories, accounts of tournaments, and novels fill bookshelves. Currently blogs,[101] discussion forums, Facebook pages, and websites permit the establishment of a community of discourse and argument. Words overwhelm.

Perhaps the line between playing and writing should not be drawn too firmly. In tournaments, each player is required to record his moves. One comes to the board with a clock, pieces, and a pad and pencil. Only a few exceptions exist. With less than five minutes on either clock the requirement to record moves is waived. The sponsoring organization owns the score sheets, which it can save or sell to collectors.[102]

Significantly, the moves are all that players are supposed to write during a game. The rules state, "The use of notes made during the game as an aid to memory is forbidden, aside from the actual recording of the moves, draw offers and clock times, and the header information normally found on a scoresheet."[103] One can eat an apple, but writing a poem could be punished. Reading is taken even more seriously, especially if the material has bearing on the game. The game is inscribed in ritualized ways, and additional information must be in one's own memory, not from a written text. Even coaches are limited in what they can communicate and are typically allowed only to answer a set of predetermined questions, such as whether a player should accept a draw based on the team's need. As a result, chess is organized differently from activities such as baseball, where it is assumed that coaches will give advice. Treating chess as a "mind game" means that the mind must be segregated from other minds. The availability of notes in over-the-board chess would eliminate players' mental isolation.

Fischer versus Fine, 1963

The written format of a chess match creates a script that permits a full reenactment. As Bruno Latour and Steve Woolgar emphasize, knowledge structures come about through their written form: the creation of science emerges from marks on paper.[104] Memory demands inscription in the form of both notation and annotation, creating a relationship between "human memory and written memory," the argument of Thierry Wendling.[105] The narrative of the game—sequential moves—is crucial. It constitutes a bridge between knowledge as used by players in a moment of action and knowledge as used by readers in a moment of contemplation, connecting past and present through words and symbols.

As a result I can replay an informal "skittles" game between Bobby Fischer and Reuben Fine, the latter retired from competitive chess since 1945, played in Fine's Manhattan apartment in 1963. The game was included by Bobby Fischer in his *My Sixty Memorable Games*.[106] As in most of these games, Fischer is victorious, in this case winning in seventeen moves. To replay the game one needs the moves, available in Fischer's book and on chess databases.[107] The database chessgames .com includes five games between Fischer and Fine, all informal, with Fischer winning four.[108] Fine has 389 games in this database, 66.9 percent of which he won. As the "game of the day" of June 13, 2009, on chessgame.com, Fisher and Fine's 1963 game was given the punning title "A Fine Line." The website gives the names of the players (white first), location, year, and opening (and the tournament if applicable). The *Encyclopedia of Chess Openings* code (C52 for this game is provided for further reference. We also learn the outcome (1–0), meaning that white won. Then the moves. Fischer moves e4 (white king pawn moves two squares), and Fine responds e5 (black king pawn moves two). I discuss notation subsequently, but notation is designed to be unambiguous. As this is an interactive database, with a click of my mouse I can watch the game unfold on my screen. I watch move by move as Fischer creates a stranglehold. Because this was the game of the day, because it was in Fischer's collection of games, and because it was one of the few games between two men who some say are the two finest American players of the twentieth century, the game has received more than two hundred comments. A large community is interested in this informal game. I return to the game shortly.

The Global Literature of Annotations

One of the central features of the chess community, found in numerous books and in all chess magazines, is the annotations of games. Setting aside works aimed at novices or a wider public, annotations are the literature of the chess community. The September 2010 issue of the United States Chess Federation's *Chess Life* contains fifteen annotated games. *New Yorker* writer and Harvard English professor Louis Menand is correct when he writes:

> Chess is not friendly to prose. Chess is, after all, a sport, but there is almost no way to convey what's exciting about it to people who are not themselves deep students of the game. "Then, on move 21, came Black's crusher: a6!"—totally opaque, as are references to the Najdorf Variation of the Sicilian Defense, the Giuoco Piano, and the Queen's Gambit Declined. You can ignore the technical stuff and write about powerful queenside attacks, hammering rook assaults, intense positional struggle, and so on; but the truth is that the game *is* the technical stuff.[109]

The examination of past games is a special form of literary analysis that depends on an appreciative audience that uses imagination to see the scene behind the words, no less than literary erotica or science fiction. Action is never friendly to prose unless and until readers have the desire and cultural experience to make it so.[110]

In annotated games either one of the players (typically the winner) or some other knowledgeable person provides commentary, assessing moves deemed decisive, brilliant, or misguided. If the annotator is the winner, the text is, implicitly, self-glorification, a less writerly form of the memoir. If the loser annotates, he accounts for failure. Fischer in *My Sixty Memorable Games* describes three defeats. As good as Fischer was, he could have filled his book with his losses, but he would have lost his audience.

Analyses vary widely, some being quite extensive and focused on explanatory narrative, some addressing the scene of play, and others focusing on alternative possibilities. Some are filled with evaluative adjectives, whereas others have only a few guiding words. Some refer to black and white, whereas others refer to players by name. In the annotations, sometimes the pieces[111] are referred to by letter (K for king, Q for queen, B for bishop, N for knight, R for rook, pawns indicated by the absence of a letter) and by the square to which the piece moves and whether it takes an opposing piece (x) or places the opposing king in check (+).The French use *roi* (R) and *dame* (D), and Russians use the Cyrillic alphabet. Castling is 0–0 or 0–0–0, depending on whether the king moves to the kingside or the queenside. Checkmate is indicated by "#." Books and magazines that wish to attract an international audience use pictograms of the pieces instead of letters.

The forms of notating moves have their own social psychology. The key feature of a formal linguistic system, especially that of a limited one like chess, is that the moves are unambiguous.[112] Once the linguistic rules are understood, communication becomes transnational, understood outside of more elaborated language systems.[113] The lack of ambiguity of notation is one reason that chess is so useful for studying and developing artificial intelligence. Several systems are possible, but the two that are most widely used are "descriptive notation" and "algebraic notation."[114] The difference is perspective. Descriptive notation, the older of the two, operates from a dual perspective: the player and his opponent can make the same move: P-K4 (say), meaning that each player moved his king's pawn ahead two squares. Readers of the notation would understand that they had to view white and black's notations from *each one's* perspective. Algebraic notation, introduced in the eighteenth century, assumes white's perspective. So the move that is designated P-K4 in descriptive notation is e4 for white and e5 for black in algebraic notation. Files (columns) in algebraic notation go from a to h (the king's file is e, based on white's view), and rows go from 1 to 8 (based on white's view). America was late in adopting algebraic notation, now the standard. The first use of algebraic notation in *Chess Life* was in 1969. One American chess coach insists that his best students learn descriptive notation to read older chess books.

At inflection points a diagram of the board is presented. This is not done for the early moves, but when the game becomes complex. For the Fischer-Fine game, four diagrams are presented (after moves 7, 9, 13, and 17). Longer games have more diagrams.

Fischer's book contains his annotation of this game. Fischer as an annotator is not literary, but he does present alternative moves that others could have followed. After Fine's move 4 (Fine's bishop takes

FINE

Position after 7 0-0

FISCHER

FINE

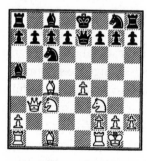

Position after 9 ♘xc3

FISCHER

FINE

Position after 13...♕g5

FISCHER

FINE

Position after 17 ♕g3!

FISCHER

Fischer's queen's knight pawn [Bxb4]) Fischer remarks "Safer is 4 ...
Bb6 [the dots mean that it is a move for black]. But that is hardly the
way to refute the gambit."[115] Later Fischer refers to black's hypothetical move Bb6 (bishop to the sixth square on the b-file), remarking that
this is "the famous Lasker's Defense, which put the Evans out of com-
mission last century."[116] Given that Fischer played the Evans gambit,
he implicitly claims that he has created it anew. The rest of the twelve
comments present alternative lines of play and his evaluations with
references to other formations (Waller's Attack) or players (Tchigo-
rin). After move 14, Fischer presents three different lines of play. Given
that Fine resigned, Fischer shows how he would have checkmated
Fine. This review requires a commitment to chess play and to history.
Fischer's annotations are revered because of his deep insight, but they
require subcultural knowledge. Top players can visualize the board, so
they "see" these alternative futures without a board in place. They are
helped in this by communal concepts. The idea of a "good pawn" or
"bad bishop" or "counter-play" or "minority attack" has meaning that
links metaphor, chess theory, and the moves themselves.

These accounts are dry, but they embody the chessic version of
emotion. Even though annotations are ritualized, based on the presentation of alternative lines of play, they incorporate style. One can
note Fischer's youthful aggressiveness. *My 60 Memorable Games* was
published in 1969 when Fischer was twenty-six. Fischer refers to one
of his moves as "the crusher" and an opponent's move as "horrible."
While this involves Fischer-speak, it juices up the analysis. In some
games Fischer (or other annotators) places evaluative markers. In his
annotation of a game against Samuel Reshevsky in the United States
Championship (1962–1963), Fischer (as white) remarks, "Reshevsky
steers for an inferior ending" and "Black's game is, at best, barely ten-

able."[117] In their dry way, these comments capture the excitement of the game as it unfolds. Emotion is also revealed through the power of punctuation. Commentators indicate good, surprising, or brilliant moves by means of exclamation points (! or !!). Questionable or bad moves are, politely, indicated by question marks (? or ??). The symbols !? and ?! stand for interesting move and dubious move, revealing an ambiguity in interpretation and uncertain emotion.

Annotation and Community

When I asked friends which annotation they most respect, I was surprised at the consensus. Many serious players named David Bronstein's *Zurich International Chess Tournament, 1953*. The account of the tournament is canonical, at least among upper-level players, and receives enthusiastic responses on Amazon.com, where thirty-four of forty-three reviewers give it five stars ("It is universally considered one of the classics in chess literature," notes one commenter; "perhaps the greatest tournament book ever written," writes another). To have read Bronstein's volume is to connect one's identity to chess culture. One Amazon reviewer writes, "The whisperings of my fellow players at the club, as if to hide a secret, first clued me in to this book.... After reading and playing through the first game, I knew ... why my fellow players did not want anyone else to find it. It's a jewel.... Find it, read it and try to keep it from your rivals." Another writes, emphasizing chess history, that Bronstein provides "a look into the minds and thoughts of some of the best players of that era."

Zurich 1953 was one of the most influential round-robin tournaments of the twentieth century. One reviewer considers it "the best tournament of all time." Fifteen of the world's top players competed (Reuben Fine had retired from active competition a few years earlier). Thirty rounds were played. Each competitor played all others once as white, once as black (with two byes). The winner, Vasily Smyslov, later became world champion. Bronstein, a world-class Ukrainian player, tied for second with two other players. Nine of the fifteen players were from the Soviet Union, and two others hailed from Eastern Bloc nations. Of the 210 games, 118 (56.2 percent) were draws, and some allege that the Soviets fixed the outcomes of crucial games.[118] Whatever the politics, within chess literature Bronstein's book is part of the canon. The work has plot and character, context and denouement.

Bronstein's annotations are impressive for detail and narrative quality. They historicize and commemorate the tournament. Bronstein does not merely provide a list of possible moves but explains how he understood the games in light of the collective wisdom of his community. I focus on the best-known game of the tournament, Paul Keres (USSR, Estonia) versus Samuel (Sammy) Reshevsky (USA) in round eleven.[119] Reshevsky as black plays the Nimzo-Indian defense against Keres's opening of d4 (the Queen's pawn moving two squares, auguring a closed game). This is a well-studied opening defense by black, using the classic Indian opening as reconceived by Aron Nimzowitsch, a leader of the Hypermodern movement in chess—thus the enchantingly esoteric name Nimzo-Indian (E40, E41 in the *Encyclopedia of Chess Openings*). The significance of the game—what the chess community calls its brilliancy—is that dominance oscillates. In the second edition of Bronstein's book, he adds the perspectives (and criticism) of others ("V. Turchuk has rightly upbraided me for uncritically accepting this analysis"), making clear that the text is part of a conversation among colleagues.

Even in translation, Bronstein is delightfully chatty, even witty. He refers to one of Reshevsky's moves as "Fierce!" and notes that Keres "concocted an astounding combination." Of a difficult position of Reshevsky, Bronstein writes, "In such situations, many players are ready to throw up their hands and play the first move that comes to mind; but Reshevsky does not despair." Later: "Under severe time pressure, with his emotions in a turmoil from the whole preceding phase of the struggle, Keres fails to find the correct maneuver."[120] Players' emotions are depicted in these pages.

Bronstein links his writing to his community. The text is implicitly dialogic. He asserts that chess knowledge is fundamentally social, not personal:

> If the reader should ask which game I liked best of all in this tournament, I would have to pass over my own two encounters with onetime American *wunderkind* Samuel Reshevsky in favor of one of the tournament's most note-worthy games from the viewpoint of its depth of conception, beauty and complexity. This game has been reproduced in chess journals in every language, and has been subjected to dissection by dozens of masters, almost all of the grandmasters, and even [world champion] Botvinnik himself—and yet

one cannot say with absolute certainty that these analyses represent the final answer. The reader will have the opportunity to examine for himself, and perhaps to add his own contribution to the collective effort of all the world's chessplayers.[121]

Many subcultural communities establish forms of literary inscription, even if abbreviated.[122] The texts build upon shared knowledge. But Bronstein goes further by demonstrating the presence of his colleagues in treating his analysis as a text to be critiqued, perhaps even referencing a Talmudic tradition. By noting the popularity of the game, he situates it as central to his public. He invokes the community of grandmasters, including world champion Mikhail Botvinnik. Finally he brings in the reader as a contributor to shared knowledge. He advises the reader how to approach texts including his: "And now the reader who would like to poke about with us through the byways of these combinations should follow the analysis, as Nimzowitsch once recommended, on two chessboards: one to make the moves of the game, and the other to examine the variations."[123] One board is for the knowable past, the other for the imagined future.

But this is not all. Bronstein brings in alternative lines of play and situates them within chess knowledge. He refers to the analysis of others, including such stars as Botvinnik, Najdorf, Euwe, and Reshevsky himself, but also the insight of R. G. Ashurov, a class-A player (well below the level of grandmaster) from Baku, Azerbaijan. Bronstein creates a mosaic of insight.

Despite its importance, the Keres-Reshevsky game lacked a winner. In 1953 games were often adjourned, and Keres sealed his forty-first move (so he could not change it and Reshevsky would not know what it is). The players retire for the evening to study the position. Bronstein reports: "Both players analyzed all night and the next day as well.... Both Keres and Reshevsky knew there was no need to play off the adjourned position beyond the opening of the sealed move; if they had known better, then at least one would not have agreed to the DRAW without playing on."[124] The game was a draw, despite being the most revered contest at the Zurich tournament, indicating that within the chess community, draws can be thrilling. It wasn't that it didn't have an outcome; it did, but that outcome reminds us that victory and defeat are not the only options. The salience of the game is such that it is listed as among the one hundred best games of the twentieth century by several chess historians and described as "miraculous," "stunning," and "brilliant." Even sixty years later players discuss the game and lines that might have led to victory.[125] Bronstein's text focused the attention of subsequent generations on the game's significance.

Shared Pasts and Sticky Culture

To understand the creation of allegiance, we must recognize that shared culture embeds people within communities. This constitutes a *sticky culture*, building affiliation. Within a cultural field one finds numerous publics with local histories, operating independently and overlapping. In this, the domain of chess, with its deep commitments, is exemplary. Chess is a bounded community with knowledge that participants can access with effort. While chess has a more self-conscious past than many fields of activity, similar to other complex communities chess publics depend on embracing tradition. As the chess public looks forward, it relentlessly gazes back. Players are not engaged in a merely slight activity but an activity that has lasting meaning and defines the self.

Social worlds and their memory entrepreneurs build pasts through heroes, events, and canonized strategies. The presence of consecrated heroes whose skills define the possibility of genius, along with the willingness of interested parties to organize commemoration, supports the claim that the activity matters. Beyond heroes, eventful moments and shared strategies build collective memory.[126] While the recording and replaying of games make chess distinctive among voluntary cultures, other cultural fields have remembered moments as well. Baseball fans treasure great games and magnificent plays, and, while not replayed, they are commemorated in shrines. Fantasy or rotisserie baseball has some of the same features of chess, in that actual games bolster the interest of audiences. Amateurs in sports, in science, and in the arts may connect themselves with professionals, basking in reflected glory.[127]

Finally, chess, like other commitments, has a subcultural literature. One not only plays chess but also reads and writes chess. From score sheets to annotations, games are narratives with philosophies, styles, and morals. While the library of chess is extensive and diverse, annotations are central to community. Perhaps the literary quality of these productions is thin, but for players who can take on the role of others, they are a rich basis for imagination. These texts are social by suggesting common emotional reactions and by making evaluation collective. The doing of chess is part of the sociality of the game, but so is chess literacy.

The history of any voluntary social world and the recognition of this history bind people and permit them to think of themselves as a public, not merely as casual bystanders. To have a history is to belong to a community. This emphasizes the connection between culture and the interaction order of which it is part. History is never unmoored but belongs to a sticky world, revealed in the interest of its publics.

In the next chapter I turn from the history and culture of chess to the creation and the use of community, exploring how the realms of chess provide inviting and supportive spaces for those who demonstrate commitment to the activity. The chessworld is a place-based social scene.

5

THE WORLDS OF CHESS

*We must make sure that Chess will not be like a dead
language, very interesting, but for a very small group.*

SYTZE FABER

Voluntary communities depend on thought, action, time, and history.
However, *social worlds* also depend on common places, an ideology
of openness, and a supportive infrastructure: sites where friends, acquaintances, and rivals meet. Members of a public often find that they
are a world apart, a world essential. Boundaries and shared outcomes
give meaning to pursuits. This recognition that leisure worlds can be
potent—and tolerant—communities stands at the heart of my argument that chess is a social world. Chess creates a space where people
can belong, and this belonging strengthens the community but also
supports the player. As an accepting world, chess constitutes what I
term a "soft community."

As a game, chess requires only two persons indifferently linked to
the activity, perhaps with an uncertain understanding of the rules.
However, as a subculture, chess demands more. The same might be
said of golf, which requires a stick and a hole in the ground. Like that
of chess, golf subculture requires an infrastructure, both cultural and
physical. Golf is society as well as exercise. In chapter 7, I discuss organizations that support competitive chess, but here I examine commitment, community, and subculture, arguing that chess as a scene
involves the intersection of multiple fields of practice, creating a welcoming presence.

Chess Hunger

When one embraces the identity of chess player, the activity becomes
a resource for self-definition.[1] I have skied twice in my life, but never

have I considered myself a skier. I played Candyland as a tyke and as a dad but never was my self wrapped in Candyland culture.

A commitment suggests that one will feel an ongoing connection with an activity and its participants. Identities are hierarchical, and those at the top produce loyalty and public show. One prioritizes that identity and its associated public and defends that involvement in moments of conflict, ceremony, or choice. People can be passionate in their interests—such as bridge, caving, or opera, passions that require study, initiation, and affiliation.[2] For the French sociologist Pierre Bourdieu, this constitutes *illusio*, an investment in a social world that is of *interest* for participants.[3] The scene becomes a transcendent universe. Participants invest time, self, emotion, and concern.[4] The chess player who persuades his wife that he must attend the club every Thursday reveals his priorities. So does the person who pays dues to the United States Chess Federation, joins a high school team, takes lessons from a master, or spends a weekend at a tournament. While some speak of this involvement as an addiction, a virus, or a drug,[5] *investment* is a better term, recognizing that the activity has outcomes and can oscillate in degree. For voluntary activities commitment is rarely all or nothing. Rather, commitment is punctuated, encouraged in contexts with social support. Following Lewis Coser's discussion of religious cults, Puddephatt refers to chess as a "greedy institution."[6] This means that the social organization of chess fosters participation and discourages distance. This is a world in which the bitter rivals Viktor Korchnoi and Anatoly Karpov can each write an autobiography titled *Chess Is My Life*. If one desires to improve, one must devote time to places in which the activity is found. One must enjoy the action, but one must also enjoy the social relations in which the activity is embedded. Indeed, a prime motivator of socialization to chess is the family, often a father-son relationship in which part of the pleasure is parental pride and juvenile admiration.

Bobby Fischer reveals the dominion of commitment. He famously remarked, "Chess is life," about as a strong a statement of commitment as one can imagine (more than "chess is *my* life"). Perhaps the competitor who was most distant from the opinions of others, Fischer became deeply engaged in chess only when at age eight he began to attend the Brooklyn Chess Club, the Hawthorne Chess Club, and the Manhattan Chess Club, taking instruction from Carmine Nigro and John Collins.[7] Tournament culture provided the glue necessary for

Fischer's passionate involvement, and he was excited when he first met Reuben Fine, because of Fine's influential chess manuals.[8] Without these shared spaces and social relations, Fischer might never have committed to chess. Eventually his interest and his success in these spaces proved reinforcing. But what would Fischer's—or anyone's—affiliation be without public spaces and warm relations? It was not simply the pleasure of winning a game, but rather winning within a community that mattered. As a boy Fischer was uncertain about playing in tournaments; it took several years before it could be said that he had a "chess career." A *career* assumes an ongoing commitment to an activity. Fischer once claimed, "I've thought of giving it up off and on, but I always considered: what else could I do?"[9] After he won the world championship, Fischer essentially resigned the title and only played one more public match in his remaining thirty-six years, remaining on the shadowy edges of the scene. His dedication to a public chessworld had vanished.

Commitment operates through an ongoing process, as people's time commitments and motivation change. My friend Boris, now a prominent chess professional, emphasized that his involvement resulted from "step-wise decisions." At several life stages he had to decide how much attention to give chess. Sometimes he was less involved, but he made choices that directed him to a life as a chess player during school and after he received a technical degree. As the case of Boris reveals, we adjust our desires as we are given alternatives.[10]

Addictive Leisure

Sometimes we can become so tied to an activity that our involvement is judged excessive. We become, in effect, "chess bums." In the nineteenth century such a pathological preoccupation was termed "monomania," an early example of the medicalization of morality. One man's monomania is another's devotion. Addiction has become the preferred metaphor in the last few decades, as when one chess teacher jokes about his strategy for building his team, "Like drugs, I get them addicted to chess" (field notes). Said another coach, "I'm a chess junkie." A third, a talented adolescent girl, linked her commitment to her identity: "Sometimes I get to the point where I want to quit, because I'm so frustrated. But I can't. It's part of who I am. I'm addicted!"[11]

For centuries chess has been seen as being all-encompassing, so much so that the Roman Catholic Church once banned priests from playing. King James I of England remarked in *Basilikon Doron* (1616): "As for the Chesse, I think it ouer fond, because it is ouer-wise and Philosophicke a folly: for where all such light playes are ordained to free mens heades for a time, from the fashious thoughts on their affairs; it by the contrarie filleth and troubleth mens heades with as many fashious toyes of the play, as before it was filled with thoughts on his affairs."[12] Albert Einstein agreed: "Chess holds its master in its own bonds, shackling the mind and brain so that the inner freedom of the very strongest must suffer."[13] The surrealist Marcel Duchamp found his interest in art and romance waning because of his leisure passion. On his honeymoon he ignored his wife, Lydie. After a week his enraged bride glued his pieces to the board.[14] An online discussant worried about the young Norwegian star Magnus Carlsen: "Magnus is going to spend his whole life living-sleeping chess . . . and when he is 60 he may regret it."[15] One strong player recognized the obsessive quality of chess in light of communal belonging: "Chess is its own world, and if you're decent at it, it's sort of its own [self-]contained world. The whole of the outside world disappears" (interview by Antony Puddephatt).

A Centripetal Life

The gravitational pull toward full engagement is set against centripetal forces that push away. Building a stable community of engaged actors is difficult in any domain, particularly when rewards are small or uncertain. The leading American player Gata Kamsky left his intense chess involvement[16] for seven years, attending medical school and receiving a law degree. When he returned, it took several years to regain his dominance. Every teacher realizes that no matter how committed the ardor of most students, even the best will cool.[17]

This pull was evident at Lakeside High School. Although several players were talented and the school traditionally maintained a very strong team, none of the players wished to continue serious chess once they graduated from high school. On one occasion half of the first-string team skipped a tournament, something unthinkable in football. Others left in the middle of the tournament, having priorities that trumped chess. Devotion to hockey, baseball, band, or video games took priority. One coach regretted the number of players "addicted" to World of Warcraft, which he insisted provides no life skills and "leaves you with nothing." There is competition in the market of voluntary activities: poker, dating, clubbing, or Ultimate Frisbee.

On occasion some high school teams lacked sufficient players for their matches and had to forfeit. Perhaps chess was seen as bolstering college applications, but mostly students played because they enjoyed the game, the instructors, and their teammates. One coach of a mediocre team sarcastically remarked about the presence of all of his players at an out-of-town tournament, "Some are here for a vacation, some for their college applications, and some to play chess" (field notes). As another coach explained, "My biggest problem is in finding kids who are serious. They don't play the tournaments. You wonder whether some kids are there because it is convenient daycare. They know how to play chess, but they are not *into chess*. They need a group. We used to have clusters of kids. There was camaraderie. The participation was minimal without it" (interview). Although students enjoy playing, they don't study, and, as chess is a voluntary extracurricular activity, the coach can do little. Being *into chess* means engaging with a chess community, making the scene a priority.

Intense chess commitment involves a lifestyle or even a life. Garry Kasparov explained, "The loss of my childhood was the price of becoming the youngest world champion in history. When you have to fight every day from a young age, your soul could become contaminated."[18] For Rafael Vaganian the bargain was not worth it. Not wishing to give up a life "filled with friends, long sessions at the dinner table often lasting far into the night, dates and parties, cards and dominoes ... he was too fond of all the joys of life ... to trade them all in for immortality in the form of his photograph hung up for posterity amongst the apostles on the chess club wall."[19] The son of a friend who ranked in the top ten in his age cohort quit chess for much the same reason (interview), following Boris Spassky, who admitted that after a time he preferred young women, tennis, and the Riviera more than he enjoyed studying. Without passion the high points of human creativity would be lost, but with this passion the broad satisfactions of a life are traded for narrow ones.

Ways In

A book is waiting to be written on how chess players are made, not born. This is not that book, but I address this topic to argue that a leisure pursuit requires social pathways, even if in time it becomes less leisurely. In chess the preferred story is often a "family romance"—an intimate and powerful bond between father and son (or occasionally daughter). This is the story that Freudians treasure. Many informants shared how their fathers taught them chess; in time they challenged the father's dominance.[20] This certainly was true for my son. When he had turned six, I felt that he was ready to be inducted into the world of chess. He and I had a chess relationship until he was nine. When a son surpasses the father, it is a moment of proud pain.[21] A prominent chess player—a woman—had a similar story: "It started out as kind of a coincidence. I found a chess set, and I got interested. My father was a chess fan. He liked chess, but he had nobody to play with, so he was very pleased when I showed interest to get involved in the game. He showed me the first moves and quite a bit beyond. I was very success-ful very early, so by the time I knew my mind, I knew I wanted to play chess" (interview).

The most famous story of the magical acquisition of chess is that of José Raúl Capablanca, one of the gifted masters of the twentieth century. There are many versions, but I select Capablanca's own tale, slightly less literary than those who have retold it:

> I was not yet five years old when by accident I came into my father's private office and found him playing with another gentleman. I had never seen a game of chess before; the pieces interested me, and I went the next day to see them play again. The third day, as I looked on, my father, a very poor beginner, moved a Knight from a white square to another white square. His opponent, apparently, not a bet-ter player, did not notice it. My father won, and I proceeded to call him a cheat and to laugh. After a little wrangle, during which I was nearly put out of the room, I showed my father what he had done. He asked me how and what I knew about chess? I answered that I could beat him; he said that was impossible, considering that I could not even set the pieces correctly. . . . I won. That was my beginning.[22]

This is an unusual tale in that Capablanca learns on his own, although he also bests his father. This hero narrative captures the belief that chess ability comes naturally—a magic gift[23] but within the circle of the family. The story emphasizes a belief in the chess prodigy (com-parable to the mathematics or music prodigy). Similar stories are

told of the young Garry Kasparov and Anatoly Karpov, who learned
the rules by osmosis from their fathers without ever having been for-
mally taught.[24] Josh Waitzkin, the central figure of *Searching for Bobby
Fischer*, tells a similar story, although not involving his actual father but
"an old man with a grey beard" playing in Washington Square Park.
Even though Josh had not played chess but had only watched schoolmates, he felt that he could do it. As Waitzkin played, he explained,
"I remembered the strange sensation of discovering a lost memory.
As we moved the pieces, I felt like I had done this before. There was a
harmony to the game, like a good song."[25] Waitzkin, at six, had found
his métier. Perhaps his story is romantic, but its romance makes sense.
The impulse is revealed in competition as the prodigy embraces the
sociality of the chessworld. Brilliance is not sufficient; social relations
are necessary for a prodigy to become heroic. Even if talents are more
divine than human, they are revealed through social relations.

Group participation cements identity. A study of girls' chess involvement demonstrates the importance of friends in creating a cli-
mate for participation. As one girl commented, "Most of my friends
were in it, so I wanted to be with them."[26] The community can be
local and limited or broad and deep. One fine New York player emphasized the importance of the community in high school: "The single
most important social group for me was the chessworld. I would go
[to clubs] every Friday night" (interview). The importance of community is evidenced by the huge success of New York schools at the 2011
Scholastic Championships. The three top-ranking high schools were
all New York public schools; at the elementary and junior high school
tournaments, New York schools won most of the sections.[27] Perhaps,
as Arpad Elo suggested, New York City is the center of American
chess because of its "cultural dynamism" and sophistication,[28] but a
more direct connection may be in the fact that New York players have
many sites of chess action, the result of a demand that creates structures for chess education and competition and draws talented players.[29] The fact that New York is the home of Jewish-American culture
and its appeal to Russian immigrants makes the chess culture stronger.
As a result of the attraction of New York chess venues, in contrast to
many American cities, the streets of New York are filled with under-
employed grandmasters.[30] Both the population and the chess culture
draw top players. Although the subculture grew from the cultural or
demographic call of the city, it also developed an intense network.

While he was a young child Bobby Fischer's mother traveled through the American West, spending time in the small town of Mobile, Arizona, a dot in the desert southwest of Phoenix with a population in the hundreds. Had Regina Fischer settled in Mobile, the possibility of Bobby Fischer's chess celebrity would have been remote, even had his sister found a chess set to purchase as she did in Brooklyn. Fischer needed the infrastructure that New York provided. Frank Brady, Fischer's biographer, noted that about 80 percent of the leading American chess masters are New Yorkers by birth or residence, adding, "It's difficult ... to imagine [Fischer] blazing the rocket trail he has against any but these particular skies."[31] The Manhattan Chess Club, Fischer's preferred setting, has since closed, but the Marshall Chess Club remains, as do other venues for children and adults. Despite increased regional diversity, New York chess is still central. Hikaru Nakamura, America's highest-rated grandmaster, grew up in New York, even though as an adult he lives in Saint Louis. If one wishes to raise a chess champion, New York remains the place to be, not because of the skies, but because of the stars.[32]

If a player, especially a child, does well in early matches, adults may provide encouragement, including offers of coaching. A group of active friends may bolster one's willingness to study, crucial in producing a chess master. Involvement begins in a personal relationship, extends to a group, and becomes further established in treating chess as part of a public self.

Community and Culture

Selves are embedded in community, a group of others who share a culture. Communities can be of various sizes from microscopic to extensive. We find communities of climbers, of cavers, of car collectors that in their thoughts, reading, online participation, and chance meetings share allegiance. These interest groups build a subculture, sharing a commitment to style.[33] A subculture is a network of groups. Within the subculture participants share a focus, and when this interest is salient, they realize that they belong together. As described by anthropologist Thierry Wendling, members share a view of the world.[34]

As a social world, chess is accepting and accommodating. It is a *soft community* in which boundaries incorporate rather than exclude. I return to the concept of soft community in discussing communal deviance, but here I note the push for inclusion. Gossip circuits exist in tight networks, such as at the higher end of chess. Inquiring minds wish to know who is sleeping with whom, who drinks too much, and who is in debt. As cohort replacement occurs, old stories die, and once-influential players are neglected. One tournament organizer explained wistfully, "We are at the edge of forgetting." Communities always are.

Divisions reveal splits within the subculture: sub-subcultures, as it were. The awareness of major tournaments (Tata Steel, Linares, London, the United States Chess Championship) and chess magazines (such as *New in Chess* and *Šahovski Informator*, a high-level Serbian publication) create an elite, distinguished from more casual players who are not so knowledgeable, illuminating internal boundaries.[35] Because of the deep knowledge necessary for elite tournament play, immersion in chess culture is tied to placement in a hierarchy. What is crucial is not ability per se but a devotion that correlates with ability. Dedication results from the satisfactions of sociability. Like most action domains, chess subcultures are filled with identity markers: T-shirts ("Do you want a piece of me," "I'm your worst knightmare," or "Your next move may be your last"), orthodontic braces (with tiny chess pieces decorating the wires), or key chains. Nonmaterial markers include insider jargon and slang—the ability to "talk chess" reveals a hierarchy within the community. One coach explained that "a culture emerges when they learn the language" (field notes). Yet divisions arise as to fluency and "dialect." While a chess subculture exists—a play "metaculture"[36] that transcends local scenes—within that culture there are divisions of age, skill, and locale.

Friends and Play

Over time those at various levels of ability and involvement become acquainted. Friendships and some enmities arise. In examining flow Mihaly Csikszentmihalyi finds that emotional bonds build social integration.[37] Discussing the Chess House in New York's Central Park, C. K. Damrosch points out that some rivalries continue for decades: "'Gary' . . . and I had an epic series in the nineties. Once, as we played a particularly fascinating series of blitz games, the rain began to fall. One by one, players fled for dry ground. Gary instead produced a Ziploc bag and put his battered Chronos inside. We gleefully continued banging the clock, as the raindrops grew in size and intensity.... I look up; water is streaming through Gary's beard, a maniacal grin as he eagerly plots my demise.... Good times."[38] Friendship and rivalry fuse, as became evident when I spent a week with a group of talented international masters at the World Open outside of Philadelphia. These young men enjoyed each other's company, but they also competed fiercely. They spoke of their "crew," in contrast to older players or immigrants from eastern Europe. The affection is real, the gossip is pungent, the shared analysis is sincere, but so is the competition.[39] These ties can continue for decades as committed players ascend the hierarchy. Whenever a cohort characterizes a community, one finds tight links, as age is treated as a moral boundary. Players note, "We grew up together." Network ties are long-standing. Age is not the only basis of friendship, as Kasparov, Kramnik, and Carlsen helped Vishy Anand prepare for one of his world championship matches,[40] at least in part because of their affection for Anand and animosity toward his opponent.

The same is true in scholastic chess. Adolescents and preteens who are most engaged in chess see the same faces. At the top echelon of scholastic chess some parents see the community as constituting an extended family. I noticed that at multiday, elite scholastic tournaments such as the Denker invitational tournament for state high school chess champions, an air of giddy camaraderie is evident.[41] Top adolescent players who compete in such tournaments recognize common interests, have attended the same high-level chess camps, and see each other repeatedly. These teens are like the high schoolers in National Circuit debate who have tight networks that less committed colleagues do not.[42] At lower levels, players tend to stick with their schoolmates, and few links are formed between schools.[43] One strong player at Lakeside High School explained that he was on a first-name basis with only two or three other players on other teams; his less-talented teammates knew even fewer. At tournaments these teens play silently and then review the games with their coach and teammates. Sometimes tournaments provide team rooms that separate schools further. The same thin network exists at the Pan-Am Intercollegiate tournament. With the exception of the stars who participate on adult circuits, players at strong, midlevel schools, such as Northwestern University, do not know others, even, in the case of Northwestern, those from the University of Chicago. A few become temporary acquaintances, but they do not expect that these relationships will last. Events are not planned that mix members of competing teams. Participants on computer websites "know" each other through their handles and participation on discussion boards, but this proves a weak basis for intimacy and social interaction. Close-knit communities can form, creating giddy cohorts, but this is by no means inevitable if the structure of chess does not routinely bring players together.

Beyond friendships, loathing can infect a community. The rivalry between Karpov and Kasparov at times became real dislike. Perhaps the most extreme example is David Bronstein. Bronstein deliberately lost a crucial match to an opponent in order to ensure that Tigran Petrosian, whom he disliked, would not win sole possession of first place at the USSR championship.[44] Social relations can force participants to take sides.

Game Spots

For a social world, one needs *places* of action: truth spots, as sociologist Thomas Gieryn calls them.[45] Someone—an entrepreneur, a club, or a school—must provide resources and space for activities.[46] Successful groups depend on the ability to mobilize resources, a point that Ugo Corte demonstrates in his description of how Greenville, North Carolina, became the center of BMX bike racing.[47] This support produces what Michael Farrell terms a "magnet place" and what others term a "scene."[48]

Places of play can be structured in various ways: closed or open, small or extended. Groups of friends may gather regularly to indulge their passion. Such communities are tiny and by invitation only. Karl Menninger was part of such a group, the Topeka Chess Club, which met in private homes and served participants popcorn and root beer.[49] The political commentator and psychiatrist Charles Krauthammer presides over the Pariah Chess Club from his home on Monday evenings with a dozen Washingtonians: journalists, writers, lawyers, an academic, and a diplomat.[50] Becoming a "Pariah" is by invitation only. These minute associations connect those with similar interests. Because chess is often played by elites, particularly among serious amateurs, it may build social relations and provide networking opportunities.

Open public spaces are the other extreme, attracting anyone who wishes to play. The diversity of participation is both an advantage and a challenge. Washington Square Park in New York's Greenwich Village is a case in point. As anyone can participate, the place attracts those that some might find undesirable. Such participants are euphemistically described as "colorful." These raffish souls are outside of the range of middle-class comfort, engaging in gambling or hustling:[51]

> Bombarded by the hustlers, your every step is measured by someone after your money, for either legal pleasures or illicit ones. On a memorable day, I played blitz at this park in Greenwich Village as the police stacked handcuffed drug dealers like cordwood behind the bushes.[52]

> Gambling $20 on a five minute game is not the only way [players in Washington Square Park] make money. The enterprising ones show up at dawn, fend off junkies to stake out a table, and then charge tourists $3 a game for the privilege of playing them. Many of the hustlers talk incessantly during the game, providing an aggressive, expletive-ridden commentary ("You think you can fuck with my queen?," ...) that is designed to rattle their mark and entertain passersby.[53]

In Chicago a well-known venue for public chess was a small shopping center in Hyde Park, near the University of Chicago campus. Merchants found the activity so disruptive that they removed the concrete chess tables. Neither Borders nor Starbucks was willing to host the games or the players, mostly African American men (field notes). After protests, chess returned to Harper Court.[54]

Between private clubs and public spaces are community clubs. Perhaps the most famous, attracting philosophes, was the Café de la Régence in Paris. The equivalent in London was Slaughter's Coffee House.[55] The café or coffeehouse provided a public sphere that welcomed not only intellectuals debating politics[56] but also chess players, groups with considerable overlap, as the interests of Denis Diderot, Gottfried Wilhelm Leibniz, or Benjamin Franklin attest. Throughout the nineteenth century chess clubs grew in number,[57] perhaps part of the same impulse that gave rise to fraternal organizations.

These places were once common in most large cities, but in the United States the main clubs are now Manhattan's Marshall Chess

Club and San Francisco's Mechanics Institute. The Marshall Chess Club, with its approximately 250 paying members (dues are $325 per year for local members, with high-ranked players charged less, as they are a draw for others) has a special place in the hearts of New Yorkers. The club is filled with photographs and other mementos, including a hallowed table on which Capablanca played. There was once a long rivalry with the older Manhattan Chess Club.[58] The Marshall Club was founded in 1915, and in 1931 it obtained its own building, the home of the great American chess player Frank Marshall. Owning this prime Greenwich Village real estate provides the club with permanence that the Manhattan Club lacked. When I attended in 2006, members spoke reverently of the building. One spoke of it as "a home for chess. I'd like to think of it as the miracle on Tenth Street, and if we take care of it, it will always be here for us." An active member reminisced about visiting at age thirteen, "I thought I was walking into the Oval Office, the Sistine Chapel. I really was scared to death. I was always awed. There is so much history here" (field notes). The club is a shrine, as I realized when I was shown about by proud members. These devotees emphasize an aura of place, made manifest through its institutional stability.

Clubs exist, but as free-standing places they are endangered by the constraining schedules of participants, as well as the current preference for speed chess, at which Internet sites excel. Many no longer need flesh-and-blood engagements that local gatherings provide. The Internet has sucked the life out of the tight-knit gathering.[59] Today most clubs are fragile, dependent on access to a library or community center. Still these places provide a "third place," a home away from home and work in which regulars can meet friends and enjoy that portion of their segmented identity. As one regular phrased it, a club is "a place to be around people. They forget about their lives out there and they walk into that room and become something else" (interview). Or as a famed chess teacher phrased it, "In the old days, the club provided all kinds of services. You'd have friendly play, you'd have the ladder where you'd work your way up to the top. You'd have tournaments on the weekend or one game during the week in the evening. There would be presentations made in the club. Most of your chess activity could revolve around that" (interview). Many clubs also served as ethnic gathering places. In Toronto separate clubs served Poles, Russian Jews, Lithuanians, Macedonians, and Estonians. In the 1980s Chicago was home to the Chicago Chess Center, open every day. This center eventually closed when its organizer died. Strong suburban clubs vanished as well, but the city and suburbs still maintain clubs, although most are open only one evening a week. As one strong Chicago player explained, a club open every day creates community: "It's something where, even if you don't show up every day, somebody would be there. It would be worthwhile showing up. That has an effect on the kind of interactions that go on" (interview). An available space makes community possible.

As the number of over-the-board players dwindles, with more players choosing Internet play, club life diminishes. From 1996 to 2006, the United States Chess Federation lost 900 club affiliates, from 2,232 in 1996, a decline of 40 percent.[60] By 2011, the number of affiliates was a mere 687. In order to survive, a social scene must provide benefits not available elsewhere with less expense or more convenience, a challenge for a club that is a physical gathering point.

Where Everybody Knows Your Name

Clubs are access points to a subculture; they are where friendships flourish. When the process works, the club serves as the agent of socialization, providing initiates with mentors and motivation.[61] However, to ensure that novices are not overwhelmed, recruitment organizations must provide a cozy entry.

Although they are structurally similar, clubs differ in tone and in the style of chess preferred. Some claim that they can tell a player's club from his style. One player speaks of "chess incest," a local idioculture that shapes how one plays:

> There is definitely sort of a club consciousness.... Your style becomes a lot more pronounced, since you're only playing a select group of people. It's like inbreeding.... After a while you do get into ruts and develop bad habits. (interview by Puddephatt)

A Canadian player explicitly distinguishes among club styles:

> If you have a very active chess club like Kitchener, you'll develop a certain style of play, stemming mostly from the stronger players. They will tend to dictate or influence a particular style of play. And it would be slightly different in London [Ontario].... London [has]

a tactical emphasis. The ability to attack, put pressure. Kitchener is more theoretical in terms of the opening, which means the attack doesn't come as readily as with the London players. (interview by Puddephatt)

Through interaction, each club creates a set of local practices.[62]

While many players now focus on Internet play, often they begin in over-the-board chess, in which personal relations spur involvement. As one club organizer informed me:

> We suffer a bit because a lot of people think it's too hot, it's too cold, it's rainy, it's snowing, it's sunny. They decide it's more convenient to stay at home in their underwear.... I think sooner or later—and I think it's changing to some degree—people are missing the human contact. Yes, they can get the game at home, [but] they still want to have a friend in the chess club. For many people who join my chess club, it's about making friends. It's about sitting face-to-face with somebody. It's the whole social act. It's not just a game of chess. (interview)

This is optimism that a sociologist can endorse. Unfortunately, his club has apparently now closed. It is no longer an affiliate of the USCF, and its webpage has not been updated since 2007.

However, this organizer is correct in what established clubs can do. I spent four months observing the Blue Hills Chess Club, located in a Chicago suburb. The club has met in a spacious room at the local community center for over twenty-five years. During my observation approximately twenty players gathered at 7:00 p.m. each Thursday. The first hour is devoted to setting up the room, placing boards on tables, playing informal games, friendly banter, and reviewing past games. Few women attend, but the diversity of the men is impressive, from preteen to elderly, including African Americans, Hispanics, eastern Europeans, and Asians. From 8:00 p.m. until about 11:00 p.m., the club sponsors multiweek tournaments that produce the club "ladder," the ranking of players. Stronger players also participate on two club-sponsored teams in the Chicago Industrial Chess League (a league created in 1957, when workers shared leisure time, representing firms such as Motorola, Illinois Bell, Johnson & Johnson, Western Electric, and Sears, Roebuck). On the Blue Hills teams participants range from beginners to experts (with ratings up to 2200). I felt warmth that was not evident in observing games on the Internet Chess Club or at open tournaments. Some lonely participants clearly desired acceptance, and this soft and accommodating world provided that welcome. A regular shared that he had only one friend (he later added me to that small list), but that the club was meaningful for him because he felt that people cared for him. Small groups, including those devoted to leisure activities, build commitment to civil society.[63] Perhaps cybergroups can have this function, but face-to-face groups permit visual and verbal sharing.

In addition to the Blue Hills Club, I also spent a year with the chess club at Lakeside High School. Lakeside had a strong tradition, arguably the strongest chess program in Illinois over thirty years. While this was not an elite chess training program like that of Brooklyn's Edward R. Murrow High School,[64] it was respected throughout the state. As at many high schools, the team and club overlapped. Students could drop in for after-school chess meetings twice a week. Two teachers served as coaches. Over the year, some thirty students participated, and perhaps fifteen attended at least one tournament. Ten players made up the core of the team. The year I observed, the team was strong but came in tied for seventh at the state tournament, with a record of 5–2. While the group was congenial, the level of commitment was modest, and top players missed important tournaments because of scheduling issues, the need to study, or a lack of motivation.

Over the season, a team culture emerged as players began to feel comfortable together. One of the younger players, a strong freshman, was teased for his cockiness and his spacey attitude. One player's love for donuts was noted, and the player whose game was weakest had to carry the large briefcase with team equipment. I saw little evidence of drugs or alcohol, and few of the players had girlfriends.[65] The team also joked about the Fried Liver opening, which was seen as a special favorite, even if the top players used other openings. The team recalled a crucial match in which the team was penalized because a coach's cell phone rang during a round.

The venues of chess gatherings are no different from other places of community. Our world in all its choice and diversity is filled with leisure events, groupings, and gatherings, and each proclaims that fun and satisfaction are to be had from participating. Those who wish to participate despite a moral or behavioral strangeness, a point discussed in chapter 6, are tolerated as part of the world. Through the structure of a soft, welcoming community, one finds that commitment to action meshes with commitment to others.

The Kids in the Hall

Scenes must expand or die. How can an organization grow? This is a problem for all organizations, but it is particularly acute when activity is out of fashion. American chess after the decline of Bobby Fischer's popularity seemed in dire straits. The hero had left the board. True, some Fischer babies became grandmasters, but the activity was contracting. For chess's survival give credit to soccer moms, so prominent in the mid-1990s, who were less committed to soccer than to the cultivation of their children. The skills that chess taught came to be seen as more useful and less dangerous than physical competition. A chess organizer reported "the migration of the soccer mom." Here was a competitive game—a game of the mind—that might translate into college application fodder. Ann Hulbert speaks of "the domestication of chess: the transformation of an abstruse game allied with innate brilliance (and madness) into an educational tool for training mental skills and attitudes."[66] Despite the absence of definitive evidence, the belief that chess makes you smart is culturally persuasive.[67] Scholastic chess grew rapidly during the 1990s and has continued to expand, just right for baby Kasparovs. As Edward Tenner points out, "When a generation of young people becomes serious about an activity—as black high-school students turned to basketball in the 1950s—a self-reinforcing 'social multiplier' of institutions that recognize and develop talent emerges, raising performance."[68] Tenner suggests that this happened with scholastic chess. In time the movement grew to include inner-city schools, just as it did in high school debate.

The growth of scholastic chess proved a financial windfall for the United States Chess Federation, which used the dues from memberships of third and fourth graders to support adult tournaments. Most of the membership income of the USCF is from children,[69] but the same proportion does not fund scholastic tournaments. Within any domain, resource allocation is sensitive. Should the USCF promote the best American chess or encourage more children to be involved? Some of those most active in scholastic chess became disillusioned with the USCF's lack of support, and for a time the organization eliminated the position of scholastic director. As one man committed to scholastic tournaments explained, the organization has not successfully connected with local schools. Another claimed that if it weren't for the fact that it was the organization's "cash cow," adults would wish that scholastic chess would disappear (field notes). To be sure, those who run the organization would disagree. The organization is torn by different goals. One critic spoke of the desire to increase scholastic members: "This seems like a part of the *conspiracy* by the scholastic committee to get their numbers high.... We keep our numbers high by finding new suckers each year" (field notes). This pungent comment reveals a critical division. Organized chess must confront a fundamental boundary between scholastic chess and adult chess, a conflict that ebbs and flows. What might seem to be an organization of members with a shared interest in a single activity is split over the allocation of its resources.

The argument about the value of chess is persuasive not only to mothers (and to fathers, who enjoy teaching their sons) but to school systems. Schools depend on local and state decisions, and as a result one finds a patchwork of programs. The Chess in the Schools program in New York City is a model for how both parents and schools could benefit. Teaching jobs became available for adult players. The New York City program serves twenty thousand students with a budget of $3,000,000 (10 percent of which is funded by the city). Miami's program is supported by the county and serves seventeen thousand students. Philadelphia, Atlanta, and Brownsville, Texas, have notable programs targeted on poorer Title I schools. But the location of these systems suggests just how random—and fragile—the programs are. Brownsville has been stable, but in a nearby city, the program was canceled as interest waned (field notes). Wealthier districts, such as academically oriented Evanston, Illinois, can fund their own programs. As in high school debate, we find a "doughnut effect," in which suburban schools have strong programs that urban and rural schools lack.[70]

In 2008 the Idaho state Department of Education approved a chess curriculum (the First Move curriculum) available to all second- and third-grade classrooms in the state, although the program required outside funding and, after the first year, support from the local school district. Tom Luna, the state's superintendent of education commented, "There are no studies that teaching chess has benefits for children, but there is anecdotal evidence."[71] According to Wendi Fischer of

America's Foundation for Chess, some 226 classrooms participated in the First Move program (about 15 percent of the eligible classrooms), even though because of budget issues the state has cut back on funding. With fifty states and thousands of school districts, the quality of programs varies. How much in the way of teaching skills must a chess master have? How much chess must a teacher know in order to be a chess teacher? One chess educator sighed, "We had one teacher who knew a lot about chess but hated kids. We had one teacher who loved the kids, but she didn't know the names of the pieces" (field notes). Finding someone who knows chess and likes kids is not always easy. Within the Chicago area fifteen organizations provide chess education to elementary schools, each with its own program and personnel. While scholastic training is an important, even essential, component of the chessworld, how and where it is organized remains fraught, problematic, and decentralized.

The Parental Presence

My first field study was of Little League baseball, a world known as much for its parents as for its players, and not always kindly. The same is true of chess. Whose world is it, the child's, the organizer's, or the parent's? Parents typically behave with caring concern. But stories, clichés, and generalizations arise from taking the rare cases and inflating them, comparing chess parents to "hockey moms," "Little League dads," or "stage mothers." In contrast to these other arenas, chess is seen as a "brain game," and so it is treated as central to middle-class success in a modern information society. One scholastic judge explained, "Chess moms make soccer moms look like wimps. I think the reason for that is in soccer if your kid isn't good, you can just say that he isn't talented, but in chess it means that he's an idiot" (field notes). Children are welcomed into the chess community, while "tiger parents" are viewed with suspicion.

At many scholastic tournaments, the floor judges told me that at their own tournaments the parents were well controlled, and then they proceeded to narrate horror stories: *échecs noir*. In one case a judge highlighted the difference between some parents and others by describing one father as "a real parent, not a chess parent" (field notes).

When a child is on a school team or reaches adolescence, parents vanish, but with younger players moms and dads are present. Emotions may be heated. Parents want their child to succeed and not to be hurt. This is intensified when a parent sees college admission or a scholarship waiting for the successful child. Having a child succeed in chess, perhaps as in ballet or piano, is a form of what Annette Lareau speaks of as "concerted cultivation," where a parent shapes a child's self in order to provide subsequent status benefits and life opportunities.[72]

A child's defeat puts several emotions in play: protectiveness, anger, resentfulness, suspicion, and even self-blame. Did the child not win because of a failing that needs correcting, is the child upset, is that upset because of self-admonishment or because of a fear of punishment? The looking-glass self, described by social psychologist Charles Horton Cooley,[73] in which one's self-image is shaped by the reactions of significant others, notably parents, is crucial. The child gains a sense of who he is and how he should feel from how parents respond to victory and defeat. Every parent wants his or her child to triumph, but hiding that feeling is not always easy or even possible. The good parent, and there are many, can fake it, telling the child that winning doesn't really matter or that learning to lose is as important as learning to win. The claim is that being part of a community matters more than where in the communal hierarchy you are placed.

It will not surprise anyone who has followed high-level chess that the archetypal bad parent is said to be Rustam Kamsky, a hostile, demanding, and controlling parent, who isolated his son Gata from friends, forcing the boy to spend twelve hours a day on a training regimen. One journalist who visited the family (his mother had left years before) when Gata was fifteen wrote: "He never watched television or read anything other than chess books. He didn't play sports with other boys, but he jogged for thirty-five minutes in the evening, which his father said was good for chess endurance. He didn't go to school."[74] This might be a private matter, but Rustam took his monomania—or his intense commitment—into public settings, forcing family dynamics on others in the community. Gata became one of America's strongest players, but every outcome was filtered through Rustam's obsession. Grandmaster Joel Benjamin explains:

> You cannot separate the chess from the atmosphere of paranoia and intimidation created by Gata's father Rustam. A large and threaten-

ing individual, Rustam employed strong-arm tactics to aid his son's cause. During the Fedorowicz-Kamsky semi-final match, Rustam noticed Fed brushed past DeFirmian and went ballistic, insisting they had discussed the game.... He would occasionally pay people to follow "suspicious" individuals..... Rustam wanted to know why Gata had not been awarded the Samford Fellowship.... [Faneuil] Adams had no choice but to meet Rustam head on. "The reason I voted against Gata," he told him, "is because of unacceptable behavior by you and your son on a number of occasions."[75]

This behavior reveals just how intensity can affect community. Perhaps the son was accepted within the community for his ability—and was pitied for his family circumstance—but no such tolerance was shown for the father. At age twenty-two, after losing to Anatoly Karpov for the FIDE World Championship, Gata quit competitive chess and distanced himself from his father. Eight years later he was welcomed back to competitive chess and is now a top American player.

Rustam Kamsky is an outlier, but other parents overstep recognized if unstated boundaries. Rejecting a child after a defeat in the final round or telling a child that he "certainly can't play any worse"[76] is worthy of gossip. In another case, a parent refused to let his undefeated son play in the final round of a tournament because he was convinced that the boy would be defeated and lose rating points, insisting that the child forfeit (field notes). These antics separate the parent from the child in the eyes of the community, which tolerates the eccentricities of players. Because of concern about parents, many scholastic tournaments close the playing room to adults. When I took my son to a national scholastic tournament, the players were on the floor of a basketball arena, the parents in the stands. The belief among many tournament organizers is that a "closed floor" protects children from parents. As one leading figure in scholastic chess told me, "What breaks my heart is seeing players, especially the very young players, six years old, who are devastated and heartbroken when they lose because Dad is going to be mad, and they are just full out crying hysterically at the board" (interview). The chessworld is protective of the kids, kindly treating them as members of the community, while creating barriers to parents, outsiders whose virtues are often their transportation and their wallets.

The Worlds of Chess

The places—physical and social—in which leisure is enacted provide an appreciation of the dynamics of community. Chess matters because it is communal. Whether we discuss private homes, city parks, or community centers, the places of action establish standards. If chess is to be possible as a collective activity, such places must be provided by some person, group, or organization. Some restaurants, bars, or coffee shops open their rooms to leisure groups. They welcome chess players as they do groups that gather to watch a television show such as *Buffy the Vampire Slayer*.[77]

Commitment and place join to form the domain of chess. Chess playing can be compelling and so intense that for some the image of addiction springs to mind. But players drift in and drift out of the activity. America's two most honored active chess players—Hikaru Nakamura and Gata Kamsky—left competitive chess to pursue higher education. But the community welcomed them home and not just as prodigal sons.

The microcommunities of chess and their openness encourage affiliation, but it is not all-powerful; participants choose the extent of their affiliation. As was clear at Lakeside High School, players lost interest and gave priority to competing activities. When chess did not match up to alternatives, participation waned. The social environment in which chess is played is crucial for encouraging continued involvement.

Even an activity as focused as chess is internally segmented in light of the motives and the investments of the participants. As a result, different groups create distinct styles of chess, establishing norms and fashions. Ultimately all cultural worlds depend on social relations. In this, chess is not an exception but an exemplar. In the next chapter, I examine divisions in chess by looking at the establishment of hierarchy, the backgrounds of players, and how chess communities are open to deviants, providing soft communities in which to dwell.

6

STATUS GAMES AND SOFT COMMUNITY

*The poets lie about orgasm. It is a small, chancy business, its
particularities immediately effaced even from the most roseate
memories, compared to the crescendo of triumph in chess, to the tide
of light and release that races over mind and knotted body as the
opponent's king, inert in the fatal web one has spun, falls on the board.*

GEORGE STEINER, *Fields of Force*

Every form of community, no matter how welcoming, requires hierarchy, a ladder of mind or body that is built on the consensual reading of social relations. In this consensus some have resources; others have influence; a few have stature. These dimensions, parallel to dimensions of wealth, power, and prestige spoken of by the early twentieth-century sociologist Max Weber, often overlap in shared evaluations, although not inevitably. Groups create leaders through these dimensions, and such persons set community standards. Others serve as a warning of the dangers of misguided involvement. Every status system belongs to an interaction order based on shared beliefs or morality, and as a result, reputation is fully social.

Chess has a special feature—the rating—discussed later in this chapter. But here I note that persons are quantified for purposes of evaluation and for providing or limiting opportunities. This is a remarkable feature of this ancient game. In its specifics it is unique, but it bears comparison to other aspects of modern life where selves are quantified for appraisal and social control.[1] This quantification is a form of what Wendy Espeland and Mitchell Stevens have termed "commensuration,"[2] whereby ostensibly different things or persons can be arrayed on a single dimension.

With the exception of its failure to involve girls and women in great numbers, chess has an enviable record of inclusion. It is a global domain. This does not mean that it is equally popular everywhere. Japanese play *shogi* and go, and Chinese play *xiangqi* (Chinese chess) and mahjong, and chess is only now making inroads into Africa. However, throughout Europe, the Middle East, South Asia, and North and South America, chess is popular. Even China has not been immune to the charms of the game. Many of the top female players, including the current women's world champion, as of 2014, are Chinese. FIDE (the World Chess Federation) has the motto "Gens una sumus" (We are one people) and comprises 180 national federations. As noted above, at large American tournaments, apart from gender, the diversity of players is impressive.

Is It Good for the Jews?

Groups are often characterized by their demography, for good or ill. In chess this is most explicitly linked to the real and imagined prominence of Jews. In twentieth-century elite chess the list of Jewish players is extensive. The two greatest stars of the century were Jewish by birth: Garry Kasparov and Bobby Fischer. Other chess luminaries like Steinitz, Lasker, Nimzowitsch, Judit Polgar, Samuel Reshevsky, Reuben Fine, and many others are Jewish by religion or birth (through at least one parent).[3] When Arpad Elo listed the highest-rated chess players in history, he discovered that approximately half were Jewish.[4] It is quicker to name non-Jewish stars: Ruy Lopez, Philidor, Morphy, Capablanca, Alekhine, and Karpov. Most important stylistic innovations over the past century were associated with Jewish players.

Why should this be? As Jewish chauvinists and anti-Semites recognize, many elite activities are dominated by Jews. If we demand that valued slots in society are to be filled by persons of all races and creeds, it often means that in practice we limit the involvement of Jews. On the other hand, we might wish to choose the best and the brightest, an approach that protects well-trained Jews.

The connection of Jews and chess was well established by 1905, when the *American Chess Bulletin* quoted *New Era Illustrated Magazine*: "If there is such a thing among the Jews as a 'National game,' surely that title belongs by overwhelming right to the royal game of chess.... For upward of 50 years there has not been a tournament of any account in Europe or America that has not had a Jew taking a prominent place therein, and today, as has been the case often before, the world's champion is one of them.... In the world of chess the Jew reigns supreme."[5] In the world of chess Jews are everywhere. When the Soviets decided to use chess to carve out a sphere of dominance, the men who led the way were certainly or likely Jewish: Bronstein, Botvinnik, Smyslov, Tal, Spassky, Korchnoi, and Kasparov.[6] In American chess, for nearly forty years every United States chess champion has been at least partially of Jewish origin.[7]

Such dominance was seen by many—Jews first of all—as reflecting positive characteristics. Wilhelm Steinitz was said to feel that "the reason why Jews are so clever at chess is because of their patience, pure breeding, and good nature. Having been the most persecuted race in the world, they have had the least power to do harm, and have become the best natured of all people."[8] But to refer to "pure breeding" is to walk in mud, even in a good cause.[9] The endowment of Jewish intelligence is given credit along with Jewish love of learning. Gerald Abrahams suggested that "a disproportionally large number of Jews are endowed with greater mental aptitude than the European average."[10] In 1910, Mendel Silber, examining "Jewish achievement," noted that intelligence—perhaps sophistry—led to Jewish dominance: "The study of Talmudic subtlety and Rabbinic sophistry has not been without wholesome effect, at least in one direction. It has constantly sharpened the intellect of the Jew and has endowed him with those qualities that make of excellence in chess playing."[11] Others suggest a psychological explanation. For Jews chess provided a satisfying alternative to military prominence.[12] In the words of Horowitz and Rothenberg, "There is a distinct possibility that Chess has symbolized for Jews the struggle inherent in their history of persecution. In short, the bloodless fight, the battle of wits, the excitement of the intellectual argument (symbolized by action on the Chessboard) . . . may well have descended to his posterity."[13]

The prominence of Jews in chess—an objective fact—has also been a source of concern to some. The most widely cited attack appeared under the byline of Alexander Alekhine, the world champion, in "Jewish and Aryan Chess," published in 1941 in *Deutscher Schachzeitung*.[14] The text is anti-Semitic, although how much was due to the pressures that Alekhine faced is uncertain: "It is becoming more and more apparent that the purely negative Jewish conception of chess . . . perverted, for half a century, the logical development of our art of battle. . . . Yes, the Jews are extremely well endowed with the ability to exploit the ideas of chess and the practical potentialities entailed; but, as yet, no real chess artist of Jewish origin has existed."[15] Some spoke of a "Jewish" style of chess. This apparently referred to complex, modernist positions, as practiced by Garry Kasparov, and some openings, such as the Grünfeld Defense, that were defined as Jewish openings. Surprisingly, I found no claims about chess as a political field. Because of its prominence in the Soviet Union and in New York, one might have expected the line that chess was "liberal" or "socialist"; perhaps the recognition that it is a military game made the claim implausible. Although Kasparov is a leading Russian dissident, political discussions are rare at tournaments.

No discussion of the role of Jews can neglect Bobby Fischer, who toward the end of his life saw Jewish conspiracy as having a global reach. But early in his career, Fischer's concern was style. He remarked in an interview in 1962, "There are too many Jews in chess. They seem to have taken away the class of the game. They don't seem to dress so nicely, you know. That's what I don't like."[16] Certainly players at Fischer's Manhattan Chess Club dressed less fashionably than those at Paris's Café de la Regence, but it is an open question whether Jews—a race of tailors—can be held responsible.

Putting aside whether there is any validity to claims of Jewish virtue or vice, institutional features link chess with religion. The presence of Jews in cosmopolitan cities contributes to their institutional dominance. We expect a correlation between the size of a city, its intellectual life, and the number of venues for chess. The social scene in New York contributed to a rich chess culture. Just as Jews dominate American chess, so do New Yorkers. Further, once a community is involved in an activity, network-based recruitment occurs. It becomes easier for similar people to feel at home in a social world and to be welcomed. Given the belief in the intellectual virtues of chess, upwardly mobile Jewish families might be particularly supportive of this particular form of "wasting time." As in many social worlds, the characteristics of participants are more a function of the organization and location of the activity than of genetic or psychological effects.

Colors beyond the Board

Jews are not the only population whose presence is noticed within chess culture. Asians and Asian Americans are becoming more prominent in competitive chess. The former men's world champion is Indian, and the women's world champion is Chinese. At American scholastic tournaments the proportion of South Asians and East Asians is high. I heard one white player remark of Asian American children, "When I play these talented juniors, I just want to kill them [defeat them], especially when it is some little Asian kid" (field notes). While many Jewish Americans still excel in scholastic competitions, increasingly the faces are Asian. Asian Americans have access to the same familial and institutional structures to which Jews have access.

African Americans have a different relation to chess. Although I don't discuss how social class affects chess, class determines what activities seem admirable or ridiculous. Chess is a luxury for the leisure class. Race serves as a stand-in for class. There are many strong African American players, but they often participate outside of formal competition venues. At tournaments one is more likely to find African American adults than children. Inner-city schools provide fewer opportunities, even though scholastic chess programs are expanding in poorer communities with considerable success, especially in New York public schools, as revealed in the recent (2012) documentary *Brooklyn Castle*, about a middle school chess team.

Anyone who visits public spaces where chess is played, such as New York's Washington Square Park, finds that many of the players are black, and often they play speed chess for money. These men are sometimes labeled hustlers, and their talk ("trash talk") is denigrated, but they are a committed, able, and distinctive community.[17]

In some instances black chess players face racism. An extreme example is a book published in 1905 that sees social order in the combat between "white" and "black" pieces, where white gets to move first. The author, Wallace Nevill, suggests that "the whites are, therefore, aggressive because they inaugurate the attack, and black men are supposed ever to act on the defensive."[18] Statements can readily be seen as racially charged, whatever their intent. Maurice Ashley, the first African American grandmaster, reported "one Grandmaster remarking while I was playing against an International Master, Jay Bonin. We were playing speed chess. And he looked at Jay after I defeated Jay a game and said, 'Are you letting this shvarts beat you?'"[19] On another occasion, a player frustrated by a defeat by a lower-rated, well-dressed African American adult, told me in frustration, "It's like playing a primitive life form. He just moves like a monkey. He just moves randomly. He doesn't respect chess. He's not capable of thinking" (field notes). I challenged these remarks, and he assured me that he was not criticizing black players in general (and he does have black chess-playing friends), but only this opponent. Still, the metaphor rankled. It is easy for black players to feel that they do not belong in the heart of the community, but only on its edges.

The point in examining leisure demography is not to read core abilities into skin and genes but to recognize how an activity fits into particular communities and institutions. A community that can provide shared spaces (ethnic chess clubs) or organizational support (school clubs) has a structural and interactional advantage over communities lacking such support. Those with access to those institutions have benefits.

Age Cultures

Age cultures stratify voluntary activity. Youngsters playing mahjong are uncommon; Ultimate Frisbee is played by the fleet. Eight- or eighty-year-old boxers are scarce. But few domains have such an age range as chess: four-year-olds compete, as do a few centenarians, sometimes against each other. Those at the older end of the spectrum have challenges of fading vision, endurance, or memory. They face "senior moments."[20] Because chess ratings have a floor below which rated players cannot slip, the ratings of aging players may suggest more ability than is warranted.

However, when chess players discuss age cultures, they emphasize younger players. It is said that mathematics, music, and chess produce prodigies: children able to compete with or surpass adults. These activities have abstract qualities less reliant upon lived experience or bodily development. When chess players become masters or grandmasters at increasingly younger ages, it may be a result of greater opportunities and stronger competition more than development. The youngest master-level player (a rating of over 2200) reached that goal while still nine years old. In 1958 Bobby Fischer became a grandmaster at age fifteen, but since 1991 his record has been broken over twenty times. Fischer, not a powerful player until he was a teenager, was not a prodigy in the traditional sense.[21] The youngest boy to become a grandmaster, Sergey Karjakin, achieved that title when he was twelve.[22] Whether the title means what it meant fifty years ago is an open question, but today preteens can reach the highest levels of chess. Perhaps this is a result of the chess boom that Fischer helped to produce, the role of computer training and competition, or the increased globalization of the chessworld.

I previously discussed the case of Capablanca, but such early giftedness was matched a century ago by Samuel Reshevsky, a true child prodigy who learned to play chess at age four and then gave demonstrations of his chess prowess, wearing a cute sailor suit, beating many adults.[23] One chess instructor teaches three-year-olds. The current world champion, Magnus Carlsen, speaking at age thirteen, said of a failure, "I played like a child!"[24]

Beyond playing like a child is playing *with* a child, a reflection of the diverse leisure world in which children participate as full members. With children playing in the strongest tournaments, there are opportunities for adult humiliation, since the victors are not merely talented opponents but children. To lose to a young child—a "ten-year-old with a pocket protector"—is humbling or, worse, "unworthy and degrading."[25] This is true for fathers and sons, but in a world of strangers the reputational danger cannot be salved by pride in one's offspring. At the suburban chess club I studied, one adult visitor never returned after being embarrassed by a nine-year-old. Other comments echo this fear:

> The other guy standing by says, well, look on the bright side, at least you didn't lose to a six-year-old! And starts to laugh. For some reason, it is just not as humiliating losing to an adult.... Getting killed in an intellectual exercise by a six-year-old, who is still learning how to count, is a harrowing experience. (Antony Puddephatt field notes)

> I once met a physicist who as a child had been something of a chess prodigy.... He took particular delight in the mortification older players felt upon losing to a kid in short pants. "Still play?" I asked. "Nope." "What happened?" "Quit when I was 21." "Why?" "Lost to a kid in short pants."[26]

Adults have strategies both on and off the board, often slowing the game so that a child's focus will wander.[27] As one player explained, "The way to beat kids is to play a long, boring game" (field notes). Another player comments that he plays the Italian Game against young players: "It's a thinking man's game. The slow Italian game makes the young snots think" (field notes). Most children prefer active games and may lack the patience for a lengthy game. I was told that the style of young players is known as the "phonebook attack," since they must sit on thick tomes to see the board.

As is true with regard to race and religion, age matters in the chess-world. The structure of scholastic chess, along with computer technology, has produced a generation that is more talented, committed, and knowledgeable than its elders. Yet adults publish books and run organizations, and as a result, the stories told are adult stories. Children are welcomed into the world of chess, admired, and seen as the future of the game, but not without misgivings, as these lads alter the "boy's club," dominated by men.

The Girl and the Game

Perhaps the first question that an outside observer asks when visiting a chess tournament is, where are the girls? Where are the women? In so many areas of American life that were once dominated by men, women are edging toward parity: medicine, law, fiction, even politics. Wherever elites gather, there are women. Extreme gender disparity is rare.

I do not explain why women are underrepresented, but I will discuss why women are *said* to be underrepresented. The evidence of that underrepresentation is clear. No woman has won the world championship, no major tournament has a female champion,[28] and only about 1 percent of all of the world's grandmasters are women. (There are, however, women's championships, tournaments, and a category of "women's grandmasters" with different criteria than for "grandmasters.") Of the United States Chess Federation's top one hundred players, two are women; this is double the number for the World Chess Federation. Of the top one hundred eleven-year-olds, seven are girls. When I attended the World Open in Philadelphia, the largest American tournament, none of the players in the open section (above 2200 rating) were women; a few women played in lower sections. While precise figures fluctuate, about 4 percent of the members of the USCF are women.[29] In first grade perhaps a third of chess players are girls, but by sixth grade that number declines to 10 percent (Field notes).

To understand the role of women in chess, it is worth noting that many of the top players—Bobby Fischer and Garry Kasparov among them—have a low opinion of female players. Not only are women not good at chess, but *by nature* they will never be good, some believe. Of course, one could also dig up antique quotations about female doctors or novelists. This view stands in contrast with research that indicates biology plays a small role in ability. While women and men might have different cognitive skills, with male skills benefitting chess ability, the more sociological view is that opportunity structures matter more. Analyses of life histories of players, as well as surveys, support the opportunity-structure theory.[30] Boys enter chess in greater numbers, and those who are successful continue. Boy culture dominates. One high school boy explained, "There are already a lot of boys, and so girls who do start would kind of feel out of place, and that would discourage them even more. I guess since chess is viewed as nerdy, and girls already care more about their appearance, that would probably discourage them" (interview). International master Irina Krush echoes this view: "A lot of things change for girls when they're thirteen, fourteen, and fifteen.... During those years, interactions ... matter more to girls. Their first crushes, their first kisses, when they first fall in love."[31] Krush might be romantic, but she shares the perspective of many players.[32]

One of the main passages is the father-child relationship, often the father-son relationship. If fathers are less inclined to teach their daughters, the parental bond is lost. In schools girls face other obstacles. An ethnographic study of a mixed-gender chess club in elementary school found that girls dropped out at a much higher rate than boys because of hostility, criticism, and distaste for the aggression of the games.[33] In second-grade talk, boys are "really mean"[34] or, later, they are "so annoying" (field notes). Despite support from the club organizer, these girls felt that the boys didn't want them there. Male chess players have the dual reputations of being nerds and boors. Perhaps chess, unlike medicine, is too trivial to be worth the bother. As anthropologist Margaret Mead remarked, "Women could be just as good at chess, but why would they want to be?"[35]

Nerds and Boors

To understand sexism I begin at the pinnacle. Bobby Fischer, who could read the board, even if he was less proficient at reading the world, commented in 1962, "They're all weak, all women. They're stupid compared to men. They shouldn't play chess, you know. They're like beginners."[36] Not to be outdone, Garry Kasparov commented in 1989 in *Playboy*, "There is real chess and women's chess.... Chess does not fit women properly. It's a fight, you know? ... Chess is the combination of sport, art and science. In all these fields, you can see men's superiority.... Probably the answer is in the genes."[37] He described female chess players as "trained dogs."[38]

But sexism goes beyond pejorative evaluations. Anyone who spends time around male chess players will hear the metaphor of chess victory as rape. As one high school player explained, "The word *rape* is thrown around a lot. It's sort of a completely inappropriate word, but a player comes back and he crushes the guy really badly, he will say, 'I raped him.' That's the lingo. If [our coach] hears it, he yells at us not to use the word. It's completely appropriate if no one else is there" (interview). The imagery is part of the game, when, as noted above, grandmaster Nigel Short announced, "I want to rape and mate him."[39] Nasty language is used toward not only men[40] but women as well. One woman prominent in American chess reported that a male opponent called her a slut after her victory (interview).

In addition, men treat women as sex objects, and some women embrace the male gaze. A few years ago a group of men organized the World Chess Beauty Contest, in which photographs of female chess players were posted online, and viewers could vote on who was the loveliest.[41] In another instance, Alexandra Kosteniuk, a grandmaster and former women's world champion, posed clothed for *Penthouse*, leading one chess journalist to jeer: "What on earth are the good readers of *Penthouse* to think of chess? It's played by stuck-up bimbos with their clothes on, that's what.... Ms K needs to take a long hard look in the mirror, reflect a little more on her obligations to the wider chess community, and bloody well get 'em off."[42] Female chess players, it is said, wish relations with those men with large ratings. As Diana Lanni pointed out, "Why not pick the strongest?"[43] One woman was accused of such preferences, claiming that she moved from man to man up the chess ladder. Of one relationship, these men suggested, "She's a siren, saying, 'please come to my room.' She's a Medusa. She sucked the lifeforce out of him. Now she's going to drop him because he lost all of his points." A young woman, a master-level player, confided, "Guys judge women more on their looks; women judge guys more on their rating" (field notes).

Then there is the baleful effect that women have on men. As noted, male players fantasize about women when they should be calculating.[44] And there is the well-endowed fifteen-year-old, known as "Jailbait." Beautiful women excuse defeat. One young adult remarked of an attractive female player that she used "the breast attack. The only solution for these types of players [well-endowed young women wearing tight shirts] is to play them blind and then you crush them" (field notes). One coach shared an account from the Illinois State High School Tournament of a male player allegedly asking his attractive girlfriend to sit behind him, wearing a low-cut dress, so that his opponent would be distracted (field notes). An Australian player complained to tournament officials that his opponent's cleavage caused his defeat.[45] One research study, based on actual games, found that men select significantly riskier strategies when playing against an attractive female opponent,[46] although this does not improve their performance. Whether or not hormones affect women's ability, they surely affect women's social relations.

Status Structures

Beyond social categories, talent cements one into a set of status structures. Finding a comfortable community of esteem is essential. Consider the story that psychiatrist Karl Menninger told about his mentor Ernest Southard, a professor of neuropathology at Harvard Medical School in the early twentieth century:

> Southard, as a college freshman, had been an unpopular, asocial individual who felt lonely and somewhat rejected because he was not taken into any of the clubs, had no athletic ability, and was not outstanding in any of his classes. He did play a little chess, however, and when a call was issued for aspirants to the Harvard Chess team to play against Yale, he responded and, to his great surprise, won a place on the team. It was not long before he was the champion of Harvard and then the champion of Massachusetts and of New England. These chess victories constituted a turning point in his life. He had discovered that he could really do something better than most other people could do it; this gave him confidence that he might also excel in something besides chess.[47]

This cheery remembrance shows the power of status to shape a life. By being venerated, one becomes confident; by being confident, one becomes successful. Success generates admiration that when solidified becomes status. The chessworld provides categories of worth, such as grandmaster, international master, master, expert, and class A, B, C, D (through J) players.[48] The categories of master, expert, and chess classes depend upon ratings (master is over 2200, expert over 2000, and the others are based on 200-point divisions). For the grandmaster and international master title, one needs not only a master rating (2500 for grandmaster) but to achieve three grandmaster or international master "norms," defined outcomes against rated players at tournaments. The rules are complex (and changeable), but rating points are not sufficient. One must succeed in competition. There are more grandmasters today than ever before, more than 1,400, in contrast to 90 in 1970, which has led some to suggest that the status of the grandmaster title has been diminished. Grandmasters used to be a community; now they are a diffused network. Still, these labels are markers of self-esteem as well as public indicators of status. One master-level player comments about a colleague, "Maury though will be very much respected by the other elite players in town for his chess ability. You know they will associate with him for sure, even though they normally wouldn't under any other circumstance."[49] Honored chess players receive deference from their peers, whatever their status outside the chess community.

At every point in a hierarchy a division between elites and those less talented emerges. At Lakeside High, a school without any player close to having an expert rating (the top player had a rating of 1600), the hierarchy was reflected in the "board order." Illinois high school chess requires teams of eight players who are arranged in order of "strength." Strength is not easy to measure and doesn't always correspond with rating. The first board is expected to be the best player and, in most cases, should have the highest rating. And boards two through eight should reveal declining talent. On the Lakeside team it was very clear who were the first and second boards, but below that opinions varied. The Lakeview coach explained:

> State rule is you play them in strength order. So how do you determine strength order? I do look at ratings, and I tend to emphasize the local ratings more than the USCF ratings. I do look a little bit

about who can beat who in the club.... Board order is a lot of things. One of them is maturity level.... I do think about personality. I had a kid who slit his wrists. He probably should have been board two or three, but I knew he couldn't handle that. He needed to be board one. (interview)

The status of playing first board outweighed the fact that, as a result, he was more likely to lose to other top players. The trade-off was striking. The construction of a status system requires negotiation, as many players believe that they are better and deserve more deference than their ratings or board positions suggest. As a result, the coach or the club must distribute rewards so that participants feel that justice has been done.

Each scene generates an elite that works to preserve the status order. In the world of chess, the label grandmaster symbolizes that elite. The term was not used until the beginning of the twentieth century at the Ostend tournament in 1907; in 1914 Czar Nicholas II awarded the title in Russia. It became an official designation in 1950 by edict of the World Chess Federation.[50]

But by whatever label, elites have privileges both social and material. To be a grandmaster—and especially what is termed a "super grandmaster"—is to have status. These men (and a few top women) are celebrities. If a tournament organizer can announce their presence, they may draw others. As a result, tournament organizers waive registration fees for grandmasters and may provide appearance fees, payments above and beyond prize money. Status carries benefits, particularly at the pinnacle, as super grandmaster Loek van Wely points out: "Everything depends on your rating. If you're rated 2600 you can say, yell or scream whatever you want, but you will be a voice crying in the wilderness.... If you want to be heard ... you have to be in the top five."[51] Both Garry Kasparov and Bobby Fischer have referred to certain fellow grandmasters as "patzers," suggesting status differentiation among the elite (field notes). A humorous tract entitled *How to Cheat at Chess* distinguishes untitled players, grandmasters, and the world champion:

Untitled Players: the competitor ... has virtually no rights whatsoever. He may be required to share a room with a similar unfortunate and to provide his own travelling expense. Feed on beans-on-toast;

coffee 10p extra.... The Grandmaster: double room to himself in four-star hotel (with lift, night porter, catering for pets, private tennis court).... No cockroaches, queers or musical plumbing. Should be given substantial appearance fee and prospect of attractive prize.... Whitebait or avocado with shrimps, coq-au-vin, fresh lychees, coffee with whipped cream.... The World Champion: just give in to all his demands and there won't be any trouble.[52]

At one tournament, the top players sat in comfortable office chairs, while the lower-ranked players had to settle for hotel lecture hall chairs.

Status divisions are evident not only at the highest levels of chess competition but in clubs as well, spaces where hierarchies are locally constituted. These communities differ in their openness, but status is considered, as when one player asks another, "Are you playing a human or some other life form?" One longtime chess player with a rating of 1900 called another, with a rating of 1500 "not a real player." Such affronts do not go unanswered. Aggrieved players comment:

> It's definitely hierarchical.... When I started at the club, nobody gave me the time of day at all. Literally, they would ignore me.... There are some ham-and-eggers [modestly talented players] ... that will go up and talk to anyone, but for the most part they stay away and keep to themselves.... It is very cliquey. (interview by Antony Puddephatt)

> I am getting so sick of this elitist attitude at the club.... They call people's moves "primitive" and all of that business. You know, in the club, they are so superior and important compared to the rest of us. Greg, I swear to god, pretends he doesn't know who I am. He has stopped me to ask my name about five times. I say to him, "I am Fred Perdue"—I am the president of the goddamned club! But since I am a lower rated player, no, he doesn't even know my name.[53]

This is the un-Cheers, a status system in which some pretend not to know your name.

However, such systems are never entirely stable, permitting claimants to argue for its revision. Weaker players take pleasure in challenging their higher-ranked colleagues, particularly if they can later claim that they held their own. One friend noted with pleasure that a grandmaster had commented at a midpoint in a game with him that it was heading for a draw. Although the friend was defeated, this comment made the game a moral victory. One player speaks about getting five "grandmaster scalps." By this he means drawn games in simuls. He figures that if a grandmaster offers a draw, the star is losing. When I asked a strong college player about his best game, he provided such a story: "Eighth grade. I was at the Florida State Scholastic Championship. It just so happened that I got paired up with the top player in Florida, and I was all bummed out, because he was really good. He was like 2100 at the time; I was like maybe 1500 or 1600. I was able to pull off a draw.... I even actually had one position that I messed up to let him get a draw. Even though that happened, that was definitely the best game I ever played" (interview). Another player told me about a victory against a player rated almost 1000 points higher. The opponent lost on time, but a win is a win, and a decade later the story is worth telling. These moral tales provide a basis of commitment. Some low-ranked players are grateful for an invitation for a draw even if they are ahead ("He offered me a draw, which I accepted because he was a grandmaster, but he was behind") or are offended if a lower-status player makes the offer ("I know I can get the draw, but it's a lack of respect. I should judge whether I should give a draw"). A delicate interaction order justifies social systems.

The Ratings Game

Every social world develops criteria by which status arrays are established, and those then determine strategies of action and identities of self.[54] Pierre Bourdieu speaks of the politics of distinction in indicating how material objects and behaviors create hierarchy.[55] These may be subtle and indistinct or open and knowable, but those inside the community will figure out who is where.

One of the distinctions that make chess fascinating for sociologists is the explicitness and the centrality of the rating system. Its apparent objectivity identifies and validates its elite and standardizes judgments across communities, providing definable goals for participants.[56] Ratings appear to create a single dimension, and this is important in how players discuss each other, but players also link ratings to other important characteristics. For instance, high schools players often focus on the ratings of other adolescents, while adults, seniors, and juveniles with the same rating are often treated as part of separate systems for purposes of judgment. This is the process that David Stark terms *heterarchy*, referring to the existence of distinct systems of evaluation or distinction within what appears to be a single status hierarchy.[57] In practice, while players of different social positions (notably age and gender, and sometimes geography) might be rated according to the same system, they are treated as belonging to different hierarchies. While for purposes of this analysis, I treat the rating system as a single dimension, individuals with similar ratings may compare themselves with others that they define as similar in other consequential ways.

Ratings are not as simple as they appear, but they make a claim for precision. Some assert that the single most important role of the United States Chess Federation is maintaining the rating system, a system that extends from 0 to about 2850. The mean rating as of 2004 for all rated members was 1068.[58] Dividing members into adult and scholastic categories (as of 2002) yielded averages of 1429 and 608.[59] These averages do not consider that higher-rated players are likely to be more active than lower-rated ones and that active players have higher ratings. In the USCF ratings Hikaru Nakamura currently has the highest rating, at 2849 (his world rating is 2775). The highest ever recorded rating in the World Chess Federation system was 2882, attained by world champion Magnus Carlsen in 2014. As players who continue to win will gain points and those who lose will drop points, theoretically (but not in practice) there is the possibility of having a negative rating[60] or an unlimited one. "God is said to be rated 3000."[61] Computer scientist Ken Regan posits that perfect play deserves a rating of 3600,[62] suggesting that perhaps God is not omniscient. The ratings of computer programs are uncertain, but as they can beat the best grandmasters, they must be competing with God. As I write this, my friend Boris has a rating of 2688, Jeremy 2527, Phil 2101, Bruce 1254, Claire 132. By the time this book is published their ratings will have changed for better or worse.

Ratings are a recent addition to chess. The London International Chess Tournament of 1851 created an international status regime, and the first world champion was crowned (not quite officially) in 1886 with the match between the two most highly regarded players in Europe, Johann Zukertort and Wilhelm Steinitz. Steinitz won. In 1907 the title of grandmaster came into use, but several decades passed before ratings were established. The goal of the ratings system is to produce an "objective" and numerical system by which individuals could be compared.[63] In 1939 a ratings system was established for correspondence (postal) chess. The USCF adopted the Harkness system in 1950 for over-the-board players and then in 1960 adopted the Elo system.[64] The system is named for Arpad Elo, a Hungarian-born professor of physics at Marquette University, a chess master and longtime chairman of the ratings committee of the USCF. Elo took previous systems and gave them a firmer statistical logic. The Elo system was later accepted by FIDE, the World Chess Federation, in 1970. It has also been applied to speed chess, and many players have a speed chess rating as well as a regular rating (Jeremy has a speed rating of 2300, 227 points below his regular rating, while Bruce has a speed rating of 1317, 63 points higher than his regular rating).[65] Recently a blitz rating has been added. Other systems have since been developed, and many states have established ratings systems for scholastic chess. In the USCF the necessary rating for master has decreased from 2300 to 2200, and for expert from 2100 to 2000.[66] The current assumption is that a strong "club player" will have a rating of about 2000.

Ratings are mathematical systems for determining status. They recognize that there is a random distribution of chess outcomes, constrained by the actual ability of the players. I do not discuss the complex statistical theory that determines the creation of ratings, other than to recognize that human authorities select the metrics based on their preferences for the distribution of the rating system, avoiding rating inflation and deflation. Ratings are adjusted continually. These are "legislative" decisions made by appointed or elected individuals.[67] I attended one meeting of the USCF Ratings Committee, where it was explained that in 2006 the committee was given the mandate to make the distribution of ratings mirror their shape a decade previously, perhaps through bonus points. The earlier assignment of players into rating categories was to be taken as the "true" distribution. At one point the ratings of middle-aged players dropped by 20–25 points per year, in part because of the influx of talented young players whose victories lowered the ratings of their seniors; that deflation was addressed through "corrective inflation."[68]

The goal is to establish rules by which chess players can be ordered, so even when mathematical equations change, the numbers should remain roughly comparable over time. In discussion of inflation and deflation, the obvious comparison is to the Federal Reserve, easing and tightening the rating supply to encourage participation. These are rules of commensuration, grounded in claims of precision that makes sense in light of the moral certainties of the community.

Much can be said about the statistics involved, but the key sociological point is that while ratings are systematic, they are not fully objective, even if they produce an ordered ranking. Players gain or lose points depending upon whether they win, lose, or draw their rated games (not all games are rated).[69] A key question is how much should each victory or defeat count. If a player ranked 2000 defeats one rated 2500, does that mean that the first player should now be rated higher than his opponent? No one would argue this, even if there is an objective outcome based on ability, because, like any sport, outcomes are variable. If player A, as expected, beats player B, should he gain as many points as he would otherwise have lost? Or should player A gain the same number of points that player B loses? In reality, the decision about point gains and losses results from the percentage difference between the players, shaped by the maximum points that can be lost or gained. At one point the maximum gain per game was 16, and the maximum loss was 30 (interview). Ultimately, these matters are determined within a community by individuals who have the authority to decide. Ratings points are not poker chips but estimates that vary over time. The assumption is that the average rating in the community should remain constant, even if players overall become more knowledgeable. Of course, the active player who has no rated games has a stable rating, whether a rapidly improving child or a fading expert. The ratings universe is created by those who envision what the ratings population should look like. Those who establish ratings speak of a "K factor" which is the adjustment that determines how many points will be gained or lost.

The World Chess Federation (FIDE) ratings are also based on the Elo system but produce different numbers, in part as a result of different games rated (many outside the United States). Typically FIDE ratings are used to determine pairings in the top division at major tournaments. Boris, whose USCF rating is 2688, has an FIDE rating of 2622, which makes him the fifth-highest-rated American player, but he is not one of the hundred best players in the world. Jeremy, at 2425, is the sixtieth-best American player, but his FIDE rating is more than one hundred points lower than his USCF rating of 2527. (FIDE ratings are generally lower than USCF ratings, but players who score well in international tournaments have higher FIDE ratings).[70]

As noted, some states have their own systems. Children (and their parents!) are enthusiastic consumers of ratings and acutely sensitive to their implications. As a result, some communities deliberately inflate the ratings of their weaker players. In one suburb, no elementary school player can ever have a rating below 800. The community organizer noted that "we try to avoid them from getting too discouraged, or too unhappy, or too embarrassed" (interview). Because of her enjoyment of the game, Claire in high school can accept her rating of 132—she has had many other successes in life—but a second-grader might not.

When children in a community play each other, ratings don't matter much as long as the system is internally consistent. The problem arises in national competitions that are based on state ratings or on ratings generated from endogenous (closed) pools of players. The weak player who beats a closed community of weaker players is likely to have a rating that is too high, and the strong player who loses in a community of very strong players will have a rating that is too low. The state of Washington is known for low ratings,[71] which underestimate players' strength as measured by USCF ratings, whereas the ratings in Illinois are higher than the players' USCF ratings would be. This means that a girl with a rating of 1200 from Yakima would likely be stronger than a boy from Peoria with the same rating. When they are paired based on their ratings, the edge would go to the Washington player, who would typically have greater ability. Thus scholastic ratings are uncertain predictors of ability in comparing communities.[72]

Some top players prefer not to play in certain tournaments, such as junior tournaments, because of the belief that many players are underrated,[73] meaning that a "truly rated" player would lose more points or gain less in a game because of the artificially low rating of his opponent. In contrast, players on the make hope to challenge strong opponents, particularly those that they feel are overrated. One international master singled out a grandmaster he hoped to beat: "I want a big fish. I want Lenderman. He's oozing with points" (field notes).

The problem of the closed ratings pool is evident in the case of Claude Bloodgood. By 1997, Bloodgood was the second-best chess player in the United States, one of the strongest players in American chess history. Or more accurately, Bloodgood had the *second-highest chess rating* in the United States, a USCF rating of 2722, but that rating did not reflect his overall chess ability. Mr. Bloodgood didn't get out much. He was a resident of Virginia's Powhatan Prison, where he was imprisoned for murdering his mother (he had been given the death sentence, but it was commuted to life imprisonment). Mr. Bloodgood taught several of his fellow inmates how to play chess, paid for their USCF memberships, and started a chess group in prison and played numerous rated games. Despite his oedipal failings, Bloodgood was a serious player, served as a chess statistician, and published books on chess openings. Even if his opponents were not highly proficient, his rating increased a few points with each victory. Was Claude Bloodgood America's best native-born chess player, second only to world champion competitor Gata Kamsky? He warned about the dangers of a closed-pool rating system, and surely he would not have beaten most grandmasters, but ratings are ratings, at least until they aren't.[74] His ratings were such that he should have been invited to the United States Chess Championship (he couldn't attend), but the USCF declined to invite him, removed him from the top fifty players list, and altered the system so that closed-pool ratings are not permitted. Still, while this change is understandable, it emphasizes the social side of statistics. These statisticians were making a *sociological*, not mathematical, judgment. The opposite argument is sometimes used by local players, as by those in New Mexico, where a closed system produces ratings that are too low: "A favorite mythology amongst New Mexican chess players is that they are all underrated. They reckon that they hone their craft against the same opponents—who are also improving. And since their rating pool is never cross-pollinated by the soft-petal daisies from the big cities, their ratings don't reflect their true progress. This belief is so ingrained that an 1800 (New Mexico rating of course) will announce himself as 1900 once he crosses the state line into Colorado."[75] These debates emphasize the centrality of local communities in chess. While there is a national and an international circuit, most chess playing is local, found in clubs or schools or prisons.

Although the chess rating appears to be a means by which the past can be gauged, its goal, as ratings committee chairman Ken Sloan explained, is to predict the future. If you do better than expected, your rating rises; if you do as expected, it moves little. Currently a player with a two-hundred-point advantage should win 76 percent of his games, useful knowledge for tournament organizers to help them ensure that tournament pairings result in fair games, with players in the early rounds having different ability but not wildly different levels.[76]

Does a rating have a stable meaning? An understandable desire exists to claim that a rating of 2785 means the same thing over decades. Bobby Fischer had that rating. Does that mean that he is equally good as Vladimir Kramnik, the fourth-best player in FIDE's list, at this writing, who has precisely the same rating? Are they both "2785s"? Fischer was clearly the greatest chess player of his era, an era with a different form of chess training; Kramnik is excellent, but not the best. But one might suggest that Kramnik builds on his knowledge of Fischer's games. Like sports, chess has "improved" over time. Despite identical ratings, one might argue that either was "better." Ultimately, ratings seem precise and objective, but their creation and meaning is communally determined, and, once again, what seems outside society is firmly embedded within an interaction order.

Identity Markers

Not only do communities have status structures, but they develop ways of distinguishing those of higher status from those of lower status. Position is made visible through uniforms, physical markings, or other forms of caste assignment. In chess, the markings are not physical, but numeric. One sign of status is where in the tournament hall one plays: the strongest players are at the front, sometimes at nicer tables with more comfortable chairs, but otherwise status is opaque. In team matches the strongest player should be on the "first board." Outside of close-knit clubs and teams, chess involves thin networks unless players, especially grandmasters, repeatedly see each other at events. But it is ratings, evident on the wall charts posted at every tournament, that make status clear. When one learns his opponent, he discovers his rating.

Ratings are organizational signals that shape self-identity and reactions by others. Perhaps not surprisingly, people indicate that this "silly" number matters more for how they think about others than how they feel about themselves. Yet, as Jennifer Shahade notes, "Top British woman player Harriet Hunt says that very early she realized that her chess rating was an important part of who she was.... Rating denotes value to such a large extent that one grandmaster compared losing ten rating points at the top level to losing ten liters of blood."[77]

One player when asked his rating responded, "1938. It's pathetic isn't it?"[78] Another of very different ability noted, "If my rating dropped and I became under 1000 that would drop my self-confidence a lot" (interview). A third asked, "Is your ego costing you your Elo?" noting, "Once I made the conscious decision to stop worrying about my rating and decided to just 'play chess,' my results improved."[79] This sensible advice is easier given than taken, particularly when others are judged by their ratings. Some players have a target rating, and when that number is reached, involvement ends.

Ratings provide a credential, visible to all concerned, even though, as the previous examples indicate, those standards of adequacy vary widely. Consistent with Bourdieu's emphasis on the importance of status markers,[80] the rating serves as a prestige marker in a circuit of exchange. As Ken Sloan, chair of the USCF ratings committee, commented, "Ratings are a stand-in for IQ scores.... One player may say, 'Why should we listen to you, you are only an XXXX player?'" (interview) One chess instructor explained, "A lot of people identify with a number. If you have a high enough rating, you don't want to play with people lower than you" (field notes). The Lakeside coach told a medium-ranked player, "When you play a 1700, you should try to draw," and another player commented, "I was up against a 1600 and then I blew it." People are known by their number, although often the ratings are rounded to the first digits; the difference between 1999 (rounded to 1900) and 2000 is powerful, a form of cognitive slicing.[81] They belong in different categories. The former is an A-level player; the latter an expert. The former plays in the U2000 class, the latter in the U2200 class. Some distinguish between 2199 and 2200 (the minimum for a master rating), the latter constituting the "Magic 2200." These masters are esteemed, invited to tournaments, required to play in the top division, and if they are instructors, they can charge more for lessons.

Antony Puddephatt quotes an expert-level player about his companions: "They are judged by their current rating. If they are clean, dirty, doesn't matter. We are aware there are people there who are nuts, or they don't dress very well, they might be poor, they might be rich.... The cliques that form and so on? It's chess skill and rating."[82] For one player, his rating is a "big stick.... It's psychology. It's clear to people what you are" (field notes).

Ratings divide those with different abilities:

One club player reports, "It is interesting how much the perception of a player drops when you find out he is among the lowest rated there at the club. I figured he might be between 1600 and 1800, as most average club players are better than me. When I find out he is well below me, I totally lost any shred of respect I might have had for him earlier." (field notes)

You heard that continuous, "Oh, he's an under 1400 player," you know, almost like he has leprosy and we are elite.... The first question your opponent will ask [is what is your rating?]. They usually don't ask it anymore, because it is on the wall. It is there for everybody to see. (interview by Puddephatt)

It is important to know where you are in the world.... If ... two 1900s [are playing] and a grandmaster goes over, he looks a little skeptical about the moves. If they are like 2700, he is not skeptical. He is really trying to understand their moves instead. (interview)

As Stacy Lom argues, based on her observations of ice skating and musical competitions, evaluative cultures affect judgments of ability: what you expect shapes what you see and hear.[83] Perhaps the moves of the 1900 and 2700 players are identical, but for the hypothetical grandmaster, they have different meaning because of the rankings of the players. Ratings organize social relations in an otherwise complex domain of action.

High status is not always desirable. Sometimes players covet lower ratings. The rationale for this strategy—termed "sandbagging"—connects to the social organization of chess. Tournaments are structured by rating classes; adult tournaments award cash prizes at each level, but the higher classes are often awarded larger prizes. A player might feel that he can win in a lower class, just as a boxer or wrestler may try to qualify for a lower weight class. A player with a 2000 rating would be forced to play against competitors rated 2000–2199. He would be the weakest player. But if his rating were 1999, he would be the best of the 1800–1999 group. One point could translate into thousands of dollars. Speaking to the metaphor as well as the competition, one player referred to this desire to be in a lower class as "playing in the mud" (field notes). While wrestlers and boxers gain or lose weight, in chess the practice of manipulating one's rating is seen as devious. I was told of a strong player who played in the Chicago Open and lost to two 600 players and drew a 900 player, a result that seemed implausible. Granted, this player could not fall far, but such a tournament result would decrease his rating (field notes). Yet no matter how poor your results (or how bad you *are*), your rating can never fall more than two hundred points (rounded to the next hundred) below what it was at its peak.[84] The question is whether one can determine who really has become weaker and properly belongs in a lower tournament division and who is merely pretending. The former should have no rating floor, but judging incompetence is a sensitive matter in a world in which ratings are seen as simultaneously true and self-defining.

One reason ratings are perceived as useful is that they serve as guides. Those who face a lower-rated player may complicate the game. As one respected chess authority explained, "You want to play a very positional game against them and try to get more into the subtleties of chess that only experience is going to bring" (interview). Recognizing this, a player explains that when he plays a higher-rated player, he wants the game to be "like crazy and tactical," dramatic and aggressive (interview). The better player relies on the cooling of experience, the weaker player on the heat of the moment. The lower-rated player is more likely to accept a draw and the higher-rated player more likely to offer one. Ratings are consequential in social relations not only before and after a match but also in the course of the game. In this, chess is like any social world in which deference organizes life.

Odd Fellows in a Soft Community

Open communities are filled with strangeness: persons of odd demeanor who find comfort among those who appear to treat them as equals. Conformity may be powerful, but it is far from absolute, and some idiosyncrasy is tolerated. One of the more influential fraternal orders in Great Britain and the United States is known as the Odd Fellows. Oddness confers some benefits, as communities must determine individually and collectively to what extent they recognize, tolerate, or encourage behavior that stands outside preferred standards. As an accepting world—a soft community—the chessworld, like other voluntary domains, tolerates strangeness as long as a commitment to the common endeavor is evident.

No metric exists for oddity. However, there is little doubt that strangeness is central to the self-perception of the chess community. While some believe that chess obsession is in itself destructive (see Vladimir Nabokov's 1930 novel *The Defense*), the assumption is that the game attracts and nurtures those who flout the standards of broader society. Chess suffers the insufferable.[85] Perhaps the chessworld is a *greedy institution* that discourages participation in other social domains.[86] But sometimes chess provides social support.

When I studied Dungeons & Dragons,[87] a few concerned parents warned that the game encouraged adolescent suicide. There were some. Was the game deadly? But how many people choose life because of communal support? Psychologist and international master William Hartston claimed, "Chess is not something that drives people mad; chess is something that keeps mad people sane."[88]

I met men who were strange by any standard. They were not people "you want to take home with you" (field notes). I also met some who were accomplished, charismatic, and socially adept. Reuben Fine, for instance, was more psychiatrist than patient.

But because of a common focus on the game, eccentricity is accepted. Like other voluntary spaces, the chessworld constitutes a *soft community*, an action arena where commitment justifies one's presence. The group tolerates a wide range of behaviors as long as chess is esteemed. As my friend Jeremy explained, emphasizing the role of community support, "Chess doesn't make you go crazy, but it provides a place for crazy people" (field notes). Put metaphorically, "There are nuts in the chess community. There are always a few filberts; some are hard shelled" (field notes). After quoting master chess teacher Bruce Pandolfini that "there are more unbalanced people in chess than in your average profession or activity," Paul Hoffman noted, "Chess culture is a haven for social misfits: it does not care how players dress or speak . . . and it offers its own rich world, in which you need only chess skills to succeed."[89] Talented loners are not alone, and devout misfits can fit in. As Puddephatt remarks, "The chess club is a perfect venue for those who want social contact but have little aptitude for it."[90] If acceptance is based on commitment to chess, poker, bridge, Scrabble, or pick-up basketball, those who embrace the leisure self can join.

Given that participation is the key membership criterion, some accept deviance. One competitor cheerfully labeled himself "the chess psycho." He wasn't psychotic, but he was sufficiently socially inept that others referred to him as "monkey boy." Another coped with Asperger syndrome, a high-functioning form of autism. He was a startlingly good player but was limited in banter. Still, he was widely accepted and admired.[91] This doesn't mean that some players aren't criticized, considered immature, or worse: "sociological scumbuckets," as one put it. These evaluations are part of the moral economy of the community, but the scorned remain members:

> Thomas, thin and lanky, wore only a light sweater and no socks. He was shivering as he responded to Turnbull's queen pawn opening with the classic Slav Defense. First Turnbull won Thomas's king pawn, then a bishop, and finally his queen.... "I have an excuse," he said. "My feet are cold. I should have worn socks but I haven't done laundry in weeks."[92]

> I am told of a middle-aged man who, while playing a younger woman, sneezed on the pieces and continued playing as if nothing had happened. While this was an account of deviance, it was told to indicate the acceptance of such deviance. (field notes)

These men belonged to the chessworld. Strange but tolerated, and perhaps treasured because they suggest that commitment is what matters. Within the game one's opponent is an enemy,[93] but after the game the community embraces all. The chessworld incorporates an explosion of cultural styles, even hip-hop or "Eurotrash." A group of international masters talked about a colleague seen as a "chess thug," far from the norms of a sport of gentlemen. At one point, I was told, he tried to kiss a tournament director in the playing hall. He often seemed on the edge of explosion. And yet he had a social community that tolerated him. Tournament directors keep a "wall of shame" in the backroom to remind them of potential problems, but those pictured on the wall are not excluded from participation (field notes). My field notes are filled with stories of attempted suicides, drunken fits, promiscuity, destructive rages (a chess star kicked in a hotel wall), and drug use (especially Adderall), but these are stories of people who *belong*.

Of course, every community eventually draws boundaries. In one club, a male was excluded because of his sexual harassment of a younger female. A larger scandal was that of Robert Snyder, a convicted child sex abuser, master-level player, and scholastic chess instructor. After his prison term, Snyder was supposed to remain on parole, but he fled to Belize. The word went out through chess networks about this predator, and the community breathed a sigh of relief when he was captured.[94] For hard cases, a soft community is not enough. Boundaries are not infinitely flexible.

The Black Rook

Deviance is tolerated in a competitive community, but cheating cuts to its heart. Even soft communities draw boundaries when their core beliefs are threatened. Most chess players act properly. Perhaps there is technical "cheating"—that is, not following the lengthy rule book—but much rule breaking is not considered cheating and is therefore not treated as a problem. But the concern with cheating—preserving moral boundaries—is such that tournament organizers hire *arbiters* or floor directors to answer questions, handle disputes, and watch games.[95] They are the beat cops of chess; their surveillance prevents gross violations.

Put aside technical rule breaking such as noting one's moves improperly or hitting one's clock before one moves. These are things that are outside the rules but are not quite cheating. Given that rules (rule 20G) outlaw annoying one's opponent (the tournament director has discretion), much tapping, coughing, grunting, or staring might be outside the rules, perhaps even, as discussed above, wearing a low-cut dress. The rules note that the director has "the right to invoke rule 20G" for coughing, but the authors recommend that "this is quite harsh if the player's actions are involuntary."[96] It is not that a sniffle is cheating, but how it is defined is locally determined. But some violations are crucial: touch-move violations, fixed games, and receiving advice during the game.

THE ETERNAL TOUCH

The most common form of cheating is to violate the touch-move rule. The touch-move rule is at the core of competitive play, as it defines the end of one turn and the start of the next. To abrogate the rule is to permit "do-overs." Players often discover an error while the piece is in air. Rule 10B states "a player on move who deliberately touches one or more pieces, in a manner that may reasonably be interpreted as the beginning of a move, must move or capture the first piece touched that can be moved or captured."[97] An exception is made for when players "merely" wish to adjust the pieces on their squares. They should say, "Adjust" or "J'adoube." This touching is not considered touching that requires a move.

But humans are klutzy clods. A separate rule (10E) says that if the touch is deemed accidental, the piece need not be moved (rule 10G says if it is dropped accidently on a legal square the drop counts). So some players newly wise to their error claim that a piece was accidently touched. Sometimes players claim that they did not even touch a piece that was grazed. Games are not video-recorded, so it is the word of the two players. If the floor director is called over, and the two hold their ground, the claim of accidental touch is usually upheld. The plaintiff is left with nothing more than a gossipy story and perhaps an emotionally intense game. Floor directors claim that adjudicating touch-move claims is the greatest problem they face, particularly in scholastic tournaments. As one scholastic tournament director explained: "You have a lot of low-level cheating with violations of the touch-move rule. Kids will touch a piece and not move it. That is endemic in any tournament, especially at the lower grade levels, and those are almost impossible to adjudicate by a director because it is one kid's word against the other, even though our suspicion is that nine times out of ten, ninety-nine times out of a hundred, the kid who is complaining about it is probably right" (interview). But sometimes the desire to cheat cannot be hidden and may be captured on video-tape.[98] A dramatic story tells of the temptation of rule breaking:

> As the child took advantage of my error and eagerly captured my pawn, he let out a loud, snotty snort.... He smiled, got up from the table, and skipped around the room. I saw no alternative than to comply with his plan. But after I made my move, I realized that I had overlooked a killer continuation that would have won his queen ... and subsequently the game. I was angry at myself for missing it. Once you make a move in tournament chess it is absolutely forbidden to retract it. But the child was still away from the table frolicking with his friends, so he didn't know that I had moved. I glanced at the players at the neighboring board, and when I saw that they were so engrossed in their own games that they would not witness what I was doing, I reached out, took back my move, and assayed the winning continuation instead. Ignorant of my infraction, the boy

returned to the board and saw that I had won his queen. He gasped, resigned the game, and left abruptly. When he gasped, I felt terrible, and my humanity returned.... I was disgusted with myself.[99]

The story reveals the power of community standards. The writer realized that he had violated a fundamental moral principle and felt self-loathing, particularly in cheating a child. It also involves surveillance. The writer concludes that he can cheat unobserved; other times the temptation is present but the concern with other eyes outweighs it.

Claims of adjusting a piece avoid the touch-move rule. The rules state that adjustments are permitted if the motive is clear *even if the adjustment has not been announced.* One need not say "I adjust" or "J'adoube." But clarity can be in the mind of the beholder. Sometimes touching a piece can falsely be claimed to be an adjustment, even at top tournaments:

> The behavior of Grandmaster Milan Matulovic of Yugoslavia ... at the 1967 Interzonal in Tunisia stands as one of the most outrageous violations of tournament rules ever perpetrated at an event of such importance [a tournament to determine the challenger for the world championship]. Matulovic moved his bishop, pressed his clock, and suddenly saw that he had made a mistake. So he took back his move, made a different move, and only then said "J'adoube." ... Until that game, all the Yugoslav players customarily took their evening meals together in the hotel, but thenceforth Matulovic dined alone, shunned by his own compatriots. And ever since that incident, he has been sneeringly referred to as "J'adoubovic."[100]

While formal procedures could not punish Matulovic, given that the only other witness was his opponent, the normally soft chessworld enforced hard control. On one level the guarantor of rules is the tournament director, but when violations are egregious, the community itself has power.

FIXED GAMES

In any competition, the animating assumption is that the outcome reflects the ability of the opponents. Some of the most revealing sports stories are from those moments at which this belief is undercut. The

1919 Black Sox scandal in which the outcome of the World Series was fixed lives with us still, immortalized in film, books, and in the saying aimed at Shoeless Joe Jackson, "Say it ain't so, Joe."

Given this, I was surprised to learn of the number of games that were "fixed" at tournaments. I don't suggest that this collusion is fully accepted, but it is understood and even sympathized with. As noted above, sometimes in the final round, two players recognize that by ensuring a draw or having one of them win, they will share a larger pot, and they agree to the outcome. They desire to maximize profit or to gain a norm for grandmaster status. Even such a powerful player as Viktor Korchnoi admitted to being involved in games that were fixed.[101] This was Bobby Fischer's (proper) complaint against his Soviet opponents: that the outcomes of their games were fixed to produce desired tournament results. After the fall of the Soviet Union, the justification for fixing games was personal, not political. I was told several times about grandmasters whose games were said to be arranged with the losers sharing the prize; such accounts have been published several times in *Chess Life*. As one writer said, "I was also aware of dealings being made and games being thrown at the boards around me in the last round of that tournament.... You know this 'cheating thing' has been around at chess tournaments for many years now."[102] US champion Hikaru Nakamura was once offered "compensation" for a draw. He refused and reported the proposal. "Penalties were assessed," but the players involved are still in good standing.[103] I was told of two distinguished players tied for first in the final round of a tournament in which first prize was a new Buick. One player made a "foolish blunder," giving the other player first place and the car, which he sold, and split the profits with the "loser." This story was not shared to attack the two players but because the narrator found the episode amusing. The reality of fixed games is evident in an instance involving world champion Garry Kasparov, which, if true, is both damning and enlightening: "Nigel [Short, a British grandmaster] told me, '[Georgian grandmaster Zurab Azmaiparashvili, Kasparov's chief second] offered [American grandmaster Nick de Firmian] a draw and $2000 if he took it. Nick declined. Kasparov went up to Nick and was very angry with him. He said that $2000 was a very generous offer for a draw and that he should accept. Of course he's a friend of Azmaiparashvili and wanted to help him.'"[104] I have no idea whether the event happened, but it is remarkable that it is seen as plausible that the world champion would suggest that a game should be drawn for a price.

Why bother showing up when the outcome is determined? Chess, like other domains in which outcomes affect the community, is based on trust in the legitimacy of a hierarchy. The rating organizations rely on the information they receive. In other words, the tournament organizer is the guarantor of trust. On occasion a player submits a score sheet that indicates that a loser won, particularly if it is unlikely that the opponent will check, a situation that happened twice in my observation. The first time it was treated as an error; in the other instance the player was ejected for turning in a score sheet with false moves. On rare occasions tournament directors submit results for tournaments that are not played and that shape the ratings of these "players." A friend well versed in eastern European chess politics explained, "There was this Ukrainian tournament that didn't occur. It's a huge thing in European chess that you buy norms [the criteria by which titles are awarded]. You might not buy a norm, but you buy key games" (field notes). These "ghost tournaments,"[105] as they are called, are said to occur in the Wild East of the Balkans or the former Soviet Union, perhaps reflecting American beliefs about their foreign counterparts.

While imaginary tournaments are rejected, it is surprising that arranged outcomes are understood. They undercut the legitimacy of the ratings system, but the communal understanding that players struggle for prizes provides some acceptance. Of course, when someone wins a prize, someone else will lose, but this recognition is ignored.

THE TROUBLES OF HELP

Given the relative lack of concern about collaboration to produce game outcomes, the deep concern about external aid was startling. In many leisure worlds players receive advice from their coaches. Perhaps in chess one can more easily use that expert advice than in baseball or golf. Moving a pawn is easy, swinging a club less so. The relationship between the advice and the follow-through varies.

Before the advent of portable electronics, the concern was personal communication—whispers and winks—a concern found primarily in scholastic chess. Players are not supposed to talk about their games, but it is legitimate for players to have unsupervised conversations with friends while wandering the floor. If the conversants talk in Russian, those who are not fluent are suspicious,[106] perhaps an outgrowth of Cold War mistrust. In the past, when games would be adjourned for the night, prior to the availability of computer databases, players could legitimately develop lines of attack with friends or assistants. A game could transform from an individual to a collective effort at night and the following morning return to individual game once again.

The real challenge today is electronic communication. As one chess organizer pointed out, "The problem is that when you are suspicious, everything looks suspicious" (field notes).[107] At times moral panic has arisen over cybercheating. While use of electronic magic is sometimes only imagined, cases have been documented—perhaps as many as one per month.[108] One Polish player was expelled from a tournament after it was discovered that his moves corresponded 98 percent with those of the chess program Rybka. No devices were discovered, but the similarity was sufficient for punishment. The most famous (unproven) charge occurred at the world championship match between Veselin Topalov and Vladimir Kramnik. Topalov charged that Kramnik used his private bathroom too often; since the room was not monitored, he might be relying on computer assistance. Many moves matched those of high-level computer programs, but, after all, Kramnik had been world champion. After accusations back and forth, locking of the restrooms, and an angry forfeit by Kramnik, the match continued—now nicknamed the "Toilet Bowl"—and Kramnik emerged victorious.[109] Today hearing devices, CD players, and cell phones are seen as sources of dishonor. In one case a group of Latvian players accused a Hungarian colleague of receiving signals from a tube of lip balm, electronically linked to a computer outside the hall.[110] My friend Jeremy, a strong international master, has been accused because he listens to an MP3 player during his games. This is permitted (until the final rounds and for the players with the best records),[111] but when his moves seem similar to those of computer programs, he is accused openly or covertly of cheating. An opponent wrote to the USCF suggesting, "Either we have a new Nakamura [the US champion] or we have a cheater." The charge went nowhere and undermined the collegiality of the community.

Ultimately, these instances are about how a community views moral propriety and how they police boundaries. Cheating is deviance, but rather than being tied to the person, it is connected to the scene. The extent to which obtaining advice from those outside the game is legitimate is a communal decision. Rules are created in and bolster status systems, part of group life.

Status Games

In this chapter I have addressed how the chessworld generates and distributes status and how it serves as an accepting community, at least provisionally. Central is the rating system. The salience of these seemingly precise, if organizationally determined, assessments of ability distinguishes chess from many voluntary activities. All systems have status hierarchies, but some rely on explicit systems to produce them. Often the hierarchy will be a ranking (as in tennis, for instance), but the ranking in chess is based on a rating. While many players claim that they are not concerned with their rating, numbers can become goals, motivating continued engagement. These numbers generate other status markers, such as titles (grandmaster, master, or expert). Here status is tied to achievements in tournament play. Once such titles are awarded, they become honorifics and create deference.

Just as many activities are socially situated, so is chess. High-level chess has been dominated by Jews and eastern Europeans, a reality that is slowly changing with the growth of chess in India and China. This reality can produce ethnic tension and bigotry with claims that ethnic presence might be destructive to the game itself. The outcome of a contest might seem objective, but it is often read through the character of participants.

Age and gender matter as well. At tournaments, young and old are immersed in a multigenerational family—a rosy picture, if not always a happy one for the adults who lose to children improving with each game. With regard to gender, many social domains have figured out how to incorporate women and girls. Chess hasn't yet, and hostility, harassment, and patronizing acts are still found. The community struggles with the recognition that all social worlds should be open, but theirs is not.

Finally, I consider moral outcasts and a welcoming community. In chess, a common belief is that the game is open to all, and that the presence of the odd and obnoxious reveals the strength of a shared commitment. Chess provides a *soft community* in which *strange persons* are accepted. They do not have equal status, but they belong. A big tent of openness depends upon embracing common rules and values. It is here that beliefs about cheating become relevant. The fundamental value in chess is that over-the-board games are determined by the individual and help from another mind—human or electronic—is unacceptable. So too is infringement of the touch-move rule, which links mind and body, eliminating the do-over.

All social worlds create status systems, and in this, chess serves as a powerful example. Games spawn winners and losers (and those who draw), and this becomes the primary basis of status, although colored by external characteristics (age, religion, nationality, gender, class, dress, hygiene). Chess is both inclusive and exquisitely sensitive to the world of minute differentiations. But chess is also part of a larger world, a world of institutions, politics, and technology, and it is this context that I address in the next chapter.

7

CHESS IN THE WORLD

There may be an analogy in totalitarian states, or states which are autocratically led even if they are democracies, but in a real democracy there should be no particular resemblance to chess.

LORD JAMES CALLAGHAN

While cultures are always locally grounded, to ignore the institutions and structures that surround communities misses how society is organized. When I examined high school debate, I watched boys and girls struggling with the creation of persuasive talk. They talked to and with each other, but they were provided the opportunity to participate because of values that were made material by school boards and principals—values of democratic discourse. Debate is not alone; social worlds are simultaneously local and extended.

With some forty million Americans who can play chess, with the United States Chess Federation having eighty thousand members, with 140 high schools in Illinois that maintain competitive chess teams, with the state of Idaho including chess instruction for second and third graders in their curriculum, chess competition is situated in a wider world. In this chapter I examine the chessworld in light of its politics, economics, and technology, but I begin by discussing the community as judged by the larger public.

Play and Public

In a media-saturated society, the public is aware of many action domains in which it has little interest. I know many things about hunting, waterskiing, snorting cocaine, knitting, and playing the violin, even though I have done none of these things. Perhaps it would be more precise to say that I have been told about these activities and their communities.

Much knowledge is spread through popular discourse, media images, and advertising. Firms routinely use images of chess to sell products, including Intel and Geico Insurance. As Reuben Fine pointed out during World War Two, we read about pawns, pieces on the board, and gambits.[1] The United States Chess Federation presents such metaphors in its publications:

> The knights, bishops, castles, and queens are maneuvering on the global chessboard. It is unclear whether the USGovt leaders are adept at chess, while Russian President Putin is a master chess player.

> The stock exchange sector's chess game of consolidation is likely to drag out longer from here, says an analyst.[2]

These metaphors are readily understood. Chess is an activity that most literate Americans know *something* about. Bobby Fischer connected chess to creativity, insanity, quirky genius, and American ingenuity, leading President Gerald Ford to declare October 9 National Chess Day. Chess served a greater function in the Soviet Union, both justifying the state apparatus and exemplifying national excellence, and also providing a space for civil society in which players could think outside of the reach of the state.[3] The game represented both the state to its people and the opposition to the state; it created a zone of private creativity on which the state depended.

The scholastic boom of the past twenty years suggests that chess is seen as helping a child build cultural capital. But on the other hand, there is a fundamental skepticism of chess. It is often treated as not fully masculine but "nerdy."[4] As one star high school player commented: "How the public views chess, it always ticks me off.... There are small comments that I know people don't respect it.... 'The nerd's here.' There are a lot of people who would be really good at chess, but won't do chess club, because they think it is all a bunch of nerds. A lot of people are deterred from chess because of the nerd stereotype" (interview). At Lakeside High School the chess team chose not to participate in the school pep rally. A varsity player explained, "You could be embarrassed by it. Because you don't want to go and say you are this huge nerd in front of the school" (interview).

This image of chess transcends high school corridors. As Garry Kasparov remarked, "Good at chess usually means bad at life" (field notes). The wife of an active player speaks of the magazines that he studies as "geek porn."[5] More to the point is the television reality show *Beauty and the Geek*, where eight socially challenged male geeks were paired with female beauties. One geek was an active chess player.[6]

More than scorning chess, much of the public rarely thinks about the chess community. The moral philosopher James Rachels, a committed player, contrasts chess with music, both domains with child prodigies and lengthy traditions, but with very different public perception:

> If chess is an art, it is hardly treated as such in the United States. Imagine what it would be like if music were as little known or appreciated. Suppose no self-respecting university would offer credit courses in music, and the National Endowment for the Arts refused to pay for any of it.... Once in a while a Mozart might capture the public imagination, and like Bobby Fischer get written about in *Newsweek*. But the general attitude would be that, while this playing with sound might be clever, and a great passion for those who care about it, still in the end it signifies nothing very important.[7]

With the prominence of Russians and eastern Europeans, it is easy to see why chess is not treated as fundamental to *American* life. Attempts by chess federation officers to gain sponsorship from large American companies such as McDonalds and American Airlines have come to naught.

When Americans feel underappreciated, they blame marketing. Over the years, there have been numerous attempts to rectify this lack of appreciation. The stories of scholastic chess are heartwarming, as in the book *Searching for Bobby Fischer* or the documentary *Brooklyn Castle*, but the *buzz* that they generate is momentary, not cemented into continuing popular fascination. The standard line is that a great and charismatic player is needed to capture American—or global—attention. As author Jennifer Shahade points out, "If there was more of a celebrity culture around the top players in this country, that would really help—so that when these young kids see the grandmasters being treated like royalty, it would make them want to be those grandmasters."[8] Many current stars are colorless, at least as far as the popular media. Perhaps the handsome young Norwegian world champion Magnus Carlsen will change that. As one prominent grandmaster pointed out:

Chess was unfortunate not being able to find those personalities to promote it.... A couple of years ago, poker was poker, and now it is all over different television stations.... Chess does have the potential; there are about forty million people just in America who play chess. A few decisions can change that overnight. If CBS or ESPN decided tomorrow we are having a chess reality show, it may have the same effect as poker or years ago golf or tennis. So one breakthrough can change the whole game. [A charismatic figure] is not necessarily a positive figure; it could be a controversial figure. (interview)

Perhaps this is a fantasy, but it is a common one. In 1972 lightning struck momentarily in the mercurial figure of Robert James Fischer. The problem, as novelist Julian Barnes has pointed out, is that once you commercialize your sport, you lose control of the message.[9] This is the dilemma of relying upon powerful allies; their support is comforting, but ultimately one is at their mercy.[10] In the case of Bobby Fischer, the problem was with not only the man himself but the fact that the media found a powerful rise-and-fall storyline, not one with which the chess community was pleased.

Publics do not merely stand outside but are bridges to the inside. The presentation of how "the public" thinks about any social domain contributes to whether individuals will join. Public evaluation creates images of activities that attract or repel those considering involvement. Ultimately the problem revolves around the boundaries of community. Chess can be comfortable in its own sheltered world, but the problem that all ambitious communities face is how to extend boundaries while preserving a desired image. Within the United States tennis has achieved this; soccer has not. Poker has, bridge has not.

An Economical Game

A social world requires an economic model in order to survive. The public position of chess produces and is produced by its finances. Playing a game of chess requires minimal investment, but creating a chess community demands more.

At the scholastic level, schools must commit resources for a chess team. Schools do this in various ways. Lakeside High School provides its team with $4,500, plus additional salary support for two teachers (somewhat under $8,000). The chess coach receives as much as the assistant football coach (interview). By standards of high schools in the state, this is generous, although it is lower than the budget for the more prestigious sports or debate teams. In some elementary schools, the chess program is entirely extracurricular, run by a hired coach. In those cases parents must pay for their child's participation, even if the school provides sponsorship and space.

For chess to be an established activity, a circuit of contests is necessary. Tournaments are central to the existence of competitive chess with their emotional and financial economy. Activities provide for collective action, requiring places where regular and committed participants meet. Tournaments can constitute celebrations of community, both in gathering people and sharing activity. When successful, tournaments "have a warm feel to them, a very rich and pleasing experience" (field notes). One friend, Marshall, spoke of the World Open in glowing terms: "I love going to those tournaments. All of the most ardent players are put into one room to compete. It is kind of like the Super Bowl. Everyone who loves the game and the best players are there. Everyone is there for chess, and it is so much more intense. Everyone is playing to win every game. It is great" (interview). While not every player would be as enthusiastic as this 1800-level player, his responses emphasize that while a tournament is an economic proposition, it is also a festive space. Referring to the National Open, Phil, a tournament organizer himself, explains that a successful tournament must attract players, distribute rewards (monetary prizes in adult tournaments and trophies in scholastic ones), function smoothly, and be fun, all leading to profit for the organizer (field notes). These times and spaces constitute the nexus of soft community and economic possibility. They provide civil society with emotionally charged, social-networked events, but entrepreneurs must make them happen. The institution of the tournament suggests that games matter, and this *mattering* draws attendance. Rather than simply playing games, participants build collective history.

But tournaments can fail. Few things anger participants more than delays. Fortunately these are less common now with computer programs that create the pairings, once the cause of many late starts. But organizers must also be ready for unpredictable attendance, a challenge because players can register on the morning of the tournament. A notoriously unsuccessful tournament was held in Chicago to determine the citywide scholastic championship. The organizer was unprepared for the crowd of children who showed up, lacked equipment, and could not create pairings. The tournament ended in chaos, with a hundred students and coaches departing in anger.[11]

Tournaments differ in their organization. Some are invitational, closed to a few select participants who compete in round-robin fashion. These select gatherings are typically sponsored by an organization, such as the World Chess Federation, or a corporation, such as Aeroflot. Other tournaments are opens, where anyone can pay an entry fee to participate. These are often run by profit-making groups. Opens, particularly in the United States, are called Swiss-system tournaments, after a tournament held in Zurich in 1895.[12] Players play others with roughly equivalent records, with the group of players with the same record divided in half on the basis of ratings and the best player in the top half playing the best player in the bottom half.

As an economic proposition, organizers must see these events as enhancing, financially or morally. Tournaments must be established by an individual or group that takes responsibility and merges their interests with their community. They then must persuade the community that this merger is equitable. Organizers determine the entry fee, the prize fund (and how it should be allocated), and the length of the event and provide playing space and inexpensive rooms. The negotiation between organizer and hotel or convention center is crucial, although smaller scholastic tournaments are held in schools. The structure of tournaments must fit the demands of the hospitality industry, which doesn't see a chess tournament as a prime draw. The Foxwoods Casino in Connecticut canceled its involvement with chess. As one player informed me, "[Players] didn't gamble, and they caused a lot of damage to the rooms" (field notes). Vandalism without gaming is not the most appealing combination for a casino. In most contracts, a minimum number of nights booked is required if a penalty is not to be levied. As one tournament organizer explained, "You wind up being a room salesman."

Fortunately chess tournaments require little in the way of public space: a tournament hall and smaller rooms for informal games (called skittles), a bookstore, and a tournament office. Still, hotels give chess tournaments low priority. One tournament director suddenly found much of the space promised assigned to a gun show. Organizers claim that chess players refuse to pay more than ninety-nine dollars for a room but want a four-star hotel. One organizer considered a tournament at a nice suburban hotel with an attached water park but rejected the idea when the hotel insisted on $144 a night per room. For those who play for cash prizes, spending $500 on a room is likely to erase their winnings.

In the United States most major tournaments are organized either by the Continental Chess Association, run by Bill Goichberg, or by the United States Chess Federation, whose former president and longtime executive board member is Bill Goichberg. American chess would look very different without Goichberg's influence. The USCF runs official tournaments, such as the United States Open, the annual national scholastic tournaments, and the invitational United States Chess Championship. A string of other tournaments, such as the prestigious World Open (with a $175,000 guaranteed prize fund in 2010, generated through registration fees and other revenue sources), the North American Open, and the Chicago Open, are run by the Continental Chess Association. There are, of course, competing tournaments, such as the National Open, held in Las Vegas every year and treated as a USCF national tournament. These major events have multiday schedules, often over holiday weekends. In addition smaller regional and local tournaments are held for a day with a modest prize fund. Goichberg's opens set the tone for American tournaments, with some higher-rated players feeling that they do not receive the respect they receive in Europe, including more generous appearance fees. But an informal analysis of the Chicago Open suggests that the tournaments as currently structured are profitable. Examining likely sources of income and expenses, a rival tournament director guessed that the Continental Chess Association might have netted $35,000 from this one tournament. The estimate of entry fees at this tournament with approximately seven hundreds players was $137,000, with $100,000 in prizes.

In contrast, as I describe in the prologue, I was invited to a new tournament, the Atlantic City Invitational Tournament, held the week prior to Christmas in a pleasant Sheraton hotel, some distance from the Boardwalk. A prize fund of $30,000 was guaranteed, with an increase to $50,000 if more than 500 entrants attended. Those attending enjoyed themselves. However, the tournament failed financially. The co-organizers dreamed of five hundred participants and hoped for three hundred in order to break even. With 162 players and despite a \$149 early registration fee and \$99 hotel rooms, they each lost approximately \$12,000. Perhaps the timing was poor, perhaps the weather hurt, perhaps a national scholastic tournament the week before or a tournament in Asbury Park on the Jersey Shore in October drew potential players, or perhaps Atlantic City was not considered child-friendly. Failure has many parents.

Like many voluntary worlds, chess is a community of communities, an action space in which diverse groups overlap or ignore each other. Many players find attending a tournament great fun, even if they do not win a monetary prize. Few participants receive prizes, and fewer cover their costs. However, some see chess as a livelihood, or at least a part of a livelihood. Once virtually all competitors, even chess champions, needed a day job, a trust fund, or an employed spouse. One chess organizer explained, "Some of the top grandmasters are married to women who have very good jobs so they can travel around the country, and the women allow them to have this occupation as a professional chess player. Like Grandmaster A's wife is a surgeon, Grandmaster B's wife is an attorney, Grandmaster C's wife is a computer programmer. So by these women having these high-powered jobs, it keeps the family going so their husbands can go around the country and play chess" (interview). In the nineteenth century Paul Morphy believed that being a "chess professional" was a mark of shame.[13]

How many people earn a significant portion of their livelihood from competitive chess? There are those players in Washington Square Park who are part of the underground economy and condescendingly termed hustlers. These men, pleasing tourists and thrill seekers, have the air of carny barkers. One man kept repeating, "Chess players. Come on over. No gambling. No clock." This mantra slid into a financial transaction, either through betting or by direct payment. Many games are three-minute blitz, spiced with trash talk, an exciting scene.[14] This world was once primarily Jewish and is now largely black and Hispanic. Those in the park belong to a chessworld, but their community barely overlaps with scholastic and tournament play.

Beyond these vivid performers stand others who hope to use chess for gainful employment. One New Yorker, familiar with chess scenes, suggested that fewer than one hundred Americans earn their living from playing or writing about chess.[15] When one adds teachers, tournament organizers, or those who sell chess equipment, the number has been estimated at fifteen hundred. With the growth of scholastic and high school chess, teaching is a growth area, even if not highly lucrative. These teachers charge whatever the market and their rating will bear. Top teachers, such as Bruce Pandolfini, can earn a comfortable living from teaching, charging at least $200 an hour and carefully selecting promising students.[16]

Today lessons are available on Internet websites, creating a global circuit of learning, particularly helpful to Russian grandmasters. Players and their teachers create an economic marketplace in which skills and ratings are monetized. At each rating level there is always someone to learn from, and even supergrandmasters hire or collaborate with others.

At the highest level, the community has achieved some measure of financial stability, and top players live comfortably, aided by writings and endorsements. With the exception of very few, such as Garry Kasparov, income is from within the community. This stands in contrast to chess champions Wilhelm Steinitz and Alexander Alekhine, who died in abject poverty in 1900 and 1946, respectively. The Soviets supported their champions in the style in which their elites were treated. In the United States, Bobby Fischer pushed for larger prizes, at one point indicating that only two players in the United States were earning a living from chess.[17] In fact, the winner of the 1969 world chess championship received less than $3,000 (in rubles); by 1993, the investment in the match was nearly $10 million (with approximately $1.5 million to the winner).[18] Today top players command a $25,000 appearance fee. As Kasparov said of one championship: "[America] is the centre of the financial world. If you want to succeed as a professional sport you must be in America.... This is where the money is.... You could see it on CNN International. That changed the rules of the game. We are a legitimate professional sport now."[19] With his gold Audemars Piguet wristwatch, Moscow apartments, and bespoke suits,[20] Kasparov embodies the financial possibilities for a champion who is willing to monetize himself. A culture of celebrity helps an activity package itself for a lay public.

The Russian Invasion

From the 1940s onward Soviet chess was dominant. This was one reason that Reuben Fine, arguably the strongest chess player of the early 1940s, decided not to contest the chess championship later that decade. Fine was heir apparent to the championship when Alexander Alekhine passed away. American players were, understandably, distraught when he left chess to practice psychoanalysis.

With the exception of the brief Fischer interregnum, the Soviets owned global chess. The story of Soviet dominance and challenges to that dominance is enlightening, particularly as documents and reminiscences emerged depicting KGB involvement.[21] The cases of Boris Gulko and Viktor Korchnoi, who escaped the Soviet regime, are dramatic.[22] Chess truly mattered for bolstering the legitimacy of the Soviet state, whereas, in contrast, it barely registered for the US security apparatus. The success of Bobby Fischer provided a momentary propaganda jolt, but the American state was only peripherally involved, in contrast to the machinations of the Soviets, who helped determine who would win major matches. If accounts in *The KGB Plays Chess* can be trusted, Soviet intelligence was involved in undercover operations of unsurpassed nastiness, such as attempting to infect a French lover of Boris Spassky with venereal disease.[23]

With the collapse of the Soviet Union, the world of chess altered. As early as the 1980s, Soviet players were migrating to the West, but after 1991, the subsidies for chess vanished, and the exodus increased. Sociologist Mariano Sana spoke of this as a case of "highly skilled migration."[24] Soviet emigration affected local chess communities including those in the United States. For a long time, the top ten US players included nine who were born in the former Soviet Union (the tenth was Hikaru Nakamura, born in Japan but raised in the United States).[25] The joke was that in team competition at the Chess Olympiad, it was "our Russians playing their Russians."[26] The possibility of migration was so established that one coach, teaching at a high school with many eastern European students, jokes that when there is a team opening, "I just go to Russia to get another kid" (field notes).

The "Russian invasion" has had multiple effects, positive and negative, for the development of American chess. That so many top players were born in the former Soviet Union suggested that native-born Americans could not compete. For about a decade, beginning in the late 1990s, no American-born player received the title of grandmaster. American chess, while existing in local communities, could not compete on the international stage. Today elite chess is a global enterprise with more international players visiting the United States.

The top dozen FIDE ratings from June 2014 belong to a Norwegian, an Indian, an Armenian, three Russians, an American-born Italian, a Bulgarian, a Frenchman, a Cuban, an Israeli, and a Japanese-born American (Nakamura). To be sure, the rankings tilt toward the former Soviet Union, but the diversity is increasing. Some weeks the four-person team that I observed in the United States Chess League comprised a Dutchman, a Romanian, a Filipino, and a Bosnian. The team at the University of Texas at Dallas included players from Serbia, India, Costa Rica, Croatia, Moldova, Poland, and Zambia.[27] Squads at urban high schools have a similarly diverse makeup.[28]

Elite American chess as a competitive community is stronger than ever, a result of what one chess organizer termed an "international brain drain." Further, some informants emphasized that these immigrants push Americans to improve and teach them advanced skills. A native-born American can learn diverse styles of play, "gaining all the positives of the immigrant player" (interview), making this public a global marketplace of ideas.

The strength of opponents improves the community. As one informant explained, "Iron sharpens iron." For Americans this migration "weakens their ego, but it sharpens their game" (field notes). As another player explained, "[Americans] may initially complain that we are not doing as well, but they will try to do better" (field notes). Immigration can be motivating. In time new immigrants and their children become Americanized. These immigrants expand the chess community at the top as players and at the bottom as teachers of the young.[29]

When a stable social system is undercut by outsiders, resentment is common. One player spoke of the influx of Eurotrash, while another suggested that these immigrants are degenerates; still another pointed to what he considered inappropriate clothing worn by eastern European women, more suitable, he thought, for a night of clubbing. One American organizer called every eastern European "Russian," whether he hailed from Latvia or Armenia or Bulgaria (field notes). Some American players felt that eastern Europeans colluded in order to win tournaments.[30] One made the bias explicit, saying simply, "I hate Russians."[31]

The hostility is not based merely on cultural conflict but on the reality of competition. In the early years of the "Soviet invasion" in the 1980s and 1990s, there was real resentment from elite players, who saw the immigrants as economic rivals. As one organizer stated, "It's devastating to some of the American players because they couldn't make a living from playing in tournaments." Joel Benjamin was most explicit, writing in his book *American Grandmaster*:

> You cannot assess American chess without addressing, as Jennifer Shahade put it to me once, the "800 pound gorilla in the room"— the domination of foreign born players.... I prefer to place value in developing homegrown talent versus importing developed products.... When Russian chessplayers first began to arrive on our shores they provided competition necessary to stimulate American talent. But the numbers have gotten so out of whack that any young player would be discouraged from a career as a professional player.... In 1989, amid the euphoria of the changes in the Soviet Union, I was asked for my opinion on *glasnost*. I replied that it was "the greatest disaster in the history of American chess."[32]

Another American grandmaster sniffed, "They are mostly rejects from the Russian school of chess whose careers blossomed only after coming to America."[33] This fear of eastern European émigrés destroying local chess communities is so well-recognized that when a Russian-born player was named grandmaster of the year by the USCF, the introducer justified the choice by saying, "He's really American and he's our brightest hope for the future" (field notes).

I do not suggest that nativism is endemic in American chess; there are real friendships and respect between native American players and immigrants. However, resentment results from different cultural traditions and competition over scarce resources. Yet, even with these debates, these "foreigners" have been incorporated into tournaments and teaching and thrive within the soft community of chess. Despite some resentments, there has been no attempt to exclude "Russians"; they belong, even as they strain national pride. Time will erase the boundary between those of eastern European descent and those who were raised in the United States; the redefinition of a once stable scene is never immediate. The fundamental reality is that this domain is composed of partially overlapping cultures that will not completely merge until interests and networks coincide, but the overlap reflects the diversity of the community of chess and the eventual incorporation of a variety of sticky cultures within the same accepting community.

The Technology of the Knight

Part of belonging to a community is embracing local technology. With time all technology becomes mundane. Every community relies on technology, even as it is taken for granted, as is true of the printing press or the sidewalk. As I noted when discussing the institutionalization of the chess clock and the speeding up of chess—altering thought over the board—chess has been tied to innovation, revealing what Mark Sussman refers to as "technological faith."[34] Whether confronting the eighteenth-century automaton or the late twentieth-century Deep Blue, we ask whether new technology is "fair," putting aside the questions of whether it makes our activities less than human and whether it creates a "new chess self,"[35] a self that is understood in light of technological support.

Some thirty years ago the chess community speculated on whether a computer could ever outperform (outthink?) a human champion. Today this question has been answered. Now we consider the effects of computer technology giving players too much knowledge with the availability of huge databases, decreasing human creativity, a creativity that is possible because we do not consider the many possibilities that complete knowledge offers. We worry about whether computers decrease face-to-face interaction, encouraging rapid games, even while encouraging a global competitive environment.

As I noted in chapter 5, local clubs face difficult times. There isn't less chess—there is surely more chess—but the players aren't in the same room or necessarily on the same continent. Increasingly players prefer to play from home. As one proprietor of a chess club told me, "Computer chess has depleted over-the-board chess. You can play in your underpants, and you don't have all of the downtime between matches" (field notes). Internet chess has appeal, especially to those who like to dress down. The strongest charge is that it makes users less social. One feature of a soft community is that it teaches ways of being, shaving some of the raw edges off those less socially adept. While computer chess is open, in that anyone, no matter how peculiar, can find an anonymous opponent, it does not create public ways of being. Computer chess is often a cyberworld that relies on games and not gossip unless these competitions incorporate personal knowledge. Sociability is ignored. Boris remarks:

The bad thing about the Internet is that you lose the social part of chess. People get together and that is why chess is such a good activity, because you are able to communicate with each other without any difficulties. You meet each other at the tournament. You first play the game, and you know each other. You really enjoy your life being in communication with other people. The Internet deprives you of that. You will find people who are addicts. They will sit home and order pizza and Coke and not leave their homes for weeks. It becomes a sickness, and we really should try to prevent that. (interview)

This is the standard argument against technologies new and old: dimmed movie palaces and darkened dens with television consoles. It is not totally false; some embrace pizza-and-Coke-fueled isolation, but so did Bobby Fischer without benefit of computers. Perhaps this shouldn't be pushed too far, as some talk about the friends—real friends—whom they first encountered on the Internet and later met at tournaments. Indeed, one father emphasized that he was convinced that his son is now more social because of his cyberfriends. The discussion boards on the Internet Chess Club are filled with camaraderie. In one case two adolescents—located in separate states and never having met in person—teamed up to win a national online championship. For better or worse, websites such as the Internet Chess Club, which went online in 1992, are now integral to chess.[36] The ICC has over thirty-thousand members who have played millions of games. As of March 1, 2010, the ICC had signed up 680 grandmasters (who could join without a fee), more than half of the total number of active grandmasters (approximately 1,200). That players feel that they can become "addicted" suggests just how compelling these contests can become.[37]

Chess was a natural sphere for the computer revolution. The choice of moves is limited and can be easily conveyed by simple imagery. As J. C. Hallman points out, "It was in computer research that chess found its neatest niche, from there helping to drive the future of technology."[38] To be sure, aspects of the game have changed, such as how one views the board. Online players no longer look down on a three-dimensional board but across at a screen, eliminating bodily and facial cues. Rules had to take into account technological disruptions ("mouse slips" or disconnections), rules about what constitutes cheating (whether one could rely on a high-power program), and time control (privileging speed chess). The computer continued the push to make the game faster and less dependent on extended calculation, more on intuition, becoming a video game. Like all social worlds, chess changed with technology, just as chess was instrumental in changing technology.

Database Heaven

As discussed in chapter 4, the chessworld cherishes moments from the past. These are not simply idle memories but are treated as the fundamental building blocks of both skill and identity. Magazines and books publish influential games that are replayed, studied, and used as the basis of innovations. Even newspaper columns include the moves of a signature game that readers can examine. The best players keep large archives of magazines. Leading American players, such as Bobby Fischer, purchased Soviet journals to learn of the latest openings of their opponents. Chess theory has spread through the printed record.

Times have changed. Databases have replaced wood pulp. Websites archive millions of games,[39] arranged by player and type of opening. The flow of information is astonishing, and the workload is unending. As former world champion Vladimir Kramnik noted nostalgically, one can no longer prepare for just an hour or two for a tournament game: recall has trumped wisdom.[40] Predrag Trajkovic, a Serbian grandmaster, sees this focus on chess theory and memorization—"turbo chess"—as destructive.[41]

Fully 389 of Reuben Fine's games are archived, and so, if I were paired against my namesake in an imaginary tournament, I could learn his favorite openings and defenses. A friend from Lakeside High School, a fan of the Fried Liver opening, told me that he had reviewed more than fifty games on one database. As I have mentioned, at major tournaments I was surprised that top masters often arrived for their games late. On occasion neither player would arrive until fifteen minutes after the lower-rated players had started their clocks. At first I thought that this indicated the casual community of elite chess, but I learned that once pairings were announced, players retreated to their rooms to study the preferred styles of their opponents. If both players did this, the game wouldn't begin until the first player arrived. Even if the clock had started, the loss of time by the late player was considered a wise investment. This, too, is an instance of clock management. Computers also eliminated overnight adjournments. As one official explained, "Computers have made it that adjournments are absurd, because you just go and the computer will spit out the lines that you need to know" (interview). Because the game must end without a "computer break," the time structure is telescoped. Onlookers rely on computers to analyze games in progress, removing the exhilaration of surprise. As one player remarks: "People with their Rybkas yelling whenever the players deviate from computer moves is very annoying. There is no entertainment value in running a computer with every move" (Internet Chess Club discussion board).

But beyond changing tournaments, the presence of huge databases has other consequences. In some regards a chess player is more like a comedian than a musician. Among the elite success and esteem depend upon novelty. A comedian who uses a routine on television is limited in its further use. Once you've heard a joke, the surprise vanishes. Once a game is published, the innovation enters the *literature* and, if remembered, loses its impact. In contrast, the musician will be asked to play her greatest hits. The more often an audience hears a song, the more they demand it. Because of the need for novelty, players hide their games. One teacher referred to a prominent player who "was really upset with the way his games would get transmitted. He said, 'I come up with a new innovation. I work hard. I practice. I learn all these clever things to do. I try them out on somebody, and six months later everybody knows it. That's no longer true. Now everybody knows it two hours later'" (interview). He felt that he could only use his innovations once. I heard one player try to persuade his opponent that they shouldn't turn in their score sheets so their game would not be published. Former world champion Vishy Anand remarks that because of databases he can no longer afford to have a favorite opening but must continually create new variations.[42] Garry Kasparov, knowing that his games will be intensively examined, arranged secret training games, a strategy that has led to spying and bribery.[43]

Yet databases have democratized chess and created more parity, allowing anyone to gain immediate access to games. Given that tournament games are now communicated to audiences in the tournament hall on large screens and online through electronic sensors that monitor the movement of pieces, audiences can evaluate the course of a game in real time. D. T. Max ironically suggests, "In a modern tournament, just about the only people who don't know precisely how well they are doing are the players."[44]

Access to computer evaluation is not the same as knowledge or ability, but it does mean that younger players can memorize openings, and the community is getting younger, as indicated by the increasing numbers of preteen masters and teen grandmasters.[45] Because of computer access, if one hopes to be competitive in tournaments, one cannot just play but must study and memorize, as happened in competitive high school debate.[46] Jeremy, himself a young international master, commented about a younger generation, "You see a lot of kids, they don't have coaches, because they have a computer which they think can tell them what the truth of a position is" (field notes). One instructor explains:

> The main change of what the computers did was to make the opening play very much more important than it used to be. We used to say you can just sort of improvise and do whatever, and put the real struggle off to the middle game. Well, this changed. Because you'd never see the middle game. You wouldn't even reach it. You would get killed out of the opening if you were playing someone who was totally booked on something and you weren't. You would be digging yourself out of a hole. So the importance of the opening has become very much greater. (interview)

A young grandmaster, skeptical about the effects of computers, asserted heatedly, "I don't dislike opening theory. I just dislike that computers came up with it." The coach quoted above makes the radical proposal that everyone should have access to a computer at least in the early stage of the game to prevent memorization from dominating action. While this proposal is not likely to be accepted, it stems from the same desire as Fischer's idea for random chess, in which pieces are randomly placed on the back row. Both are attempts to make memorization less important and to restore creativity. As Boris explained, "Everyone who is not lazy can be well-prepared in the opening. Everyone checks innovations now with the computer" (interview). Still, without the computer by one's side, the human must judge which line of play is best. In the final analysis, the human player must feel the moves, not just remember them.

The Computer as Master

The famous claim, sometimes attributed to computer scientist Donald Michie, asserts, "Chess [is] the Drosophila Melanogaster [the fruit fly] of artificial intelligence."[47] Whatever is true of fruit flies, chess proved an appealing model for artificial intelligence research.[48] The original challenge was to determine how proficient a computer program could become and whether it could play "like" a human, mirroring human thought. At first the possibility that a computer program could beat a human was laughable. In 1963, Horowitz and Rothenberg wrote: "That a richly endowed robot will one day be able to play a highly skillful game of Chess leaves no room for doubt. On the other hand, in the absence of a fantastic superspeed electronic brain, the Chess championship of the world is likely to be retained by humans for centuries to come."[49] In 1989, Garry Kasparov, then world champion, announced: "A machine will always be a machine.... Never shall I be beat by a machine!"[50] His defeat by IBM's Deep Blue in 1997 made Kasparov the cyber age's John Henry. Artificial intelligence had ultimately triumphed.[51] As Bob Bales pointed out, "Kasparov is the greatest player that ever lived; and 'Deep Blue' is the greatest player that never lived.... It is not difficult to be sucker-punched by an anti-strategy, robotic-zombie!"[52] When asked which strategy to choose against a computer opponent, the Dutch grandmaster Jan Hein Donner joked, "I would bring a hammer."[53]

As it turned out, the outcome of the Kasparov–Deep Blue matchup had less impact on chess than might have been imagined at the time. The match gained more publicity than any since the Fischer-Spassky duel, but it was as if the Russians had won. Life moved on. Soon it was no longer of interest whether a computer could beat the world champion. It is likely that the version of Fritz on my laptop could triumph. We don't organize races between runners and bicyclists; as long as the power is on, the computer will triumph. Kasparov himself remarked, "Today a computer could give a simul to grandmasters, but grandmasters wouldn't accept the insult" (field notes). His loss still rankles, as he claims that "on his best day the best human can defeat the best machine."[54] But how to find that one day? Perhaps computer programmers will create machines that "solve" chess, providing a set of moves that—as in tic-tac-toe and now checkers—can never lose, but that day is not here yet.[55]

At this point computers have neither the charisma nor the moral failings of champions,[56] and it is unlikely today that there would be much interest in a match between two computers (one from China versus one from the United States might, perhaps, be an exception). While the original assumption—and fear—was that the computer would be able to "outthink" humans, this is not precisely what happened. The programs, as they have developed, do not mirror human thought, such as human pattern recognition skills, but rather use "brute force" computing to examine a larger range of possibilities than humans can. Kasparov emphasized that his loss was a human achievement by the IBM team, and he distinguished Deep Blue from its human handlers, noting that "Deep Blue was only intelligent the way your programmable alarm clock is intelligent. Not that losing to a $10 million alarm clock made me feel any better."[57] Both humans and computers depend on calculation and evaluation, but humans focus on a few possibilities that "make intuitive sense" and are able to incorporate their own experiences. The reality is, as Kasparov came to recognize, that computers aid human chess play.[58] The question becomes how to bring them—and their programmers—into chess communities.

When writers contrast human play with computer play, they sometimes suggest that as good as the computer might be, its play lacks the "aesthetic attraction of the human game."[59] We strive to discern a boundary between technology-made-human and humanity-made-aesthetic. Computers are said to make moves that are less "humane" or more "robotic," whatever these metaphors might mean in practice. Can moving a knight to the left be mechanical, to the right civilized? Columnist Charles Krauthammer, describing the defeat of grandmaster Bent Larsen by a computer opponent, regretted that "art and intuition lost to brute mechanical force."[60] The word *brute*, as in "brute force computing" suggests a moral evaluation, a form of *metalism*, a deep suspicion of the *motives* and *agency* of technical objects, found in other domains as well, as these objects are actants that, in essence, interact with humans.[61] Can chess players tell which moves were made by computer if they judged them blind? Once one knows who moved, the aesthetics seem obvious. I have heard that humans are more likely to play "random moves" or "aggressive moves," while computers are said to prefer "very complicated" or "extremely subtle" strategies and "wild positions." Everyone *knows* that computers do not think *like* humans, but no consensus exists on what this means. The realization that computers do not "model" the human mind makes the triumph of computers over chess champions hollow.[62]

Still, the success of chess programs makes rejecting computer advice difficult, even if it removes artful surprise. Chess journalist Andy Soltis recognized the deference shown to computer analysis:

> While White was thinking here, spectators following on the Internet asked the universal question of 21st century chess: "WWFD?" (What would Fritz do?) They were stunned when their computers answered 8.Ke2! [white king ahead one square]. It's actually a perfectly good move. Yet it's one almost no carbon-based player would consider. That's beginning to change. The generation of players who grew up on computers has now reached the world's top 10 and it is proving that "computer moves" are perfectly good. As Gata Kamsky said in a Sport day by day interview, "When you constantly prepare with computers, you begin to think like a computer."[63]

Perhaps Kamsky's claim that young players "think like a computer" is strained, but the difference between computer style and human style may be narrowing,[64] creating a new "chess self" for young players. Like professional meteorologists in the digital age, chess players allow their machines to influence their style.[65] I was startled when one player announced that in his opinion Fritz, the most commonly used program, has "mood swings. This is great. This is awful" (field notes). Echoing actor-network theory,[66] another distinguished between personal moves and computer moves, transforming the machine into a social actor: "[The computer] gives you the moves, but they're not your moves. It's the computer's moves. In the past they were really your moves" (field notes).

The belief that a concordance between human and computer moves reveals that the influence of the machine is powerful. One player explained with exasperation that he was accused of cheating in a tournament because his moves were similar to those of a computer program. It was said that he "just played like the computer" and that he must have had access to one. The accuser had no evidence other than the sharp play of the winner and the belief that a computer was a know-it-all. Like many young players, the accused tests his ideas against computer models, learning what the computer "thought" about strategies that he developed, but this does not necessarily indicate access during the game itself (field notes).

Thinking like a computer is a moral claim. The trope suggests the existence of conventions of action, as in other organized social worlds. But it is hard, if not impossible, to know when that charge suggests the similarity of the human and the computer, given that computers must be programmed. To think like a computer is to rely upon a certain style, a style that members of a social world think they know. Ultimately, shared domains are based on choices of which technologies are legitimate, and these can be the technologies of books, cameras, or computers. But a community of action always depends on technology: quills, type, or CPUs. As knowledge creates outcomes, technologies create knowledge.

Chess in the World

No community is an island, no matter how isolated participants may feel at times. External domains shape cultural fields, permitting bridges of power to influence local publics.

Few worlds, however humble, are so obscure as to be unknown in societal discourse. While the Lakeside chess team does not receive the attention that the school's football team does, despite the greater success of the former, the media occasionally visit to produce feel-good features. With forty million casual players, an audience exists for nontechnical reports. The public is open to chess narrative. Richard Peterson and Roger Kern suggest that the American upper middle class is composed of "omnivores," tourists in many cultural domains.[67] People will not only eat Thai food, go to the ballet, listen to jazz, or see a foreign film but will read or listen to accounts of worlds separate from their routines. Feature journalism is often pop anthropology. With many having some chessic knowledge, curiosity is possible, even if commitment rarely lasts. It is not that chess necessarily receives good press; the game may be treated as strange, compulsive, or obscure, but it is potentially story-worthy.

In order to continue their involvement, chess communities must adjust to economic realities and find spaces to gather. With the exception of the highest level of the activity, most amateurs are meagerly rewarded; participation costs rather than pays. Winners ride on the shoulders of losers, with the house taking its cut. For a domain of excellence there must be benefits for professionals, as well as amateurs and an inquiring public.

No matter how tenuous, activities on a global stage have links to political realities. At one point this meant that nations, notably the Soviet Union, utilized chess as a marker of nationalism. This is an extreme case, but perhaps not so unique as revealed by episodes of *leisure trauma*, as when a national soccer or cricket team stumbles in international competition. Public ecstasy explodes when national sportsmen triumph. When Americans win unexpectedly in ice hockey or in chess, citizens treat the victory as validating national worth. Even issues of migration speak to national identity. If there are too many immigrants from eastern Europe, "our" chess players feel threatened by "their" chess players. If there are too many Jews, some players may fear the game can become "polluted." Games are linked to the moral images of participants. The soft community that invites everyone in can be upended by political and moral divisions from outside.

Finally, activities gain meaning from technology. Chess unknowingly changed the world by inspiring extensive research in artificial intelligence. The activity is suitable for modeling. As a game of intellectuals, chess appealed to cognitive scientists; studying their own interests seems pleasant and natural.

In turn, computer technology shapes the chessworld and its varied communities. It is no longer of much interest that a programmed computer can defeat the world chess champion. That is true, but mundane. Rather, technology changes the structure of the activity. Through the Internet, networks are global, not tied to place, a reality with implications for local clubs, once bastions of chess involvement. Even high school coaches find that their students play most of their games online. Further, the games have changed. Most online contests are brief— more video game than deliberately considered. Then there are debates about whether and in what way computer programs have distinct styles and whether players borrow these metallic styles, incorporating those styles into their own play. Players *confront* technology, uncertainly incorporating it, according to the perspectives of local communities.

Subcultures are composed of tiny publics, and every public is shaped by the communal demands that preserve the activity and the action. Recognizing the power of a public, an economy, and a technology, the chessworld reveals that external forces shape what happens within.

Conclusion

PIECE WORK

A reader might be forgiven for believing that this book is about chess. This claim is true, in part. Chess is my example. My goal is to understand the complexities of a leisure world, an expansive, knotty world of voluntary action. I strive to learn how smaller communities fit into a larger community and how this larger community organizes itself to provide for allegiance and affiliation.

The dense world of chess, my research home for five years, is ideal for this purpose, but I could have selected other domains as well. Any location in which individuals and groups voluntarily gather in common commitment would suffice, especially if subgroups with different skills and varying networks overlap.

My interest is not in the games themselves, but what surrounds them in the minds and bodies of players, in their interaction, in the community, and in the interaction orders that make the community possible. Most observational studies focus on one tightly knit group, not examining the existence of an intersecting set of groups that together constitute the community. My argument is that chessworlds are, in every particular, social worlds.

Cultural Models

Much attention has been given to how social systems create their worlds, producing boundaries of similarity and difference. This process is essential for creating categories that make sense given core values. Within communities things never stand for themselves; they stand for larger things. In other words, local actions are transformed into moral claims.

What kind of *thing* is chess? In considering an activity, we place it in a category of similar activities. It is true that everything is unique, but it is also true that everything is similar to everything else. In the introduction I ask how chess is labeled. While many possible labels might be used, I focus on three that have been taken as central. Specifically I examine the analogies between chess and art, science, and sport. These categories are not absolute, but they make categorical sense and, in some measure, are not overlapping. Features of chess permit individuals and groups to place the game into these categories in ways that make sense to the community. The choice depends on whether one emphasizes the creativity of the activity, its systematic logic, or the centrality of competition. The realms of art, science, and sport do not exist apart from the way communities create boundaries to classify domains of action. These categories become salient when groups emphasize some feature of a complex domain in order to claim a relationship between the activity and other valued spheres.

Presents and Futures

Chess is a game of thought and of thoughts. Perhaps the argument has been made with too much panache, creating distance from those who do not consider cognitive engagement central to their self-image. Still, chess depends on calculations and evaluations. However, these are special kinds of cognitions. What a chess player must do is examine the future, as judged through the eyes of another. The essential purpose of thinking within the game is to determine those moves that one should make in the present and in the future, not to examine the past. Playing chess is a form of *futurework*,[1] the preparation and formatting of events to come.

To examine the role of cognition is to recognize that thought is something that belongs not to a mind but to a community. It must be described, as Eviatar Zerubavel has pointed out, through the sociology of thinking.[2] These forms of calculation must be taught and are only learned with practice and in competition with others. In time the process by which one selects one's moves becomes intuitive. In other words, the form of calculation is erased, even while the content is central. This erasure is most evident in the increasing popularity of short games, such as blitz or bullet chess.

In most social worlds, one's actions depend on the actions that one expects from others. Actions are contingent upon the thoughts (and subsequently the actions) of others. Behaviors do not merely exist but build on each other, in effect creating a conversation. Within a social scene there is more than neurocognition, no matter how social those neuron transfers. Games depend on bodies and emotions situated in a social world. Bodily feelings result from how matches and tournaments are organized. How directors set up a tournament—including the sound baffles in a playing hall, the carpeting, the chairs, or the height of the table—influence how bodies respond. The temporal order of chess also affects bodies, but the amount of time permitted to each game and the number of games during the day strains bodies. As Michel Foucault argues, bodies are disciplined by states and by voluntary communities.[3]

Emotions are channeled by their social placement. We err if we conceive of emotions as things that belong to persons and not to communities. Emotions are performances that affect interpretations of the future. In other words, they contribute to futurework. Because chess is competitive, continually generating winners and losers, it is filled with emotions that stem from these outcomes and from preparing for these outcomes. However, emotions never just appear but are guarded, guided, and revised to fit social scenes.

Whether we consider thoughts, embodiment, or emotions, they are the outcomes of community. Voluntary activities, worlds that serve as "third places"[4] away from work and home, have a freely chosen patina. This is so even if, in practice, they arise from the commitments of participants to their chosen worlds.

Selves in Action

The discussion of thinking, being, and feeling hides another—crucially important—piece of the world. This is the realization that internal states are known through action. Social life is ultimately a form of performance; it is a performance even if no others are present. Of course, competitive games require an opponent. As a performance, chess with its board; its clock; its websites, magazines, and books;

and its tables has a material reality. Performances require a stage and props.

First and foremost, chess is a game. As a result, it depends on a sequence of moves, bolstered by a system of turn taking. Of course, not all games have pairs of opponents, but many have structured sequences of turn taking. Poker or darts can be played with a variable number of persons and still remain recognizably the same game, as the turns are ordered and equalized. As a result, the sociality of games is fundamental. Beyond this is the presence of surveillance. Chess is a game of full knowledge, so, in contrast to poker or bridge, but like go or backgammon, one's opponent has equal information. Pieces cannot be hidden. Where strategy matters is in the prediction—guessing—of what the opponent is thinking, a process that depends on role taking.

However, action is not only relevant to the participants themselves; action can be viewed by others. Action is transformed into history if the event is deemed worthy of attention from an audience. This viewability especially applies to elite activities that are often recorded for posterity. The audience gives meaning to what happens on the board, as pieces move, and over the board, as players move. These are layers of the social.

With the recognition that games are a form of competitive engagement, strategies become central. The psychology of action is ultimately the *sociology* of action. Chess involves role taking, used to generate strategic action. While a player might assert that all that matters are good moves, the good move is tethered to a belief in the opponent's response. Part of what occurs within chess games is the establishment of conditions under which the other will follow one's lead down a line of action: the game involves a set of interpersonal traps that, taken together, constitute the game as a two-person drama. Strategies are embedded within social engagement.

The Temporal Dance

Social worlds are always temporal worlds. Every realm of action depends on beliefs about the proper duration for an engagement. Again the feature of a game that is most defining is the reality that a game requires an alternation of action, demanding the active engagement of the participants. Therefore time must be allocated in a fair and technologically supported fashion. The chess clock was a crucial innovation that created chess as we know it, even while clocks have evolved. While the movement of pieces has not changed since the medieval period, competitive chess changed through the institutionalization of the clock. The clock measures duration. Once the first moves occur, each player has the challenge of clock management. Clock management results from a system in which time is controlled to create coordination, equity, and order. Managing time is a skill that chess coaches emphasize soon after novices learn basic tactics.

The modern temporal order is revealed in the increasing popularity of short events: blitz or bullet chess. Chess has been telescoped over the decades, but this temporal squeeze was not fully evident until the development of a digital clock, capable of displaying seconds. It became possible to play competitive short games in which the clock determines the outcome: losing on time. The institutionalization of brief games permitted players to engage in numerous events rather than focusing on a few longer engagements. This allowed each individual contest to have less consequence in the status battle between competitors.

The temporal order of any activity must fit the larger organizational environment. In a world that has sped up, fitting more activities within the same diurnal reality, how a community allocates time is shaped by the desires of those who wish to participate.

Sticky Culture

Central to my argument—and linked to research on collective memory—is the recognition that every social field has a history that unites participants in common cause. I label this *sticky culture*, emphasizing that the recognition and the valuation of a shared past builds an ongoing community. The history may be autobiographical, a group tradition, or a subcultural commemoration. Each contributes to allegiance between person and activity. While this history cannot override centrifugal forces that limit participation, as people do exit communities, recognition of common knowledge builds cohesion.

Although memory shapes all voluntary communities, few domains have the depth of recall of chess. Every player has a personal gaming career, linked to remembered games, revealed in the fact that informants readily describe or document triumphs. Retaining score sheets creates this personal past. History is linked to self. But history goes beyond the personal to those groups—tiny publics—that bolster community. Aside from the cemented chess tables in public parks, most participants compete against known others or those within an extended network: friends, colleagues, and those with a shared membership in an established organization. If one plays at a local club, such as Lakeside High School or the Blue Hills Chess Club, the relationships among players define the gathering as a stable group.

Even on a ritual occasion, such as a tournament in which people do not know each other personally, they are friends of friends of friends and share similar values.[5] Each game is a moment available for remembrance and narration. If the game or its outcome proves notable, it enters into memory. At a tournament each participant has stories to tell. When the event is of more than local interest, such as major tournaments with competing grandmasters, the games are published and annotated.

Finally there is the history—what becomes collective memory—of the activity itself. More than most voluntary domains, chess is drenched in the past. For centuries players have remembered the great players, games, and tournaments. And they create a literature of recall. As the core event is the game, players keep games alive. The games are replayed as learning tools, and the annotations from considering the games and alternative lines of play are crucial to *chess as community*. Not every activity has this storehouse of history, but in being an extreme case—an ideal type—chess provides a model of how the past affects the future and affects our sense that we belong together.

Soft Community

Whenever one finds a group of individuals who commit to the same activity or share the same perspective, we can claim that they constitute a community. But how much openness is present? Is the world willing to accept all comers, no matter if they violate some valued norms? Is the community open to all who wish entrance, even those who might be considered strange or peculiar? Perhaps commitment alone is sufficient, even for difficult people.

I term chess a *soft community*: a space where, if a participant accepts the core activity and values, much otherwise unusual or deviant action is accepted. Chess is not alone in this. There is within chess a

belief that in contrast to many other domains there are more participants who are mentally ill, asocial, or socially inept. However, Scrabble, poker, programming, poetry, hacking, and other specialized publics seem to be soft communities as well. These activities, especially
those not requiring extensive conversation, provide a welcoming
home. Quirks and violations validate the intensity of the community.
What matters is ability and motivation. These stand apart from what
we might label—for lack of a better phrase—*hard communities*. These
are instrumental worlds, such as workplaces, in which deviance from
rules or rejection of institutional policies or revealing bizarre speech
or acts can provoke censure or exclusion. To be sure, communities are
never absolutely open, and boundaries for acceptance and exclusion
are a matter of degree.

Numerous communities exist within the chessworld spiral: different spatial and social scenes, defined by skill, gender, ethnicity, age,
and location. These domains allow one to select a community of comfort and access. Tiny publics overlap only at certain ritual events, such
as open tournaments, and otherwise may be unaware of each other.
One sees the same process in the worlds of bridge, tennis, philately,
and car collecting. While occasions permit temporary merging, the
groups operate in their own local spaces.

Perhaps chess is more accepting than many leisure worlds, but it
is one whose specialness reveals how communities can embrace an
array of special souls—edgy or fragile—who might be excluded from
other domains that lack a common focus as evidence of commitment.
As Robert Putnam has emphasized, and as chess demonstrates, a community generates social capital, which, while it may not transform a
participant into a better person, provides an embrace that permits
individuals to gain benefits that result from long-term relations.[6]

The Status Game

To engage with a voluntary world, one inserts oneself in a status
system, operating through hierarchical relations. Every community
establishes criteria of expertise and leadership: bestness and worst-
ness. This evaluation transforms a band of equals into a vertical order
whereby some are recognized for their skills and knowledge and are
often shown deference. In cases in which this order is granted communal legitimacy, the ladder of esteem creates interpersonal stability.

Recognition of expertise validates the social field in that it makes explicit that what is at issue is communal standards. Those lacking talent can, at least to some degree, improve through the learning that comes with commitment. The creation of a status system depends both on selection effects (individuals enter the system with variable capacity) and treatment effects (some acquire capacity through involvement). Recruitment and training establish hierarchy, rank, and reputation.

Groups develop strategies for validating hierarchy. One of the features that make chess a distinctive world is that, in addition to the ranking systems or informal evaluations, chess creates both a categorical system of status and also a rating system. Although every player is assigned to a category, these categories are tied to ratings (masters, experts, A- and B-level players, and so forth). The only exceptions are grandmasters and international masters, who must also score well at events, capturing "norms." Further, to challenge the world champion, a set of tournaments selects the current champion's opponent every three years. At this level the highest-rated player is not necessarily chosen, but competitive matches determine the challenger.

The centrality and the motivating force of these ratings provide chess with a status system that is more public and more complex than other cultural fields. Everyone knows where he stands and can determine how much to invest in gaining higher status. While the peculiarities of ratings are localized to this historic game, the general phenomenon of status marking is found in all communities that require a recognized hierarchy. The world is insistently hierarchical, and the challenge for any community is how to establish the hierarchy in a way that creates consensus and dampens conflict. This is the achievement of those who fought to establish a rating system that transforms people into numbers.

Worlds and Extensions

One of the challenges that the student of any social world faces is the reality that worlds are situated inside larger worlds—worlds within worlds. If a community comprises a set of tiny publics, as most do, the community itself is set within an extended civil society. An interaction order is viewed by those outside its boundaries, shaping the recruitment of potential aspirants. These public attitudes determine the connections outside the core community that are possible. Beyond this are economic, organizational, and political worlds that shape the forms of voluntary communities.

The central task for a community within a larger world is to generate a sense of what is at stake for participants in that community. What core emotions, beliefs, and actions characterize that community? No community can be known in detail by the wider public, but the perspective of the public establishes images or stereotypes that have consequences for how the community knows itself and how it can build allegiance and create ties with other groups.

Chess is part of the cultural capital of knowledgeable adults and their children, a game whose acquisition is recognized as having virtues linked to the widespread belief in its cognitive sophistication described in chapter 1. However, the virtues of chess need not require a more intense involvement beyond rudimentary knowledge. Too much commitment is threatening, passing from the possibility of being perceived as a "nerd" to that of being perceived as monomaniacal. Over the course of his career, Bobby Fischer served as hero and as warning as he developed from brilliant child to nerdy adolescent to patriotic warrior to insane compulsive.

Whatever placement emerges situates an activity within an economic arena, as in the case of poker, golf, or skiing. Because of the belief in Baby Kasparovs and the belief that chess, when not taken to "extremes," creates moral and educated citizens, sufficient support exists for chess in the twenty-first century for establishing elementary and high school clubs. The positive public attitude toward chess permits a push for inner-city programs, despite the small number of collegiate scholarships or career opportunities for chess players. The United States Chess Foundation provides valuable support for scholarships, but the funds do not meet the potential need. The number of grants is growing, if more slowly than committed players wish. Top events—the world championship, for instance—can gather sufficient financial support to permit the strongest and most celebrated players to earn a comfortable living. This doesn't mean that the support either bubbles up or trickles down to provide extensive support for a wide cadre of professionals, but the community trades on its cultural and social cachet to generate modest economic support.

These realities create a space for the linkage of community to politics. Voluntary activities are markers of virtue, indications of deep knowledge, and sources of cultural authority. This was most evident

during the Cold War, when chess meant *something big* in the global political struggle. In some corners of the globe in which chess is gaining a
foothold (notably India and China), chess still has meanings that stand
above and apart from pushing pawns. It can reflect national dignity.
The game is part of a societal toolkit that, when conditions are ripe
and a narrative can be fashioned, becomes a source of public pride.

Finally, I refer at several points to the relationship between activity and technology. All activities constitute themselves in light of the
costs, benefits, and moral choices that technology provides. We must
bow to technological limits, even when a community sponsors or
encourages innovations. Technology is not necessarily destiny, but
choices of technology can provide smoother paths or rougher walks,
depending upon communal desires.

The growth of speed chess, now so integral to the chessworld in
its new home on the Internet, not only reflects a temporal preference
but is a decision that affects the structure of this voluntary activity,
creating a global playing field of visual anonymity that only slowly
becomes an arena of friendship, even if that friendship depends on
information that partners choose to share. Technology indirectly but
powerfully decreases the necessity of face-to-face interaction, replac-
ing handshakes with emoticons.

Communities are internally organized through selves, dyads, and
groups. Through these forms of organization they are linked to larger
communities in consequential ways. The lesson of examining a complex voluntary world—an ecology of games—is that both inside and
outside matter.

The Poetics of Possibilities

Sociologists have often neglected domains in which voluntary action has priority. Worlds of leisure and of fun are seen as secondary
to spaces that are explicitly economic, political, or familial. But, as I
suggest, through the analysis of this complex leisure world, a domain
composed of networked groups sheds light on other social systems.

At first blush the chessworld appears to be a tight-knit community,
and one can readily recognize its communal features. On some level,
this is accurate, but only partially so. Chess in its complexity is not
a unified community, but it is constituted through a multiplicity of
communities—of tiny publics—that at times recognize their similarity

but often do not. A nation of forty million chess players can hardly be considered a single community. We find enthusiasts in schools, colleges, clubs, dens, tournaments, and chat rooms, occasionally meeting, but often playing in separate spheres. When viewed from afar, they may be seen as one community, but up close they are differentiated and divided. People wish to have fun, and they discover friends and classmates and neighbors to help them.

Even an activity seemingly as private—as thoughtful and as emotional—as chess is at each moment and in each move a social space. In this we recognize that all expansive domains create an interaction order from local settings and cultural metaphors.

Chess reveals the power of a world to build a game and the power of a game to build a host of worlds. The global presence of chess is revealed in its local presence. This is its glory as humanity's greatest game and as the glue that binds fathers and sons, friends and nations. On the board and over the board, chess organizes social life and creates a sticky culture and a soft community.

ACKNOWLEDGMENTS

In this research I have had many congenial conversations with important figures in the world of American chess (I do not examine international chess tournaments, except from written accounts). My contacts include those who train young children, those who play tournament chess at the highest levels, and those who organize events. I have also talked with many whose commitment is to the game, not to the organizations that surround it. While I do not identify informants when recounting their perspectives, I thank Les Bale, Robert Bales, Betsy Dynako, Marc Esserman, Bill and Brenda Goichberg, Bill Hall, Jerry Hanken, Tim Just, Ken Lewandowski, Sevan Muradian, Tom Panelas, Glenn Panner, Daniel Parmet, Susan Polgar, Tim Redman, Brad Rosen, Jennifer Shahade, Yury Shulman, Ken Sloan, Sam Sloan, Jim Smallwood, Peter Spizzirri, Jeff Wiewel, and Harold Winston. Chess players sometimes have sharp tongues and sharper political divisions. The frequent crises at the United States Chess Federation and FIDE (the World Chess Federation) serve as cases in point. I have tried to be a sympathetic listener to all involved. Among fellow scholars I appreciate the help of Robert Desjarlais, Todd Fine, Michael Flaherty, David Grazian, James Jasper, John Loy, Philip Manning, David Peterson, Howard Sandler, Paul Widdop, and especially Antony Puddephatt.

Portions of this manuscript have appeared in other forms in Gary Alan Fine, "Time to Play: The Temporal Organization of Chess Competition," *Time & Society* 21 (2012): 395–416; Gary Alan Fine, "Sticky Cultures: Memory Publics and Communal Pasts in Competitive Chess,"

Cultural Sociology 7 (2013): 395–414; Antony J. Puddephatt and Gary Alan Fine, "Chess as Art, Science, and Sport," in *A Companion to Sport*, ed. David Andrews and Ben Carrington (Oxford: Wiley Blackwell, 2013), 390–404; and Gary Alan Fine, "The Mind, the Body, and the Soul of Chess," *American Journal of Play* 6 (2014): 321–44.

NOTES

Prologue

1. I met these men during the course of my research, and they offered to let me examine the mechanics of organizing a tournament from its start to finish, including the finances. Although this tournament was not a financial success, both men have run successful events in the Chicago area and are well known in national chess circles.

2. At one infamous national scholastic tournament, the final round was three hours late because of delays in pairing, and the award ceremony was held after midnight, causing many families to miss their flights.

3. In an examination of nearly 575,000 games archived on a computer database, 37.2 percent were won by white, 27.2 percent by black, and 35.6 percent were draws. Of the games where there was a winner (excluding draws), 57.8 percent were won by white. See http://www.chessgames.com/chessstats.html (accessed January 23, 2011). Of course, these are high-level games. The average rating for players places them in the "master" category, so the statistic might not apply more generally. Further, these games were played over centuries (1475 to 2011), and as a result changes over time are possible. Jeremy, who is an international master, informed me that in his experience, out of a hundred games, fifty are won by white, thirty-five are draws, and fifteen are won by black. He believes that when you draw as white, you have "wasted" your game, and he is less likely to offer or accept a draw as white, even if the position might be the same as when he is black (field notes). One grandmaster explained that you learn to play the black pieces, but the white pieces play themselves (interview). At any tournament with an odd number of rounds, half of the players will be disadvantaged. Proposals have been made for avoiding the bias, such as by only permitting white to move a pawn one square on the first move or permitting black to select white's first move from a limited set of possibilities. See Paul Lillebo, "Another Rule Change Proposal," *Chess Life*, May 2007, 6. This would likely change some outcomes, but there is no certainty that it would reach parity.

Introduction

1. Reuben Fine, *The Psychology of the Chess Player* (New York: Dover, 1967).

2. J. Patrick Williams, "Consumption and Authenticity in the Collectible Strategy Games Subculture," in *Gaming as Culture: Essays on Social Reality, Identity and Experience in Fantasy Games*, ed. J. Patrick Williams, Sean Q. Hendricks, and W. Keith Winkler (Jefferson, NC: McFarland, 2006), 77–99.

3. David Unruh, "The Nature of Social Worlds," *Pacific Sociological Review* 23 (1980): 271–96.

4. Dennis H. Holding, *The Psychology of Chess Skill* (Hillsdale, NJ: Lawrence Erlbaum Associates, 1985), 2.

5. H. J. R. Murray, *A History of Chess* (Oxford: Oxford University Press, 1913); Harry Golombek, *Chess: A History* (New York: G. P. Putnam, 1976).

6. Golombek, *Chess*, 12.

7. Karl Menninger, "Chess," *Bulletin of the Menninger Clinic* 6, no. 3 (1942): 80–83, at 81.

8. Richard Eales, *Chess: The History of a Game* (London: B. T. Batsford, 1985).

9. Norman Reider, "Chess, Oedipus, and the Mater Dolorosa," *International Journal of Psycho-Analysis* 40 (1959): 320–33. Murray raises some questions about these sources. *A History of Chess*, 510, 531.

10. Marilyn Yalom, *Birth of the Chess Queen: A History* (New York: HarperCollins, 2004).

11. David Shenk, *The Immortal Game: A History of Chess* (New York: Doubleday, 2006), 112.

12. Susan Polgar, "Staggering Chess Numbers," *Susan Polgar Chess News and Information*, January 31, 2007, http://susanpolgar.blogspot.com/2007/01/staggering -chess-numbers.html, accessed March 11, 2013.

13. Belindalevez-ga, "Chess Player Demographics," Google Answers, August 5, 2006, http://answers.google.com/answers/threadview/id/752764.html, accessed January 8, 2011.

14. Annette Lareau, *Unequal Childhoods: Class, Race, and Family Life* (Berkeley: University of California Press, 2003).

15. Randy Banner, "Chess Official Trying to Keep Children in the Game," *New York Times*, August 27, 2003, http://query.nytimes.com/gst/fullpage.html?res= 9B00E0D61339F934A1575BC0A9659C8B63, accessed January 8, 2011.

16. Eleanor Rosch, "Principles of Categorization," in *Cognition and Categorization*, ed. Eleanor Rosch and Barbara Lloyd (Hillside, NJ: Lawrence Erlbaum, 1978), 27–48.

17. Strictly speaking, this claim is not accurate. As David Peterson (personal communication, 2012) points out, many games end in the "scholar's mate." Some grandmaster games end in identical positions, although they may reach that position through different routes.

18. Paul Hoffman, *King's Gambit: A Son, a Father, and the World's Most Dangerous Game* (New York: Hyperion, 2007), 76; Garry Kasparov, "The Chess Master and the Computer," review of *Chess Metaphors: Artificial Intelligence and the Human*

Mind, by Diego Rasskin-Gutman, trans. Deborah Closky, *New York Review of Books*, February 11, 2010, http://www.nybooks.com/articles/archives/2010/feb /11/the-chess-master-and-the-computer, accessed January 11, 2011.

19. Erving Goffman, *Encounters: Two Studies in the Sociology of Interaction* (Indianapolis: Bobbs-Merrill, 1961); Eric Leifer, "Trails of Involvement: Evidence for Local Games," *Sociological Forum* 3 (1988): 499–524; Benjamin DiCicco-Bloom and David Gibson, "More Than a Game: Sociological Theory from the Theory of Games," *Sociological Theory* 28 (2010): 247–71, at 248.

20. Pal Benko and Burt Hochberg, *Winning with Chess Psychology* (New York: David McKay, 1991).

21. Marci Reaven and Steve Zeitlin, *Hidden New York: A Guide to Places That Matter* (New Brunswick, NJ: Rivergate, 2006), 117, 123.

22. Robert Benford and David A. Snow, "Framing Processes and Social Movements: An Overview and Assessment," *Annual Review of Sociology* 26 (2000): 611–39.

23. For an extensive elaboration of this metaphor see Franklin K. Young, *The Grand Tactics of Chess* (Boston: Little, Brown, 1898).

24. I. A. Horowitz and P. L. Rothenberg, *The Personality of Chess* (New York: Macmillan, 1963), 16.

25. W. R. Hartston and P. C. Wason, *The Psychology of Chess* (New York: Facts on File Publications, 1984), 18.

26. Julian Barnes, *Letters from London* (New York: Vintage, 1995), 244.

27. Alexander Cockburn, *Idle Passion: Chess and the Dance of Death* (New York: New American Library, 1974), 25–26. The works of Ernest Jones, Isador Coriat, Norman Reider, and Reuben Fine raise similar themes about sublimated homosexuality and father murder. This theory doesn't fit female players but could explain their relative absence in contrast to bridge.

28. Ernest Jones, "The Problem of Paul Morphy: A Contribution to the Psycho-Analysis of Chess," *International Journal of Psycho-Analysis* 12 (1931): 1–23; Isador Coriat, "The Unconscious Motives of Interest in Chess," *Psychoanalytic Review* 28 (1941): 30–36.

29. Fine, *Psychology of the Chess Player*, 1967.

30. ChessQuotes.com, http://www.chessquotes.com/player-kortchnoi, accessed August 23, 2014.

31. Cockburn, *Idle Passion*; David Melamed and Emanuel Berman, "Oedipal Motives in Adolescent Chess Players," *Journal of Adolescence* 4 (1981): 173–76.

32. Alfred Binet, "Mnemonic Virtuosity: A Study of Chess Players," *Genetic Psychology Monographs*, 74 (1966): 127–62.

33. George A. Huaco, review of *Idle Passion: Chess and the Dance of Death*, by Alexander Cockburn, *Sociological Quarterly* 17 (1976): 130–33.

34. Johan Huizinga, *Homo Ludens: A Study of the Play-Element in Culture* (Boston: Beacon, 1955): ix.

35. Willard Fiske, *Chess Tales and Chess Miscellanies* (New York: Longmans, Green) 170–71.

36. Yalom, *Birth of the Chess Queen*, 104.

37. Pope Innocent III, "A Morality on Chess," in *Chess in Literature*, ed. Marcello Truzzi (New York: Avon, 1974), 20–21, at 20. The morality is now commonly attributed to John of Wales.

38. Jenny Adams, *Power Play: The Literature and Politics of Chess in the Late Middle Ages* (Philadelphia: University of Pennsylvania Press, 2006), 1–4; see also William Poole, "False Play: Shakespeare and Chess," *Shakespeare Quarterly* 55 (2004): 50–70.

39. Shenk, *The Immortal Game*, 72.

40. Adams, *Power Play*, 3.

41. Ari Luiro, "Chess Pieces in Different Languages," ReoCities, March 30, 2009, http://reocities.com/TimesSquare/metro/9154/nap-pieces.htm, 2009, accessed February 21, 2011. Luiro presents the names of chess pieces in seventy-three languages.

42. Cockburn, *Idle Passion*, 123.

43. Antony J. Puddephatt and Gary Alan Fine, "Chess as Art, Science, and Sport," in *Blackwell Companion to Sport*, ed. Ben Carrington and David Andrews (Oxford: Blackwell, 2013), 390–404.

44. Howard S. Becker, *Art Worlds* (Berkeley: University of California Press, 1982).

45. Quoted in Truzzi, *Chess in Literature*, 160.

46. David Bronstein and Georgy Smolyan, *Chess in the Eighties*, trans. Kenneth P. Neat (Oxford: Pergamon, 1982), 26.

47. Quoted in Antony J. Puddephatt, "Chess Playing as Strategic Activity," *Symbolic Interaction* 26 (2003), 263–84, at 275.

48. Belinda Wheaton, *Understanding Lifestyle Sports: Consumption, Identity, and Difference* (New York: Routledge, 2004).

49. William James, *The Meaning of Truth* (New York: Longmans, Green, 1909).

50. Stuart Rachels, "The Reviled Art," in *Philosophy Looks at Chess*, ed. Benjamin Hale (Chicago: Open Court, 2008), 209–22, at 213.

51. Assiac, *The Delights of Chess* (London: Macgibbon and Kee, 1960), 10.

52. Larry Evans, *This Crazy World of Chess* (New York: Cardoza, 2007), 256.

53. Amatzia Avni, *The Grandmaster's Mind* (London: Gambit, 2004), 158.

54. Fine, *Psychology of the Chess Player*.

55. Andy Soltis, "Defining 'Brilliancy,'" *Chess Life*, June 2008, 10–11, at 10.

56. Mihaly Csikszentmihalyi, *Beyond Boredom and Anxiety: Experiencing Flow in Work and Play* (San Francisco: Jossey-Bass, 1975).

57. Ibid., 66; Puddephatt, "Chess Playing as Strategic Activity," 274.

58. In contrast to high school debate coaches, who typically teach social science courses, chess coaches often teach math or science.

59. Reuben Fine, *Bobby Fischer's Conquest of the World's Chess Championship: The Psychology and Tactics of the Title Match* (1973; repr., New York: Ishi, 2008).

60. Howard Sandler, personal communication, 2013.

61. Aron Nimzowitsch, *Chess Praxis* (1936; repr., New York: Dover, 1962).

62. Harry Collins and Robert Evans, *Rethinking Expertise* (Chicago: University of Chicago Press, 2007).

63. Max Euwe and John Nunn, *The Development of Chess Style* (Seattle: International Chess Enterprises, 1997), 8.

64. Anthony Saidy, *The Battle of Chess Ideas* (New York: RHM, 1972).

65. Paul Hoffman, *King's Gambit*, 385.

66. Bronstein and Smolyan, *Chess in the Eighties*, 2.

67. Antony J. Puddephatt, "Incorporating Ritual into Greedy Institution Theory: The Case of Devotion in Amateur Chess," *Sociological Quarterly* 49 (2008): 155–80, at 168.

68. Eales, *Chess: The History of a Game*, 11; Paul Hoffman, "Castling in the Square," *Harvard Magazine*, November–December 2002, http://harvardmagazine.com /2002/11/castling-in-the-square.html, accessed January 10, 2011; S. Banchero. "Chess: School Official Apologizes to Children," *Chicago Tribune*, March 17, 2007, 1–2, at 2. The high school chess coordinator also coordinated the school golf program, and the person selected in 2007 for the position had a golf background and no experience in chess. This organizational structure led to concern among some chess coaches as to whether their players would have to get preseason physicals, just like football players.

69. Wendy Espeland and Mitchell Stevens, "Commensuration as a Social Process," *Annual Review of Sociology* 24 (1998): 313–43, at 314.

70. Stacy Lom, "'Sometimes Less Is More': The Development and Effects of Evaluative Cultures" (PhD diss., Northwestern University, 2013).

71. David Peterson (personal communication, 2012) points out that while "anomalies" can be put aside in scientific research for the moment, in a competitive game, they need a response.

72. Gary Alan Fine, *With the Boys: Little League Baseball and Preadolescent Culture* (Chicago: University of Chicago Press, 1987).

73. Gary Alan Fine, *Authors of the Storm: Meteorology and the Culture of Prediction* (Chicago: University of Chicago Press, 2007).

74. Richard Peterson and Roger Kern, "Changing Highbrow Taste: From Snob to Omnivore," *American Sociological Review* 61 (1996): 900–907.

75. Erving Goffman, "The Interaction Order," *American Sociological Review* 48 (1983): 1–17.

Chapter One

1. Eviatar Zerubavel, *Social Mindscapes: An Invitation to Cognitive Sociology* (Cambridge, MA: Harvard University Press, 1997).

2. Dennis H. Holding, *The Psychology of Chess Skill* (Hillsdale, NJ: Lawrence Erlbaum Associates, 1985), 245.

3. George Herbert Mead, *Mind, Self & Society from the Standpoint of a Social Behaviorist* (Chicago: University of Chicago Press, 1934), 177–78.

4. Walter Coutu, "Role-Playing vs. Role-Taking," *American Sociological Review* 16 (1951): 180–87; Paul Hoffman, *King's Gambit: A Son, a Father, and the World's Most Dangerous Game* (New York: Hyperion, 2007), 260.

5. Paul Hoffman, *King's Gambit*.

6. Karl Menninger, "Chess." *Bulletin of the Menninger Clinic* 6, no. 3 (1942): 80–83, at 82.

7. David Bronstein and Georgy Smolyan, *Chess in the Eighties* (Oxford: Pergamon, 1982), 42.

8. Low-rated players or those who do not participate in tournaments have an unexpected advantage in that their games are not available on these databases.

9. Paul Hoffman, *King's Gambit*, 294.

10. Bronstein and Smolyan, *Chess in the Eighties*, 33, 41.

11. This quotation appears to be apocryphal. It has been attributed to Richard Réti and to Al Jaffe. Stuart Rachels, "The Reviled Art," in *Philosophy Looks at Chess*, ed. Benjamin Hall (Chicago: Open Court, 2008), 209–25, at 223.

12. James Jasper, *Getting Your Way: Strategic Dilemmas in the Real World* (Chicago: University of Chicago Press, 2006), 79.

13. Gary Alan Fine, *Authors of the Storm: Meteorology and the Culture of Prediction* (Chicago: University of Chicago Press, 2007).

14. Eric M. Leifer, "Interaction Preludes to Role Setting: Exploratory Local Action," *American Sociological Review* 53 (1988): 865–78; Benjamin DiCicco-Bloom and David Gibson, "More Than a Game: Sociological Theory from the Theories of Games," *Sociological Theory* 28 (2010): 247–71, at 249.

15. W. K. Wimsatt, "How to Compose Chess Problems, and Why," in *Game, Play, Literature*, ed. Jacques Ehrmann (Boston: Beacon, 1971), 65–85, at 71.

16. Paul Hoffman, *King's Gambit*, 11.

17. Bronstein and Smolyan, *Chess in the Eighties*, 41.

18. H. A. Kennedy, *Chips, Waifs, and Strays: Anecdotes from the Chess-Board* (London: Dean and Son, 1862), 3.

19. Herbert A. Simon and William G. Chase, "Skill in Chess," *American Scientist* 61 (1973), 394–403, at 394.

20. Christopher F. Chabris and Mark E. Glickman, "Sex Differences in Intellectual Performance," *Psychological Science* 17 (2006): 1040–46, at 1040; Nathan Ensmenger, "Is Chess the Drosophilia of Artificial Intelligence?" *Social Studies of Science* 42 (2012): 5–30. This metaphor might be particularly powerful because of the number of scientists who are also avid chess players.

21. Rachels, "The Reviled Art."

22. Adriaan D. de Groot, *Thought and Choice in Chess* (The Hague: Mouton, 1965).

23. William Chase and Herbert Simon, "Perception in Chess," *Cognitive Psychology* 4 (1973): 55–81.

24. Amatzia Avni, *The Grandmaster's Mind* (London: Gambit, 2004), 7.

25. Edward J. Kelly, "The Personality of Chessplayers," *Journal of Personality Assessment* 49 (1985): 282–84, at 284.

26. Avni, *The Grandmaster's Mind*, 8; Michael Polanyi, *Personal Knowledge: Towards a Post-Critical Philosophy* (Chicago: University of Chicago Press, 1958).

27. Paul Hoffman, "Castling in the Square," *Harvard Magazine*, November–December 2002, http://harvardmagazine.com/2002/11/castling-in-the-square.html, accessed January 13, 2011; Gerd Gigerenzer, *Gut Feelings: The Intelligence of the Unconscious* (New York: Vintage, 2007).

28. Tom Mueller, "Your Move," *New Yorker*, December 12, 2005, 62–69, at 64.

29. Dominic Lawson, *End Game: Kasparov vs. Short* (New York: Harmony Books, 1994), 50.

30. Here my analysis of strategy is bounded by the game itself. Strategies can involve tournaments or careers and can operate across games. For instance, in some cases players may wish to lose a game in order to have their ratings decrease to permit them to play in a lower division in which they are more likely to win or to place themselves in an easier bracket in a tournament. Such incentives to win by losing are also found in horse racing, as described by Marvin Scott in *The Racing Game* (Chicago: Aldine, 1968).

31. Garry Kasparov, *How Life Imitates Chess: Making the Right Moves, from the Board to the Boardroom* (New York: Bloomsbury, 2007), 17–18.

32. Fine, *Authors of the Storm*.

33. Murray Davis, *Smut: Erotic Reality, Obscene Ideology* (Chicago: University of Chicago Press, 1985); Leigh Thompson, *The Truth about Negotiations* (Upper Saddle River, NJ: Pearson Education / FT Press, 2008); Black Hawk Hancock, *American Allegory: Lindy Hop and the Racial Imagination* (Chicago: University of Chicago Press, 2013); Jack Katz, *Seductions of Crime: Moral and Sensual Attractions of Doing Evil* (New York: Basic Books); Robert Lejeune, "The Management of a Mugging," *Urban Life* 6 (1977): 123–48.

34. Daniel Johnson, *White King and Red Queen: How the Cold War Was Fought on the Chessboard* (London: Atlantic, 2007), 227.

35. Kasparov, *How Life Imitates Chess*, 48.

36. The same process occurs in other strategic domains, such as protest and politics, when one's opponent must select among bad moves (James Jasper, personal communication, 2014).

37. George Koltanowski, *Chessnicdotes*, vol. 2 (Corapolis, PA: Chess Enterprises, 1981), 54.

38. Quoted in Ralph Ginzburg, "Portrait of a Genius as a Young Chess Master," http://bobbyfischer.net/Bobby04.html, accessed August 23, 2014.

39. Quoted in Reuben Fine, *Bobby Fischer's Conquest of the World's Chess Championship: The Psychology and Tactics of the Title Match* (1973; repr., New York: Ishi, 2008), 36.

40. Players may also treat clothing as talismans, and some refuse to change their shirts when they have a winning streak. See W. R. Hartston and P. C. Wason, *The Psychology of Chess* (New York: Facts on File Publications, 1984), 98.

41. Alexandra Kosteniuk, "Abolish Women's Titles? Ridiculous," *Chess News Blog* http://www.chessblog.com/2009/10/abolish-womens-itles-ridiculous.html, October 17, 2009, accessed July 20, 2010.

42. Paul Hoffman, *King's Gambit*, 7.

43. Quoted in ibid.

44. Quoted in Pal Benko and Burt Hochberg, *Winning with Chess Psychology* (New York: David McKay, 1991).

45. Allan Mazur, Alan Booth, and James M. Dabbs Jr., "Testosterone and Chess Competition," *Social Psychology Quarterly* 55 (1992): 70–77.

46. Vishy Anand, "Chess Is like Acting," interview in *Der Spiegel*, September 29, 2008, http://www.chessbase.com/newsdetail.asp?newsid=4933, accessed April 21, 2011.

47. Lawson, *End Game*, 98.

48. Harvey Lerman, "Four Fischers and Chess Plumbers Tie for First at USAT South," *Chess Life*, May 2007, 27–29, at 27.

49. Benko and Hochberg, *Winning with Chess Psychology*, 108.

50. Quoted in David Shenk, *The Immortal Game: A History of Chess* (New York: Doubleday, 2006), 112.

51. Michael Potts, "The Peripatetic Caissa: Chess as a Supplement to Teaching Aristotle's *Ethics*," in *Chess and Education: Selected Essays from the Koltanowski Conference* (Dallas: Chess Program at the University of Texas at Dallas, 2006), 66–79, at 71.

52. Pierre Bourdieu, *The Rules of Art: Genesis and Structure of the Literary Field* (Stanford, CA: Stanford University Press, 1996), 227–28. See also Matthew Desmond, *On the Fireline: Living and Dying with Wildland Firefighters* (Chicago: University of Chicago Press, 2007), 194; and Robert Desjarlais, *Counterplay: An Anthropologist at the Chessboard* (Berkeley: University of California Press, 2011).

53. Mihaly Csikszentmihalyi, *Beyond Boredom and Anxiety* (San Francisco: Jossey-Bass, 1975), 36, 38.

54. Puddephatt, "Chess Playing as Strategic Activity." Rock climbing might occur in isolation, but typically climbers bring friends with them for reasons of sociality as much as safety. Richard G. Mitchell Jr., *Mountain Experience: The Psychology and Sociology of Adventure* (Chicago: University of Chicago Press, 1983). Some activities, such as "being lost in a good book" may produce flow without a clear sense of social presence.

55. Bourdieu, *The Rules of Art*, 228.

56. Desjarlais, *Counterplay*, 14.

57. Csikszentmihalyi, *Beyond Boredom and Anxiety*, 39, 40.

58. D. Alan Aycock, "Gens Una Sumus: Play as Metaculture," *Play and Culture* 1 (1988): 124–37, at 128.

59. After a brief break to clean the floor and to put on sweatpants, the young man, despite the embarrassment, won the game.

60. Anthony E. Santasiere, *Essay on Chess* (Dallas: Chess Digest, 1972), 6.

61. Csikszentmihalyi, *Beyond Boredom and Anxiety*, 56.

62. Arlie Hochschild, *The Managed Heart: Commercialization of Human Feeling* (Berkeley: University of California Press, 2003).

63. Fred Waitzkin, *Mortal Games: The Turbulent Genius of Garry Kasparov* (New York: Putnam, 1993), 140.

64. Antony J. Puddephatt, "Advancing in the Amateur Chess World," in *Doing Ethnography: Studying Everyday Life*, ed. Dorothy Pawluch, William Shaffir, and Christine Miall (Toronto: Canadian Scholar's, 2005), 300–311.

65. Quoted in Csikszentmihalyi, *Beyond Boredom and Anxiety*, 64.

66. Paolo Maurensig, *The Lüneburg Variation*, trans. Jon Rothschild (New York: Farrar, Strauss and Giroux, 1997), 81.

67. J. C. Hallman, *The Chess Artist: Genius, Obsession, and the World's Oldest Game* (New York: St. Martin's, 2003), 1.

68. Quoted in Dirk Jan ten Geuzendam, *The Day Kasparov Quit and Other Chess Interviews* (Alkmaar, the Netherlands: New in Chess, 2006), 64.

69. Josh Waitzkin, *The Art of Learning: A Journey in the Pursuit of Excellence* (New York: Free Press), 2007, 44.

70. Fred Waitzkin, *Mortal Games*, 199; David Edmonds and John Eidinow, *Bobby Fischer Goes to War: How the Soviets Lost the Most Extraordinary Chess Match of All Time* (New York: HarperCollins, 2004), 22; transcribed video, http://www.chessvideos.tv/forum/viewtopic.php?t-2372, accessed March 18, 2010.

71. Erving Goffman, *Encounters: Two Studies in the Sociology of Interaction* (Indianapolis: Bobbs-Merrill, 1961), 17.

72. Carol Z. Stearns and Peter N. Stearns, *Anger: The Struggle for Emotional Control in America's History* (Chicago: University of Chicago Press, 1986).

73. Norbert Elias, *The Civilizing Process* (New York: Urizen Books, 1978).

74. Joel Lautier, quoted in Paul Hoffman, *King's Gambit*, 128.

75. Larry Evans, *This Crazy World of Chess* (New York: Cardoza, 2007), 278.

76. Paul Hoffman, "Castling in the Square."

77. Quoted in Bronstein and Smolyan, *Chess in the Eighties*, 71.

78. Mark G. Frank, "Thoughts, Feelings, and Deception," in *Deception: From Ancient Empires to Internet Dating*, ed. Brooke Harrington (Stanford, CA: Stanford University Press, 2009), 55–73.

79. Josh Waitzkin, *The Art of Learning*, 29.

80. Brad Rosen (chessdad64), "64 Square Jungle," http://chessdad64.com/, entry 31, November 16, 2004, accessed August 10, 2008.

81. Michael Weinreb, *The Kings of New York: A Year among the Geeks, Oddballs, and Geniuses Who Make Up America's Top High School Chess Team* (New York: Gotham, 2007), 58.

82. Desjarlais, *Counterplay*, 135.

83. Weinreb, *The Kings of New York*, 85–86.

84. Annette Lareau, *Unequal Childhoods: Class, Race, and Family Life* (Berkeley: University of California Press, 2003).

85. Internet chess raises different issues, discussed later.

Chapter Two

1. Quoted in Michael Gelb and Raymond Keene, *Samurai Chess: Mastering Strategic Thinking through the Martial Art of the Mind* (London: Aurum, 1997), 23. Strictly speaking, Arrabal meant Noh theater rather than Kabuki, a quite different form of performance.

2. Thomas Henricks, *Play Reconsidered: Sociological Perspectives on Human Expression* (Urbana: University of Illinois Press, 2006).

3. Gary Alan Fine, *Shared Fantasy: Role-Playing Games as Social Worlds* (Chicago: University of Chicago Press, 1983); Tom Boellstorff, *Coming of Age in Second Life: An Anthropologist Explores the Virtually Human* (Princeton, NJ: Princeton University Press, 2008).

4. See Stuart Rachels, "The Reviled Art," in *Philosophy Looks at Chess*, ed. Benjamin Hale (Chicago: Open Court, 2008), 209–25, at 223. The standard Stanton wooden boards have tan (or buff) and dark brown squares, although chess sets and boards may be white and black, buff and black, or light colored and dark colored.

5. Tim Just and Daniel B. Burg, eds., *U.S. Chess Federation's Official Rules of Chess*, 5th ed. (New York: Random House, 2003). A sixth edition is scheduled to be published in August 2014.

6. The World Chess Federation (FIDE) published its first chess laws in 1929. See ibid., xxiii.

7. Ibid., xxi.

8. Antony J. Puddephatt, "Incorporating Ritual into Greedy Institution Theory: The Case of Devotion in Amateur Chess," *Sociological Quarterly* 49 (2008): 155–80, at 159.

9. Randall Collins, *Interaction Ritual Chains* (Princeton, NJ: Princeton University Press, 2004).

10. D. Alan Aycock, "Finite Reason: A Construction of Desperate Play," unpublished manuscript, 1991.

11. D. Alan Aycock, "Gens Una Sumus: Play and Metaculture," *Play & Culture* 1 (1988): 124–37, at 131; Puddephatt, "Incorporating Ritual," 160.

12. Gary Alan Fine, *With the Boys: Little League Baseball and Preadolescent Culture* (Chicago: University of Chicago Press, 1987), 20–25.

13. Fine, *Shared Fantasy*, 181–204.

14. Just and Burg, *Rules of Chess*, 12, 15.

15. In golf, for instance, there are complex rules for when moving a ball causes a penalty and when it does not (such as when searching for a ball in muddy water).

16. Just and Burg, *Rules of Chess*, 13, 23.

17. In my research, the violation was unseen, but sometimes it is "seen." Antony Puddephatt saw a fight almost break out because a player touched his rook first in castling. His opponent complained, and the judge decided that he had to move the rook, costing him the game. The player was livid and confronted his opponent after the game.

18. Harold Garfinkel, *Studies in Ethnomethodology* (Englewood Cliffs, NJ: Prentice-Hall, 1967), 73.

19. Aycock, "Finite Reason."

20. In most chess sets, particularly the Stanton type, only the knights have different fronts and backs, but some specialty sets have other pieces that have different fronts and backs.

21. Just and Burg, *Rules of Chess*, 20.

22. Michael Carroll, "A Structuralist Looks at Chess," *Semiotica* 31 (1980): 273–87.

23. Marilyn Yalom, *Birth of the Chess Queen: A History* (New York: HarperCollins, 2004).

24. J. C. Hallman, *The Chess Artist: Genius, Obsession, and the World's Oldest Game* (New York: St. Martin's, 2003), 7.

25. Pal Benko and Burt Hochberg, *Winning with Chess Psychology* (New York: Random House, 1991), 6; Waitzkin quoted in Michael Weinreb, *The Kings of New York:*

A Year among the Geeks, Oddballs, and Geniuses Who Make Up America's Top High School Chess Team (New York: Gotham Books, 2007), 265.

26. Jerry Sohl, *Underhanded Chess: A Hilarious Handbook of Devious Diversions and Stratagems for Winning at Chess* (New York Hawthorn Books, 1973), 6.

27. Rene Chun, "Bobby Fischer's Pathetic Endgame," *Atlantic*, December 2002, http://www.theatlantic.com/doc/200212/chun, accessed December 22, 2008.

28. Quoted in Dominic Lawson, *End Game: Kasparov vs. Short* (New York: Harmony, 1994), 9.

29. Kenneth Mark Colby, "Gentlemen, the Queen," *Psychoanalytic Review* 40 (1953): 144–48, at 146; Karl Menninger, "Chess," *Bulletin of the Menninger Clinic* 6, no. 3 (1942): 80–83, at 83; Alexander Cockburn, *Idle Passion: Chess and the Dance of Death* (New York: New American Library, 1974), 47.

30. Mihaly Csikszentmihalyi, *Beyond Boredom and Anxiety* (San Francisco: Jossey-Bass, 1975), 45.

31. Paul Hoffman, *King's Gambit: A Son, a Father, and the World's Most Dangerous Game* (New York: Hyperion, 2007), 85.

32. Al Horowitz, quoted in Larry Evans, *This Crazy World of Chess* (New York: Cardoza Press, 2007), 178.

33. Dirk Jan ten Geuzendam, *The Day Kasparov Quit and Other Chess Interviews* (Alkmaar, the Netherlands: New in Chess, 2006), 71.

34. Jerry Hanken, "Shulman Shines in the 107th U.S. Chess Open," *Chess Life*, November 2006, 19–27, at 25.

35. Part of the hatred was political. Karpov was the darling of the Soviet state, while Kasparov was a dissenter and Jewish. In 2010 Kasparov supported Karpov in his unsuccessful attempt to gain the presidency of the World Chess Federation.

36. Fred Waitzkin, *Mortal Games: The Turbulent Genius of Garry Kasparov* (New York: Putnam, 1993), 10–11.

37. Paul Hoffman, *King's Gambit*, 68.

38. Eric M. Leifer, "Trails of Involvement: Evidence for Local Games," *Sociological Forum* 3 (1988): 499–524, at 500.

39. Erving Goffman, *Encounters: Two Studies in the Sociology of Interaction* (Indianapolis: Bobbs-Merrill, 1961), 17.

40. Quoted in Csikszentmihalyi, *Beyond Boredom and Anxiety*, 66.

41. Jennifer Shahade, *Chess Bitch: Women in the Ultimate Intellectual Sport* (Los Angeles: Siles Press, 2005), 5.

42. Quoted in ibid., 6.

43. Quoted in ibid., 5.

44. Just and Burg, *Rules of Chess*, 339.

45. D. Alan Aycock, "Play and the Rule of Silence," unpublished manuscript, ca. 1990.

46. Ibid., 3.

47. David Bronstein and Georgy Smolyan, *Chess in the Eighties* (Oxford: Pergamon, 1982), 13.

48. Richard Schechner, *Performance Theory*, rev. and exp. ed. (New York: Routledge, 2003), 8–19.

49. Ibid., 8.

50. Andrew Leibs, *Sports and Games of the Renaissance* (Westport, CT: Greenwood Press, 2004), 92; Steven G. Hoffman, "How to Punch Someone and Remain Friends: An Inductive Theory of Simulation," *Sociological Theory* 24 (2006): 170–93.

51. Schechner, *Performance Theory*, 14.

52. Julian Barnes, *Letters from London* (New York: Vintage, 1995), 233.

53. Frank Brady, *Endgame: Bobby Fischer's Remarkable Rise and Fall—from America's Brightest Prodigy to the Edge of Madness* (New York: Crown, 2011), 188.

54. Barnes, *Letters from London*, 234.

55. Brady, *Endgame*, 189.

56. Bruno Latour, *Reassembling the Social: An Introduction to Actor-Network-Theory* (New York: Oxford University Press, 2005).

57. George Steiner, *Fields of Force: Fischer and Spassky in Reykjavik* (New York: Viking), 1974.

58. Barnes, *Letters from London*, 233.

59. Victor Turner, *From Ritual to Theatre: The Human Seriousness of Play* (New York: Performing Arts Journal Publications, 1982), 14.

60. David Edmonds and John Eidinow, *Bobby Fischer Goes to War: How the Soviets Lost the Most Extraordinary Chess Match of All Time* (New York: HarperCollins, 2004); Daniel Johnson, *White King and Red Queen: How the Cold War Was Fought on the Chessboard* (London: Atlantic Books, 2007).

61. Feng-Hsiung Hsu, *Behind Deep Blue: Building the Computer that Defeated the World Chess Champion* (Princeton, NJ: Princeton University Press, 2002); Bruce Pandolfini, *Kasparov and Deep Blue: The Historic Chess Match between Man and Machine* (New York: Simon and Schuster, 1997).

62. Turner, *From Ritual to Theatre*, 11.

63. Puddephatt, "Incorporating Ritual," 171.

64. Gregory Bateson, *Steps to an Ecology of Mind* (Chicago: University of Chicago Press, 1972).

65. Erving Goffman, *Strategic Interaction* (Philadelphia: University of Pennsylvania Press, 1969); Stephen Potter, *The Theory and Practice of Gamesmanship* (London: Hart-Davies, 1947), 92–95.

66. David Shenk, *The Immortal Game: A History of Chess* (New York: Doubleday, 2006), 151.

67. W. R. Hartston and P. C. Wason, *The Psychology of Chess* (New York: Facts on File Publications, 1984), 98.

68. Johnson, *White King and Red Queen*, 70.

69. David Hayano, *Poker Faces: The Life and Work of Professional Card Players* (Berkeley: University of California Press, 1983).

70. Mikhail Tal, *The Life and Games of Mikhail Tal* (New York: RHM), 124.

71. Peter Fuller, *The Champions: The Secret Motives in Games and Sport* (London: Allen Lane, 1978), 92.

72. Jeremy tells me about a match against a prominent grandmaster: "I offered a draw and he snickered at me. It was despicable. I broke a rule and I said, 'OK, go snicker.' They do that in street chess. In two moves he offered me a draw" (field notes).

73. Unpublished college application essay, 2009.

74. Eviatar Zerubavel, *Social Mindscapes: An Invitation to Cognitive Sociology* (Cambridge, MA: Harvard University Press, 1997), 35–52.

75. Andy Soltis, "Asking God for Help," *Chess Life*, July 2008, 14–15, at 14.

76. Erving Goffman, *The Presentation of Self in Everyday Life* (Garden City, NY: Anchor, 1959).

77. Soltis, "Asking God for Help," 14.

78. Edward Rothstein, "Fischer versus the World: A Chess Giant's Endgame," *New York Times*, January 19, 2008, 1, 22, at 22.

79. Hartston and Wason, *The Psychology of Chess*, 82.

80. Lawson, *End Game*, 140.

81. Nikolai Krogius, *Psychology in Chess* (Albertson, NY: RHM, 1976), 6.

82. Benko and Hochberg, *Winning with Chess Psychology*, 29

83. Sohl, *Underhanded Chess*, 5.

84. Eric Leifer, "Trails of Involvement: Evidence for Local Games," *Sociological Forum* 3 (1988): 499–524, at 499–500.

85. J. L. Austin, *How to Do Things with Words* (1962; repr., Oxford: Oxford University Press, 1975). Thus the game can end before it ends. But this also leaves some room for ambiguity, such as whether the handshake indicates a draw or a resignation, or the frame in which the verbal resignation occurred, as in a possibly apocryphal story, told in several versions:

> Blackburne [a leading British chess player] was once playing here with a very irascible old gentleman, who was most particular in enforcing all rules of the game and, when in a certain humour, could not take a joke. It was his own first move, and he played P-K3. "Ah," said Blackburne, "now I resign." "All right," said his touchy opponent, "that's one game to me," and nothing, as Blackburne knew, would alter that determination, so it was duly scored. This is the shortest game on record. Blackburne was beaten in one move. (*British Chess Magazine*, May 1891, 232)

86. Evans, *This Crazy World of Chess*, 285.

87. In golf tournaments, in contrast to chess tournaments, there are no gimmes.

88. Rachels, "The Reviled Art," 218.

89. In some cases a draw can help a team win a match, as teammates' points are combined.

90. Hartston and Wason, *The Psychology of Chess*, 125.

91. Internet Chess Club discussion boards, 2010.

92. Interview with Hikaru Nakamura, in Geuzendam, *The Day Kasparov Quit*, 319. Nakamura is known to disdain draws, and he comments, " If you really love chess, you really should play fighting chess and not just draw every game."

93. Peter Doggers, "Experimental Draw at Dutch Championship," June 16, 2010, http://www.chessvibes.com/?q=reports/experimental-draw-at-dutch-championship, accessed August 23, 2014.

94. Joel Benjamin, *American Grandmaster: Four Decades of Chess Adventures* (London: Everyman Chess, 2007), 260.

95. Just and Burg, *Rules of Chess*, 38–55.

96. C. K. Damrosch, "Chessonomics," *Chess Life*, December 2009, 36–41, at 36.

97. Bronstein and Smolyan, *Chess in the Eighties*, 30.

98. Benjamin, *American Grandmaster*, 140.

99. Kenneth Sloan, e-mail message to author, November 7, 2008.

100. Fred Waitzkin, *Mortal Games*, 218–19. Joel Benjamin takes an opposite perspective, calling all draws a "naturally agreed upon result." See *American Grandmaster*, 260.

101. Mike Klein, "Yeager Has the Right Stuff," *Chess Life*, August 2008, 32–36, at 32; Shahade, *Chess Bitch*, 250.

102. Benko and Hochberg, *Winning with Chess Psychology*, 185.

103. Benjamin, *American Grandmaster*, 260.

104. Albert O. Hirschman, *Exit, Voice, and Loyalty: Responses to Decline in Firms, Organizations, and States* (Cambridge, MA: Harvard University Press, 1970).

Chapter Three

1. David Gibson, "Taking Turns and Talking Ties: Networks and Conversational Interaction," *American Journal of Sociology* 110 (2005): 1561–97; Avery Sharron, "Dimensions of Time," *Studies in Symbolic Interaction* 4 (1982): 63–89.

2. Norbert Elias, *Time: An Essay* (Oxford: Blackwell, 1992), 4.

3. Eviatar Zerubavel, "Easter and Passover: On Calendars and Group Identity," *American Sociological Review* 47 (1982): 284–89.

4. Pitirim Sorokin and Robert K. Merton, "Social Time: A Methodological and Functional Analysis," *American Journal of Sociology* 42 (1937): 615–29; Eviatar Zerubavel, *Social Mindscapes: An Introduction to Cognitive Sociology* (Cambridge, MA: Harvard University Press, 1997).

5. Greg Shahade, "Mechanics Wrench Victory from New York," *Chess Life*, February 2007, 28–33, at 30.

6. Erving Goffman, *Encounters: Two Studies in the Sociology of Interaction* (Indianapolis: Bobbs-Merrill, 1961).

7. Eviatar Zerubavel, *Patterns of Time in Hospital Life: A Sociological Perspective* (Chicago: University of Chicago Press, 1979).

8. Elias, *Time*; Harmut Rosa, "Social Acceleration: Ethical and Political Consequences of a Desynchronized High-Speed Society," *Constellations* 10 (2003): 3–33; Paul Glennie and Nigel Thrift, "Revolutions in the Times: Clocks and the Temporal Structures of Everyday Life," in *Geography and Revolution*, ed. David N. Livingstone and Charles Withers (Chicago: University of Chicago Press, 2005), 160–98.

9. Michael Flaherty, *The Textures of Time: Agency and Temporal Experience* (Philadelphia: Temple University Press), 2010.

10. Dirk Jan ten Geuzendam, *The Day Kasparov Quit and Other Chess Interviews* (Alkmaar, the Netherlands: New in Chess, 2006), 339.

11. Barbara Adam, *Timescapes of Modernity: The Environment and Invisible Hazards* (New York: Routledge, 1998); Allen C. Bluedorn, *The Human Organization of Time: Temporal Realities and Experience*. Stanford, CA: Stanford University Press, 2002.

12. Elias, *Time*, 13.

13. J. C. Hallman, *The Chess Artist: Genius, Obsession, and the World's Oldest Game* (New York: St. Martin's, 2003), 144; see Rosa, "Social Acceleration."

14. Anthony Saidy, "Bronstein: I Played Chess for My Dad's Jailers," *Chess Life*, December 2007, 25–27, at 26.

15. Dirk Jan ten Geuzendam, "Everything That I Want or Dream of Actually Happens," *New in Chess*, 2006, no. 7, 26–33, at 31.

16. Julian Barnes, *Letters from London* (New York: Vintage, 1995), 247.

17. John Robinson, "The Time Squeeze," *American Demographics* 12 (1990): 30–33; Dale Southerton, "'Squeezing Time': Allocating Practices, Coordinating Networks and Scheduling Society," *Time & Society* 12 (2003): 5–25.

18. I. A. Horowitz and P. L. Rothenberg, *The Personality of Chess* (New York: Macmillan, 1963).

19. Paul Hoffman, *King's Gambit: A Son, a Father, and the World's Most Dangerous Game* (New York: Hyperion, 2007), 49; Richard Eales, *Chess: The History of a Game* (London: B. T. Batsford, 1985): 145.

20. Paul Hoffman, *King's Gambit*, 50.

21. David Bronstein and Georgy Smolyan, *Chess in the Eighties* (Oxford: Pergamon, 1982), 51–52.

22. Paul Hoffman, *King's Gambit*, 50.

23. Larry Evans, *This Crazy World of Chess* (New York: Cardoza, 2007), 157; "Game Clock," *Wikipedia, the Free Encyclopedia*, http://en.wikipedia.org/wiki/Game_clock, accessed January 29, 2011. The chess clock or game clock has spread to other games, including go and Scrabble.

24. Alexander Cockburn, *Idle Passion: Chess and the Dance of Death* (New York: New American Library, 1974), 55.

25. Bruno Latour, *Reassembling the Social: An Introduction to Actor-Network-Theory* (New York: Oxford University Press, 2005).

26. Gata Kamsky, quoted in Macauley Peterson, "Kamsky Struggles to Find His Old Form," *Chess Life*, April 2006, 20–23, at 21.

27. Michael Flaherty, *A Watched Pot: How We Experience Time* (New York: New York University Press, 1999).

28. Flaherty, *The Textures of Time*.

29. Gary Alan Fine, *Kitchens: The Culture of Restaurant Work* (Berkeley: University of California Press, 1996), 77; Robert Lauer, *Temporal Man: The Meaning and Uses of Social Time* (New York: Praeger, 1981).

30. Benjamin DiCicco-Bloom and David Gibson, "More Than a Game: Sociological Theory from the Theories of Games," *Sociological Theory* 28 (2010): 251.

31. Antony J. Puddephatt, "Incorporating Ritual into Greedy Institution Theory: The Case of Devotion in Amateur Chess," *Sociological Quarterly* 49 (2008): 155–80.

32. D. Alan Aycock, "The Perfect Wave: A Search for the Empty Gesture of Play," unpublished manuscript, 1991, 31.

33. Mikhail Tal apparently used time for psychological purposes. In a game against Fischer in the Chess Olympiad, Tal spent ten minutes staring at the board before

making his first move. See Frank Brady, *Endgame: Bobby Fischer's Remarkable Rise and Fall—from America's Brightest Prodigy to the Edge of Madness* (New York: Crown, 2011), 132.

34. Bronstein and Smolyan, *Chess in the Eighties*, 50.

35. George Herbert Mead, *Mind, Self & Society from the Standpoint of a Social Behaviorist* (Chicago: University of Chicago Press, 1934); Michael Flaherty and Gary Alan Fine, "Present, Past and Future: Conjugating Mead's Perspective of Time," *Time & Society* 10 (2001): 147–61.

36. Pal Benko and Burt Hochberg, *Winning with Chess Psychology* (New York: Random House, 1991), 57.

37. Barnes, *Letters from London*, 247.

38. Jon Jacobs, "Timing Is Everything," *Chess Life*, December 2007, 16–19, at 16. One player noted that in blitz chess, some players place their pieces on the board closer to their clocks to avoid losing time in making their moves and then pressing their clock. Even a few milliseconds can matter.

39. Tom Braunlich, "The U.S. Women's Championship," *Chess Life*, August 2008, 25–27.

40. Flaherty, *A Watched Pot*.

41. Benko and Hochberg, *Winning with Chess Psychology*, 251.

42. Michael Flaherty, personal communication, 2012.

43. Quoted in Hallman, *The Chess Artist*, 145.

44. Daniel Kahneman, *Thinking, Fast and Slow* (New York: Farrar, Strauss and Giroux, 2011).

45. Garry Kasparov, *How Life Imitates Chess: Making the Right Moves, from the Board to the Board Room* (New York: Bloomsbury, 2007), 41.

46. There is also a quick rating for games between ten and sixty minutes per side. Games with thirty minutes per side (action chess) are rated in both the regular and quick rating systems.

47. Arlie Russell Hochschild, *The Managed Heart: Commercialization of Human Feeling* (Berkeley: University of California Press, 1984).

48. Thierry Wendling, *Ethnologie des joueurs d'échecs* (Paris: Presses Universitaires de France, 2002), 175.

49. Horowitz and Rothenberg, *The Personality of Chess*, 12.

50. Hikaru Nakamura and Bruce Harper, *Bullet Chess: One Minute to Mate* (Milford, CT: Russell Enterprises, 2009).

51. Kahneman, *Thinking, Fast and Slow*.

52. Reprinted in Willard Fiske, *Chess Tales and Chess Miscellanies* (New York: Longmans, Green, 1912), 13. From the context it is unclear whether he is referring to each move being five seconds or the entire game being that length.

53. Horowitz and Rothenberg, *The Personality of Chess*, 12.

54. Danny Kopec, "Steroid Chess," *Chess Life*, October 2007, 41–45, at 42. Emphasis added.

55. Bronstein and Smolyan, *Chess in the Eighties*, 50.

56. Robert Desjarlais, *Counterplay: An Anthropologist at the Chessboard* (Berkeley: University of California Press, 2011), 2.

57. Charles Krauthammer, "The Pariah Chess Club," Townhall.com, December 27, 2002, http://townhall.com/columnists/CharlesKrauthammer/2002/12/27/the_pariah_chess_club, accessed September 28, 2009.

58. DiCicco-Bloom and Gibson, "More Than a Game."

Chapter Four

1. Robert Stebbins, *Serious Leisure: A Perspective for Our Time* (New Brunswick, NJ: Transaction, 2006).

2. Tamotsu Shibutani, "Reference Groups as Perspectives," *American Journal of Sociology* 60 (1955): 562–69.

3. Anselm Strauss, *Negotiations: Varieties, Contexts, Processes, and Social Order* (San Francisco: Jossey-Bass, 1978); David Unruh, "The Nature of Social Worlds," *Pacific Sociological Review* 23 (1980): 271–96; Daniel Silver, Terry N. Clark, and C. J. N. Yanez, "Scenes: Social Context in an Age of Contingency," *Social Forces* 88 (2010): 2293–324; David Grazian, *On the Make: The Hustle of Urban Nightlife* (Chicago: University of Chicago Press, 2007).

4. Gerald Suttles, "The Cumulative Texture of Local Urban Culture," *American Journal of Sociology* 90 (1984): 283–304.

5. Gary Alan Fine, *Tiny Publics: A Theory of Group Culture and Action* (New York: Russell Sage Foundation, 2012); Nina Eliasoph and Paul Lichterman, "Culture in Interaction," *American Journal of Sociology* 108 (2003), 735–94; Malcolm Gladwell, *The Tipping Point: How Little Things Can Make a Big Difference* (Boston: Little, Brown, 2000).

6. Ann Mische and Harrison White, "Between Conversation and Situation: Public Switching Dynamics across Network Domains," *Social Research* 65 (1998): 295–324; Eiko Ikegami, "A Sociological Theory of Publics: Identity and Culture as Emergent Properties in Networks," *Social Research* 67 (2000): 989–1029.

7. Jeffrey Olick and Joyce Robbins, "Social Memory Studies," *Annual Review of Sociology* 24 (1998): 105–40; Gary Alan Fine and Sherryl Kleinman, "Rethinking Subculture: An Interactionist Analysis," *American Journal of Sociology* 85 (1979): 1–20.

8. Gary Alan Fine and Brooke Harrington, "Tiny Publics: Small Groups and Civil Society," *Sociological Theory* 22 (2004): 341–56; Michael Warner, *Publics and Counterpublics* (New York: Zone Books, 1995).

9. Pierre Nora, ed., *Realms of Memory: Rethinking the French Past*, trans. Arthur Goldhammer (New York: Columbia University Press, 1996).

10. H. J. R. Murray, *A History of Chess* (Oxford: Oxford University Press, 1913); Harry Golombek, *Chess: A History* (New York: G. P. Putnam, 1976); Calvin Olson, *The Chess Kings*, vol. 1 (Victoria, BC: Trafford, 2006); Jenny Adams, *Power Play: The Literature and Politics of Chess in the Late Middle Ages* (Philadelphia: University of Pennsylvania Press, 2006); Marilyn Yalom, *Birth of the Chess Queen: A History* (New York: HarperCollins, 2004).

11. Pierre Bourdieu, *The Field of Cultural Production: Essays on Art and Literature* (New York: Columbia University Press, 1993).

12. Norton Long, "The Local Community as an Ecology of Games," *American Journal*

of Sociology 64 (1958): 251–61; Erving Goffman, *Interaction Ritual: Essays on Face-to-Face Behavior* (New York: Anchor, 1967).

13. Amazon lists over a million books in response to a request for religion and half that number for medicine.

14. Antony J. Puddephatt, "Incorporating Ritual into Greedy Institution Theory: The Case of Devotion in Amateur Chess," *Sociological Quarterly* 49 (2008): 155–80, at 159.

15. Thierry Wendling, introduction to *Ethnologie des joueurs d'échecs* (Paris: Presses Universitaires de France, 2002).

16. Puddephatt, "Incorporating Ritual," 159.

17. J. C. Hallman, *The Chess Artist: Genius, Obsession, and the World's Oldest Game* (New York: St. Martin's, 2003), 39.

18. David Pillemer, *Momentous Events, Vivid Memories* (Cambridge, MA: Harvard University Press, 1998), 3.

19. Robert Desjarlais, *Counterplay: An Anthropologist at the Chessboard* (Berkeley: University of California Press, 2011), 56.

20. There is an extensive Wikipedia page on Candyland that includes startling facts about the changes in the rules and the characters since the game was first produced by Milton Bradley in 1949; Plumpy has been replaced by Mamma Ginger Tree. A movie version of the game was optioned in 2009, and warnings exist against using material from the game on any adult website. See "Candy Land," *Wikipedia, the Free Encyclopedia* http://en.wikipedia.org/wiki/Candy_Land, accessed February 13, 2011.

21. Stefan Fatsis, *Word Freak: Heartbreak, Triumph, Genius, and Obsession in the World of Competitive Scrabble Players* (Boston: Houghton Mifflin, 2001).

22. Reuben Fine, *Bobby Fischer's Conquest of the World's Chess Championship: The Psychology and Tactics of the Title Match* (1973; repr., New York: Ishi, 2008), 52.

23. Just as chess champions can become celebrities, celebrities become chess players and are noted within the community: Napoleon, Rousseau, Marx, Tolstoy, George Washington, Benjamin Franklin, Robert Oppenheimer, Sting, and Madonna are all known to be chess players. See Paul Hoffman, *King's Gambit: A Son, a Father, and the World's Most Dangerous Game* (New York: Hyperion, 2007), 65. The psychoanalyst Norman Reider suggests that "participation with the great via their hobbies both lessens the sense of guilt ... and at the same time enhances the pleasure via the indulgence thereby bestowed from on high." "Chess, Oedipus, and the Mater Dolorosa," *International Journal of Psycho-Analysis* 40 (1959): 320–33, at 331.

24. Reuben Fine, *Fischer's Conquest*, 53.

25. Nora, *Realms of Memory*.

26. Fred Reinfeld, *The Human Side of Chess: The Great Chess Masters and Their Game; The Story of the World Champions, Their Triumphs and Their Illusions, Their Achievements and Their Failures* (New York: Pellegrini and Cudahy, 1952), viii.

27. Charles Horton Cooley, *Social Process* (New York: Scribner's), 1918.

28. Sigmund Freud, *Group Psychology and the Analysis of the Ego* (New York: Boni and Liveright, 1922); Randall Collins, *Interaction Ritual Chains* (Princeton, NJ: Princeton University Press, 2004).

29. Fred Waitzkin, *Moral Games: The Turbulent Genius of Garry Kasparov* (New York: Putnam, 1993), 298.

30. Al Lawrence, "Fischer: Fame to Fallout," *Chess Life*, September 2007, 18–25, at 23.

31. Hans Böhm and Kees Jongkind, *Bobby Fischer: The Wandering King* (London: B. T. Batsford, 2004), 45.

32. Frank Brady, *Profile of a Prodigy: The Life and Games of Bobby Fischer* (New York: David McKay, 1965).

33. Frank Brady, *Endgame: Bobby Fischer's Remarkable Rise and Fall—from America's Brightest Prodigy to the Edge of Madness* (New York: Crown, 2011).

34. Böhm and Jongkind, *Bobby Fischer*, 21.

35. Kerry Ferris and Scott Harris, *Stargazing: Celebrity, Fame, and Social Interaction* (New York: Routledge, 2011).

36. Fred Waitzkin, *Searching for Bobby Fischer: The World of Chess, Observed by the Father of a Chess Prodigy* (New York: Random House, 1988).

37. Garry Kasparov, "The Bobby Fischer Defense," review of *Endgame: Bobby Fischer's Remarkable Rise and Fall—from America's Brightest Prodigy to the Edge of Madness*, by Frank Brady, *New York Review of Books*, March 10, 2011, http://www.nybooks .com/articles/archives/2011/mar/10/bobby-fischer-defense/?pagination=false, accessed August 5, 2012.

38. Michael Weinreb, *The Kings of New York: A Year among the Geeks, Oddballs, and Geniuses Who Make Up America's Top High School Chess Team* (New York: Gotham Books, 2007), 200.

39. Brady, *Endgame*, 64.

40. Brady, *Profile of a Prodigy*, 2.

41. Hallman, *The Chess Artist*, 48.

42. While chess—and other leisure worlds—produce heroes, they do not emphasize villains. It is the greats who are recalled. While troublesome and troubled players— such as Fischer, Alekhine, Morphy, and perhaps some Soviet champions—are recalled with their troubles intact, they are not viewed as evil or destructive to the activity itself. Certainly some criminals populate the chessworld; however they are not long remembered.

43. Al Lawrence, "Remembering Bobby Fischer," *Chess Life*, March 2008, 20–24. The phrase "the pride and sorrow of chess" typically refers to the other great American chess celebrity, Paul Morphy. One grandmaster honored Fischer by playing one of Fischer's favorite openings at a major chess tournament in tribute.

44. Richard Eales, *Chess: The History of a Game* (London: B. T. Batsford, 1985, 149).

45. Cary Utterberg, *The Dynamics of Chess Psychology* (1980; repr. Dallas: Chess Digest, 1994), 214.

46. David Shenk, *The Immortal Game: A History of Chess* (New York: Doubleday, 2006), 100.

47. Hallman, *The Chess Artist*.

48. Quoted in Desjarlais, *Counterplay*, 96.

49. Stuart Rachels, "The Reviled Art," in *Philosophy Looks at Chess*, ed. Benjamin Hall (Chicago: Open Court, 2008), 209–25, at 216.

50. Andy Soltis, "The Lasker Rook," *Chess Life*, April 2008, 10–11, at 10.

51. D. Alan Aycock, "The Check Is in the Mail: A Preliminary View of Play as Discourse," *Play & Culture* 2 (1989): 142–57, at 145.

52. Garry Kasparov, *How Life Imitates Chess: Making the Right Moves, from the Board to the Board Room* (New York: Bloomsbury 2007), 110.

53. Larry Evans, *This Crazy World of Chess* (New York: Cardoza, 2007), 249.

54. Andrew Soltis, "The Marshall Variations of the Sicilian and French Defenses," *Chess Life*, August 2006, 8–9, at 9.

55. Desjarlais, *Counterplay*, 91, see also 86–94.

56. Ibid.

57. Shenk, *The Immortal Game*, 81.

58. The closest to a standard reference for the endgame is a 530-page tome, Jeremy Silman, *Silman's Complete Endgame Course: From Beginner to Master* (Los Angeles: Siles, 2007). But it doesn't present named "closings."

59. Quoted in Kasparov, *How Life Imitates Chess*, 119.

60. Joel Benjamin, "Building Blocks to Master," *Chess Life*, June 2007, 42.

61. One player explained that he had planned to study chess for three hours, an hour each for the opening, middle game, and endgame. He explains that after three days he gave up on the endgame, finding it not very interesting and hoping that his opponents would resign before they reached that point.

62. Jonathan Rowson, "The Nervous Elevator Man," *New in Chess*, 2007, no. 2, 87–91, at 87.

63. Reuben Fine, *Fischer's Conquest*, 55.

64. Kasparov, *How Life Imitates Chess*, 111.

65. Thierry Wendling, "The Invention and Transmission of Chess Knowledge: For an Anthropological Study of Chess Concepts," in *Step by Step: Proceedings of the Fourth Colloquium on Board Games in Academia*, ed. Jean Retschitzki and Rosita Haddad-Zubel (Fribourg, Switz.: Editions Universitaires, 2002), 113–20, at 114.

66. Dylan Loeb McClain, "Two Young Players Take a Risk by Relying on One Opening," *New York Times*, September 14, 2008, 42. The leading players have personal choices. As black, Anand often plays the Najdorf Sicilian; Kramnik, the Petrov; and Carlsen, the Dragon.

67. Saif Patel, "Fischer-Random, Anyone?" *Chess Life*, February 2009, 6.

68. Jim Edwards, "Re-Fried Liver," *Chess Life*, July 2009, 32–34.

69. Nina Eliasoph and Paul Lichterman, "Culture in Interaction," *American Journal of Sociology* 108 (2003): 735–94.

70. Antony J. Puddephatt and Gary Alan Fine, "Chess as Art, Science, and Sport," in *A Companion to Sport*, ed. David Andrews and Ben Carrington (Oxford: Wiley Blackwell, 2013), 390–404.

71. Anthony Saidy, *The Battle of Chess Ideas* (New York: RHM, 1972).

72. Ibid., 33.

73. Herbert Butterfield, *The Whiggish Interpretation of History*. London: G. Bell and Sons, 1931.

74. Robert K. Merton, *The Sociology of Science: Theoretical and Empirical Investigations* (Chicago: University of Chicago Press, 1973).

75. Thomas S. Kuhn, *The Structure of Scientific Revolutions* (Chicago: University of Chicago Press, 1962); Trevor Pinch, "The Sociology of Science and Technology," in *21st Century Sociology: A Reference Handbook*, vol. 2, ed. Clifton Bryant and Dennis Peck (Thousand Oaks, CA: Sage, 2007), 266–75.

76. Kuhn, *The Structure of Scientific Revolutions*.

77. See Imre König, *Chess from Morphy to Botvinnik: A Century of Chess Evolution* (New York: Dover, 1977).

78. Max Euwe and John Nunn, *The Development of Chess Style: An Instructive and Entertaining Trip through the Heritage of Chess* (London: B. T. Batsford, 1997).

79. Ibid., 8.

80. König, *Chess from Morphy to Botvinnik*, xiv.

81. Euwe and Nunn, *The Development of Chess Style*, 14–15.

82. Ibid., 19.

83. Pal Benko and Burt Hochberg, *Winning with Chess Psychology* (New York: Random House, 1991), 3.

84. Ibid., 3–4.

85. George Steiner, *Fields of Force: Fischer and Spassky in Reykjavik* (New York: Viking Press, 1974), 30.

86. Euwe and Nunn, *The Development of Chess Style*, 44–45.

87. Murray, *A History of Chess*, 889.

88. Euwe and Nunn, *The Development of Chess Style*, 114–17; Olson, *The Chess Kings*, 112.

89. Shenk, *The Immortal Game*, 236.

90. Dirk Jan ten Geuzendam, *The Day Kasparov Quit and Other Chess Interviews* (Alkmaar, the Netherlands: New in Chess, 2006), 207.

91. David Remnick, "The Tsar's Opponent," *New Yorker*, October 1, 2007, 64–77, at 72.

92. Fred Reinfeld, *The Human Side of Chess*, 4.

93. Quoted in Daniel Johnson, *White King and Red Queen: How the Cold War Was Fought on the Chessboard* (London: Atlantic, 2007), 337.

94. H. A. Kennedy, *Chips, Waifs, and Strays: Anecdotes from the Chess-Board* (London: Dean and Son, 1862), 65.

95. Karl Menninger, "Chess," *Bulletin of the Menninger Clinic* 6, no. 3 (1942): 80–83, at 83.

96. Comments from the Internet Chess Club discussion forum, 2010. The queen pawn opening (d4) is considered "girly" in this discussion, whereas the king pawn opening (e4) is considered macho. Not only does this evaluation consider the piece behind the pawn, but the e4 opening traditionally leads to an open, more active game, and the d4 opening leads to a closed, more defensive game.

97. Geuzendam, *The Day Kasparov Quit*, 16. I was told that the early twentieth-century chess master Richard Réti suggested that chess style is linked to the life cycle and that over the course of one's chess career one recapitulates the development of style: from a wild romanticism to a constrained classicism (interview).

98. Isador H. Coriat, "The Unconscious Motives of Interest in Chess," *Psychoanalytic*

Review 28 (1941): 30–36, at 33; Ernest Jones, "The Problem of Paul Morphy: A Contribution to the Psycho-Analysis of Chess," *International Journal of Psycho-Analysis* 12 (1931): 1–23, at 7.

99. Quoted in Geuzendam, *The Day Kasparov Quit*, 37.

100. Simon Webb, *Chess for Tigers* (London: B. T. Batsford, 2005), 22–23.

101. See for instance Mig Greengard's *The Daily Dirty Chess Blog*, http://www.chessninja.com/dailydirt/, accessed February 22, 2011.

102. It has been alleged that officials of the World Chess Federation have sold original score sheets of important games to collectors. See Evans, *This Crazy World of Chess*, 243.

103. Just and Burg, *Rules of Chess*, 79.

104. Bruno Latour and Steve Woolgar, *Laboratory Life: The Social Construction of Scientific Facts* (London: Sage, 1979).

105. Wendling, *Ethnologie des joueurs d'échecs*, 184.

106. Bobby Fischer, *My Sixty Memorable Games* (London: B. T. Batsford, 2008), 276–79.

107. This Fischer versus Fine game is archived at http://www.chessgames.com/perl/chessgame?gid=1043992, accessed February 21, 2011).

108. Fischer's mother Regina worried about her thirteen-year-old son's furious attention to chess and asked Fine, then a trained analyst, to meet with her son. The two met in Fine's apartment on several occasions to play chess. When Fischer discovered the deception, he left in anger. Fine wrote, "It becomes one of the ironic twists of history that of the two leading American chess masters of the twentieth century one almost became the psychoanalyst of the other." *Fischer's Conquest*, 24.

109. Louis Menand, "Game Theory," *New Yorker*, March 1, 2004, 87–90, at 87.

110. For an example of how, for knowledgeable tennis players, prose can enrich action, see John McPhee, *Levels of the Game* (New York: Farrar, Straus and Giroux, 1969).

111. There is a tradition in chess to distinguish between pawns and pieces. While Philidor believed "pawns are the soul of chess," they still get no respect, even lacking a letter designation.

112. George A. Miller, *Language and Communication* (New York: McGraw-Hill, 1951), 108–10; James A. Mason and Gordon E. Peterson, "On the Problem of Describing the Grammar of Natural Languages," *Language and Speech* 10 (1967): 107–21.

113. D. Alan Aycock, "Gens Una Sumus: Play and Metaculture," *Play & Culture* 1 (1988): 124–37, at 134.

114. Harry Golombek, *Chess: A History* (New York: G. P. Putnam's Sons, 1976), 240–41.

115. Fischer, *My Sixty Memorable Games*, 276.

116. Ibid.

117. Ibid., 269–75.

118. Blunderprone, "Zurich 1953: Possible Conspiracies and Controversies," Chess.com, October 4, 2009, http://www.chess.com/blog/Blunderprone/zurich-1953-possible-conspiracies-and-controversies, accessed February 21, 2011.

119. David Bronstein, *Zurich International Chess Tournament, 1953*, trans. Jim Marfia (New York: Dover, 1979), 128–32.

120. Ibid., 131.

121. Ibid., 128.

122. Gary Alan Fine, *Authors of the Storm: Meteorology and the Culture of Prediction* (Chicago: University of Chicago Press, 2007), 135–72.

123. Bronstein, *Zurich International Chess Tournament*, 129.

124. Ibid., 132.

125. "Paul Keres vs. Samuel Reshevsky," chessgames.com, http://www.chessgames .com/perl/chessgame?gid=1072453, accessed April 30, 2012.

126. This is similar to Robert Faulkner and Howard S. Becker's description of the improvisational routines of jazz musicians. Improvisation is possible because of a shared awareness of "standards." See *Do You Know . . . ? The Jazz Repertoire in Action* (Chicago: University of Chicago Press, 2009).

127. Robert Stebbins, *Serious Leisure*.

Chapter Five

1. The term "chess hunger" comes from Mikhail Botvinnik's autobiography, *Achieving the Aim* (Oxford: Pergamon, 1981). See W. R. Hartston and P. C. Wason, *The Psychology of Chess* (New York: Facts on File Publications, 1984), 13.

2. Claudio E. Benzecry, "Becoming a Fan: On the Seductions of Opera," *Qualitative Sociology* 32 (2009): 131–51, at 131.

3. Pierre Bourdieu, *The Rules of Art: Genesis and Structure of the Literary Field* (Stanford, CA: Stanford University Press, 1996), 227–28.

4. David Unruh, "The Nature of Social Worlds," *Pacific Sociological Review* 23 (1980): 271–96.

5. Robert Desjarlais, *Counterplay: An Anthropologist at the Chessboard* (Berkeley: University of California Press, 2011), 2–3.

6. Lewis Coser, *Greedy Institutions: Patterns of Undivided Commitment* (New York: Free Press, 1974); Antony J. Puddephatt, "Incorporating Ritual into Greedy Institution Theory: The Case of Devotion in Amateur Chess," *Sociological Quarterly* 49 (2008): 155–80, at 160–62.

7. Frank Brady, *Endgame: Bobby Fischer's Remarkable Rise and Fall—from America's Brightest Prodigy to the Edge of Madness* (New York: Crown, 2011), 19–20, 38–39, 50; John W. Collins, *My Seven Chess Prodigies: Bobby Fischer, Robert E. Byrne, William J. Lombardy, Donald Byrne, Raymond A. Weinstein, Salvatore J. Matera, Lewis H. Cohen* (New York: Simon and Schuster, 1974), 34–44.

8. Brady, *Endgame*, 33.

9. Alexander Cockburn, *Idle Passion: Chess and the Dance of Death* (New York: New American Library, 1974), 162.

10. Antony J. Puddephatt, "Advancing in the Amateur Chess World," in *Doing Ethnography: Studying Everyday Life*, ed. Dorothy Pawluch, William Shaffir, and Christine Miall (Toronto: Canadian Scholar's, 2005), 300–311.

11. Elizabeth Vicary, "America's Top Scholastic Players Shine in Orlando," *Chess Life*, March 2007, 24–25, at 24.

12. Quoted in H. J. R. Murray, *A History of Chess A History of Chess* (Oxford: Oxford University Press, 1913), 839.

13. David Shenk, *The Immortal Game: A History of Chess* (New York: Doubleday, 2006), xvi.

14. I am uncertain if this is an apocryphal story, but it is certainly appealing to the psychoanalytic mind. See Arturo Schwartz, *The Complete Works of Marcel Duchamp* (New York: Abrams, 1969), cited in Cockburn, *Idle Passion*, 187.

15. Internet Chess Club discussion board, June 21, 2010.

16. Fred Waitzkin, *Mortal Games: The Turbulent Genius of Garry Kasparov* (New York: Putnam, 1993), 90–92.

17. Mike Klein, "Where Have You Gone, Rachels, Shaked & Rao?" *Chess Life*, September 2008, 24–29, at 29.

18. Quoted in Dominic Lawson, *End Game: Kasparov vs. Short* (New York: Harmony, 1994), 19.

19. Genna Sosonko, *The Reliable Past* (Alkmaar, the Netherlands: New in Chess, 2003), 73.

20. This is not always the case. Adults do learn chess on occasion, often through the intervention of friends. One friend explained that his chess career began after he was diagnosed with severe myeloma and needed something to occupy his mind (field notes).

21. William O'Fallon, "Checkmate! When the King Is Dethroned," *Newsweek*, September 10, 2001, 15.

22. José Raúl Capablanca, *My Chess Career* (New York: Macmillan, 1920), 4.

23. Kenneth Kiewra, Thomas O'Connor, Matthew McCrudden, and Xiongyi Liu, "Developing Young Chess Masters: A Collective Case Study," in *Chess and Education: Selected Essays from the Koltanowski Conference* (Dallas: Chess Program at the University of Texas at Dallas, 2006), 98–112, at 99–100.

24. Paul Hoffman, *King's Gambit*, 39.

25. Josh Waitzkin, *The Art of Learning: A Journey in the Pursuit of Excellence* (New York: Free Press, 2007), 4.

26. Ingrid Galitis, "Stalemate: Girls and a Mixed-Gender Chess Club," *Gender and Education* 14 (2002): 71–83, at 76.

27. Jill Caryl Weiner, "Why NYC Kids Rule the Chess World," *Wall Street Journal*, May 13, 2011, n.p.

28. Arpad E. Elo, "Chess: A Cultural Phenomenon," in *Lore (Friends of the Milwaukee Public Museum)*, n.d., 36–42, at 40, 42.

29. One friend told me that he felt that there is a distinctive midwestern style of play: "It is very organic. It is homegrown. It is indigenous." He contrasts this to the more international style of New York play, noting that there is "less of an immigrant idea about chess here" (interview).

30. Weiner, "Why NYC Kids Rule the Chess World."

31. Frank Brady, *Profile of a Prodigy: The Life and Games of Bobby Fischer* (New York: David McKay, 1965), 3.

32. Garry Kasparov explained that different cities have different chess cultures, and he feels that in the former Soviet Union the highest levels of chess culture are to be found in the Caucasus—in Baku, Erevan, and Tbilisi (field notes).

33. Dick Hebdige, *Subculture: The Meaning of Style* (London: Routledge, 1979); David Muggleton, *Inside Subculture: The Postmodern Meaning of Style* (Oxford: Berg, 2000).

34. Thierry Wendling, *Ethnologie des joueurs d'échecs*, 49.

35. D. Alan Aycock, "The Perfect Wave: A Search for the Empty Gesture of Play," unpublished manuscript, 1991, 34.

36. D. Alan Aycock, "Gens Una Sumus: Play and Metaculture," *Play & Culture* 1 (1988): 124–37, at 134.

37. Mihaly Csikszentmihalyi, *Beyond Boredom and Anxiety* (San Francisco: Jossey-Bass 1975), 68.

38. C. K. Damrosch, "Sunday in the Park with Maurice," *Chess Life*, December 2007, 32–35, at 32.

39. Macauley Peterson, "Get Ready for the Next Generation," *Chess Life*, June 2007, 16–23, at 19; Jennifer Shahade, *Chess Bitch: Women in the Ultimate Intellectual Sport* (Los Angeles: Siles, 2005), 166.

40. Dylan Loeb McClain, "In High-Stakes Games, Rivals Can Suddenly Become Allies," *New York Times*, April 23, 2010, 24.

41. Jonathan Hilton, "Denker Deconstructed," *Chess Life*, November 2006: 28–29, at 28.

42. Gary Alan Fine, *Gifted Tongues: High School Debate and Adolescent Culture* (Princeton, NJ: Princeton University Press, 2001), 260–66.

43. Michael Weinreb, *The Kings of New York: A Year among the Geeks, Oddballs, and Geniuses Who Make Up America's Top High School Chess Team* (New York: Gotham Books), 2007, 87.

44. Viktor Korchnoi, *Chess Is My Life: Autobiography and Games* (New York: Arco, 1978), 38–39.

45. Thomas F. Gieryn, "Three Truth-Spots," *Journal of the History of the Behavioral Sciences* 38 (2002): 113–32.

46. Gary Alan Fine, *Morel Tales: The Culture of Mushrooming* (Cambridge, MA: Harvard University Press, 1998), chapter 5.

47. Ugo Corte, "A Refinement of Collaborative Circles Theory: Resource Mobilization and Innovation in an Extreme Sport," *Social Psychology Quarterly* 76 (2013): 25–51.

48. Michael Farrell, *Collaborative Circles: Friendship Dynamics and Creative Work* (Chicago: University of Chicago Press, 2001), 19; John Irwin, *Scenes* (Beverly Hills, CA: Sage, 1977); Kimberly Creasap, "Social Movement Scenes: Place-Based Politics and Everyday Resistance," *Sociological Compass* 6 (2012): 182–91.

49. Karl Menninger, "Chess," *Bulletin of the Menninger Clinic* 6, no. 3 (1942): 80–83, at 80–81.

50. Charles Krauthammer, "The Pariah Chess Club," townhall.com, December 27, 2002, http://townhall.com/columnists/CharlesKrauthammer/2002/12/27/the _pariah_chess_club, accessed September 28, 2009.

51. "Mink," *New Yorker,* June 12, 1989, 38–39. Other parks in New York also have a chess culture, including Battery Park, Central Park, and Bryant Park, behind the public library. Each has its own feel.

52. C. K. Damrosch, "Sunday in the Park with Maurice," 32.

53. Paul Hoffman, *King's Gambit*, 64–65.

54. Shia Kapos, "Move to Compromise." *Chicago Tribune*, September 26, 2003, sect. 5, pp. 1–2.

55. Richard Eales, *Chess: The History of a Game*. London: B. T. Batsford, 1985, 109.

56. Jürgen Habermas, *The Structural Transformation of the Public Sphere* (Cambridge, MA: MIT Press, 1989).

57. Eales, *Chess: The History of a Game*, 141, 149; H. A. Kennedy, *Chips, Waifs, and Strays: Anecdotes from the Chess-Board* (London: Dean and Son, 1862), 59.

58. I was told that the Marshall Club was considered slightly tonier than the Manhattan Club, although for many years the Manhattan Club had more and stronger members, including Wilhelm Steinitz and Bobby Fischer. But in New York real estate is destiny.

59. Desjarlais, *Counterplay*, 194, 198.

60. Dylan Loeb McClain, "Even in an Age of Online Play, Some Clubs Continue to Thrive," *New York Times*, December 17, 2006, 39.

61. Puddephatt, "Incorporating Ritual," 169–70.

62. Gary Alan Fine, *With the Boys: Little League Baseball and Preadolescent Culture* (Chicago: University of Chicago Press, 1987).

63. Gary Alan Fine and Brooke Harrington, "Tiny Publics: Small Groups and Civil Society," *Sociological Theory* 22 (2004), 341–56.

64. Weinreb, *Kings of New York*.

65. Only two girls attended, only one regularly.

66. Ann Hulbert, "Chess Goes to School," *Slate*, May 2, 2007, http://www.slate.com/id/2165369, accessed May 2, 2007.

67. Hilary Levey, "Pageant Princes and Math Wizards: Understanding Children's Activities as a Form of Children's Work," *Childhood* 16 (2009): 195–212.

68. Edward Tenner, "Rook Dreams," *Atlantic*, December 2008, http://www.theatlantic.com/doc/200812/chess-software, accessed December 22, 2008.

69. Dylan Loeb McClain, "In Children's Chess, Umbrage over Rating System," *New York Times*, June 16, 2010, A16.

70. Gary Alan Fine, *Gifted Tongues*, 238.

71. Dylan Loeb McClain, "Idaho Turns to Chess as Education Strategy," *New York Times*, March 20, 2008, A14.

72. Annette Lareau, *Unequal Childhoods: Class, Race, and Family Life* (Berkeley: University of California Press, 2003).

73. Charles Horton Cooley, *Human Nature and the Social Order* (New York: C. Scribner and Sons, 1902).

74. Fred Waitzkin, *Mortal Games*, 90.

75. Joel Benjamin, *American Grandmaster: Four Decades of Chess Adventures*. London: Everyman Chess, 2007, 53, 78–79.

76. Fred Waitzkin, *Mortal Games*, 27; Paul Hoffman, *King's Gambit*, 62.

77. Gerry Bloustien, "Buffy Night at the Seven Stars: A 'Subcultural' Happening at the 'Glocal' Level," in *After Subculture: Critical Studies in Contemporary Youth Culture*, ed. Andy Bennett and Keith Kahn-Harris (New York: Palgrave, 2004), 148–61.

Chapter Six

1. Sarah Igo, *The Averaged American: Surveys, Citizens, and the Making of a Mass Public* (Cambridge, MA: Harvard University Press, 2007); Theodore Porter, *Trust in Numbers: The Pursuit of Objectivity in Science and Public Life* (Princeton, NJ: Princeton University Press, 1995).

2. Wendy Nelson Espeland and Mitchell Stevens, "Commensuration as a Social Process," *Annual Review of Sociology* 24 (1998): 313–43.

3. As I write this (June 2014) the former world champion, Viswanathan Anand, and the current one, Magnus Carlsen, are not Jewish. The player with the second-highest rating, Levon Aronian, is part Jewish.

4. Arpad E. Elo, *The Rating of Chessplayers, Past and Present* (New York: Arco, 1978).

5. Edward Winter, "Chess and Jews," *Chess Notes*, 2003, http://www.chesshistory .com/winter/extra/jews.html, accessed March 1, 2011.

6. There is debate as to whether Smyslov or Spassky is Jewish. Spassky has signed anti-Semitic petitions, but this doesn't differentiate him from his most famous opponent.

7. I. A. Horowitz and P. L. Rothenberg, *The Personality of Chess* (New York: Macmillan, 1963), 32. Almost all of them were from New York.

8. "Dr. Hermann Adler and Steinitz," *Chess Amateur*, September 1911, 367, quoted in Edward Winter, "Chess and Jews," 2003, http://www.chesshistory.com/winter /extra/jews.html, accessed August 23, 2014.

9. Horowitz and Rothenberg, *The Personality of Chess*.

10. Gerald Abrahams, *Not Only Chess: A Selection of Chessays* (London: George Allen and Unwin, 1974), 201.

11. Mendel Silber, *Jewish Achievement* (St. Louis: Modern View, 1910), 119.

12. William D. Rubinstein, "Jews in Grandmaster Chess," *Jewish Journal of Sociology* 46 (2004): 35–43, at 39.

13. Horowitz and Rothenberg, *The Personality of Chess*, 32.

14. Some doubt existed as to whether Alekhine had authored the diatribe, but subsequently a handwritten copy of the manuscript was found in his papers.

15. W. R. Hartston and P. C. Wason, *The Psychology of Chess* (New York: Facts on File Publications, 1984), 115.

16. Quoted in Alexander Cockburn, *Idle Passion: Chess and the Dance of Death* (New York: New American Library, 1974), 176.

17. Paul Hoffman, "Castling in the Square," *Harvard Magazine*, November–December 2002, http://harvardmagazine.com/2002/11/castling-in-the-square.html, accessed March 7, 2011.

18. Wallace E. Nevill, *"Chess-Humanics," A Philosophy of Chess, A Sociological Allegory: Parallelisms between the Game of Chess and Our Larger Human Affairs* (San Francisco: Whitaker and Ray, 1905), 73.

19. "Chessville Plays '20 Questions' with GM Maurice Ashley," http://www.chessville .com/Editorials/Interviews/20Questions/Ashley.htm, accessed November 25, 2006. *Shvarts* is a derogatory term in Yiddish.

20. Lev Alburt, "An 'Iffy' Sacrifice," *Chess Life*, November 2006, 54–55.

21. Arthur Bisguier, quoted in George Steiner, *Fields of Force: Fischer and Spassky at Reykjavik* (New York: Viking, 1974), 29.

22. Garry Kasparov, "The Chess Master and the Computer," review of *Chess Metaphors: Artificial Intelligence and the Human Mind,* by Diego Rasskin-Gutman, trans. Deborah Closky, *New York Review of Books,* February 11, 2010, http://www.nybooks.com/articles/archives/2010/feb/11/the-chess-master-and-the-computer/, accessed March 3, 2011.

23. Calvin Olson, *The Chess Kings,* vol. 1 (Victoria, BC: Trafford, 2006), 103–4.

24. Macauley Peterson, "Get Ready for the Next Generation," *Chess Life,* June 2007, 16–23, at 20.

25. Pal Benko and Burt Hochberg, *Winning with Chess Psychology* (New York: Random House, 1991), 215.

26. Charles Krauthammer, "The Pariah Chess Club," townhall.com, December 27, 2002, http://townhall.com/columnists/CharlesKrauthammer/2002/12/27/the_pariah_chess_club, accessed September 28, 2009.

27. Although younger players may lack focus or discipline, older players may lack energy for lengthy battles. Concentration may dip for those who are either younger or older than young adults. Older players are certainly more conscious of the effects of age, and this informs their chess practices.

28. The national high school Denker Championship was won by a girl once.

29. "Searching for Bobbie Ann Fischer," *Atlantic,* June 2007, 36; Jerry Hanken, "Fun and Games in Oklahoma," *Chess Life,* May 2007, 16–19; Dylan Loeb McClain, "In Tucson, Women and Girls Are Finding a Place at the Chessboard," *New York Times,* December 25, 2009, A16; Jennifer Shahade, *Chess Bitch: Women in the Ultimate Intellectual Sport* (Los Angeles: Siles, 2005), 3.

30. Christopher F. Chabris and Mark E. Glickman, "Sex Differences in Intellectual Performance: Analysis of a Large Cohort of Competitive Chess Players," *Psychological Science* 17 (2006): 1040–46; Merim Bilalic and Peter McLeod, "Participation Rates and the Difference in Performance of Women and Men in Chess," *Journal of Biosocial Science* 39 (2007): 789–93; Neil Charness and Yigal Gerchak, "Participation Rates and Maximal Performance: A Log-Linear Explanation for Group Differences, Such as Russian and Male Dominance in Chess," *Psychological Science* 7 (1996): 46–51; Linda Carol Gilbert, "Chessplayers: Gender Expectations and Self-Fulfilling Prophecy" (PhD diss., California School of Professional Psychology, 1989).

31. Paul Hoffman, *King's Gambit: A Son, a Father, and the World's Most Dangerous Game* (New York: Hyperion, 2007), 265. One female chess coach told me that she started attending her high school club because of a crush on a male player. When he left the club—and her life—she stayed.

32. The case of "Chesslady" Miss Lisa Lane received much publicity when she suddenly quit a major (women's) tournament, announcing that she was in love and unable to concentrate on the game. The *New York Herald Tribune* warmly endorsed the institution of love, for women at least. See Horowitz and Rothenberg, *The Personality of Chess,* 328.

33. Reuben Fine's argument that chess is "a play-substitute for war" is a curious one; the game as it is now organized is more about political process than about warfare. See Shahade, *Chess Bitch*, 11.

34. Ingrid Galitis, "Stalemate: Girls and a Mixed-Gender Chess Club," *Gender and Education* 14 (2002): 71–83, at 76.

35. Shahade, *Chess Bitch*, 156.

36. Quoted in Ralph Ginzburg, "Portrait of a Genius as a Young Chess Master," *Harper's,* January 1962, http://www.bobbyfischer.net/bobby04.html, accessed March 6, 2011.

37. "Playboy Interview: Garry Kasparov," by David Sheff, *Playboy,* November 1989, http://www.playboy.com/articles/garry-kasparov-1989-interview/index.html ?page=2, accessed March 6, 2011.

38. Larry Evans, *This Crazy World of Chess* (New York: Cardoza Press, 2007), 255.

39. Julian Barnes, *Letters from London* (New York: Vintage, 1995), 244.

40. Reuben Fine believed that "overt homosexuality is almost unknown among chess players," despite—or because of—the gratification of latent homosexuality that he believed was present. *The Psychology of the Chess Player* (New York: Dover, 1967), 22. One young adult international master confided in me, after asking for anonymity, that there was a homosexual player in the last tournament. He explained, "Homosexuals tend to give off that vibe. He was wearing flamboyant clothes." Another said that when he said that he liked the romantic style of chess, a listener thought that he was gay (field notes).

41. "World Chess Beauty Contest," February 2005, http://www.1wbcb.com/contest /index.php, accessed January 15, 2007. The website no longer exists, but as of September 1, 2006, there were 550 participants.

42. The Poisoned Pawn, "Kibitzing," *Kingpin,* Spring 2007, 2–6, at 5.

43. Shahade, *Chess Bitch*, 65–67.

44. Paul Hoffman, *King's Gambit,* 411.

45. Shahade, *Chess Bitch*, 71.

46. Anna Dreber, Christer Gerdes, and Patrik Gränsmark, "Beauty Queens and Battling Knights: Risk Taking and Attractiveness in Chess," *Journal of Economic Behavior & Organization* 90 (June 2013): 1–18.

47. Karl Menninger, "Chess," *Bulletin of the Menninger Clinic* 6, no. 3 (1942): 80–83, at 80.

48. Although references to class A or class B players are common, references to class E players (much less class J players) are rarer. Because class E players are less proficient, they are given less consideration individually and as a class.

49. Antony J. Puddephatt, "Incorporating Ritual into Greedy Institution Theory: The Case of Devotion in Amateur Chess," *Sociological Quarterly* 40 (2008): 155–80, at 167.

50. Olson, *The Chess Kings,* 95.

51. Dirk Jan ten Geuzendam, *The Day Kasparov Quit and Other Chess Interviews* (Alkmaar, the Netherlands: New in Chess, 2006), 194.

52. William Hartston, *How to Cheat at Chess* (London: Cadogan Chess, 1994), 77–78.

53. Antony J. Puddephatt, "Advancing in the Amateur Chess World," in *Doing Ethnography: Studying Everyday Life*, ed. Dorothy Pawluch, William Shaffir, and Christine Miall (Toronto: Canadian Scholar's, 2005), 300–311, at 302.

54. Lom, "'Sometimes Less Is More': The Development and Effects of Evaluative Cultures" (PhD diss., Northwestern University, 2013).

55. Pierre Bourdieu, *Distinction: A Social Critique of the Judgement of Taste*, trans. Richard Nice (Cambridge, MA: Harvard University Press, 1984).

56. D. Alan Aycock, "Gens Una Sumus: Play and Metaculture," *Play & Culture* 1 (1988): 124–37, at 133.

57. David Stark, *The Sense of Dissonance: Accounts of Worth in Economic Life* (Princeton, NJ: Princeton University Press, 2011).

58. "What Is the Average Rating in the USCF?" Chess.com, http://www.chess.com/forum/view/general/what-is-the-average-rating-in-the-uscf, accessed March 5, 2011.

59. Steven Craig Miller, "The USCF Elo Rating System," Renaissance Knights Chess Foundation, http://www.renaissanceknights.org/IL Scholastic/Handouts/Handouts PDFs/EloRatingSystem.pdf, accessed March 5, 2011.

60. I was told of a player who had a negative number, but I cannot verify this.

61. Paul Hoffman, *King's Gambit*, 18.

62. Howard Goldowsky, "How to Catch a Chess Cheater: Ken Regan Finds Moves Out of Mind," *Chess Life*, June 2014, 22–30, at 22.

63. David Bronstein and Georgy Smolyan, *Chess in the Eighties* (Oxford: Pergamon, 1982), 7.

64. Arpad E. Elo, *The Rating of Chessplayers, Past and Present* (1978; repr., New York: Ishi, 2008).

65. The Elo system has also been applied to Scrabble, go, and backgammon.

66. Sam Sloan, introduction to *The Rating of Chess Players, Past and Present*, by Arpad Elo (New York: Ishi, 2008), 1–12, at 1.

67. Ibid., 8.

68. Michael J. Moody, "Membership and Titles," *Chess Life*, December 2006, 6.

69. Not only informal or skittles matches but even the matches in the United States Chess League are unrated.

70. Macauley Peterson, "Fabulous Fabiano," *Chess Life*, January 2008, 30–35, at 32.

71. Dylan Loeb McClain, "In Children's Chess, Umbrage over Rating System," *New York Times*, June 16, 2010, A16.

72. Elizabeth Vicary, "Crowning K–12 Kings," *Chess Life*, April 2009, 27–28, at 27.

73. Peterson, "Fabulous Fabiano," 32.

74. For more on the Bloodgood case see "Claude Bloodgood," *Wikipedia, the Free Encyclopedia*, http://en.wikipedia.org/wiki/Claude_Bloodgood, accessed March 5, 2011; Paul Hoffman, *King's Gambit*, 169–70; J. C. Hallman, *The Chess Artist: Genius, Obsession, and the World's Oldest Game* (New York: Thomas Dunne Books, 2003), 263–96.

75. Jesse Kraai, "The Bathhouse and the Indian," *Chess Life*, July 2008, 26–29, at 27.

76. Because of the variability in game outcomes, it takes about twenty rated games for a rating to become "established" as opposed to provisional.

77. Shahade, *Chess Bitch*, 66.

78. Puddephatt, "Incorporating Ritual," 166.

79. Michael Jeffreys, "Is Your Ego Costing You Your Elo?" *Chess Life*, October 2008, 22–25, at 25.

80. Pierre Bourdieu, *The Field of Cultural Production: Essays on Art and Literature* (New York: Columbia University Press, 1993). See also Puddephatt, "Incorporating Ritual," 166.

81. Mariano Sana, "When Foreigners Take Over: A Case Study of Highly Skilled Migration," unpublished manuscript, 2009; Eviatar Zerubavel, *Social Mindscapes: An Invitation to Cognitive Sociology* (Cambridge, MA: Harvard University Press, 1997).

82. Puddephatt, "Incorporating Ritual," 165.

83. Lom, "Sometimes Less Is More."

84. Kirby Compton, "Break Out the Sandbags," *Chess Life*, April 2008, 6.

85. Many chess champions have been seen as insufferable. Bobby Fischer was by no means alone. Alexander Alekhine had a similar reputation, once urinating at the chessboard during a tournament. Peter Fuller, *The Champions: The Secret Motives in Games and Sport* (London: Allen Lane, 1978), 69.

86. Puddephatt, "Incorporating Ritual," 162.

87. Daniel D. Martin and Gary Alan Fine, "Satanic Cults, Satanic Play: Is Dungeons & Dragons a Breeding Ground for the Devil?" in *The Satanism Scare*, ed. James Richardson, David Bromley, and Joel Best (New York: Aldine de Gruyter, 1991).

88. Quoted in David Edmonds and John Eidinow, *Bobby Fischer Goes to War: How the Soviets Lost the Most Extraordinary Chess Match of All Time* (New York: Harper-Collins, 2004), 78.

89. Paul Hoffman, "The Pandolfini Defense," *New Yorker*, June 4, 2001, 65–73, at 72.

90. Puddephatt, "Incorporating Ritual," 163.

91. For a similar case, see Jonathan Hilton, "Pulling Himself Up by His Bootstraps," *Chess Life*, December 2007, 8.

92. Paul Hoffman, "Castling in the Square," *Harvard Magazine*, November–December 2002, http://harvardmagazine.com/2002/11/castling-in-the-square.html, accessed March 7, 2011.

93. Charles Krauthammer, "Did Chess Make Him Crazy?" *Time*, April 26, 2005, http://content.time.com/time/magazine/article/0,9171,1053672,00.html, accessed September 28, 2009.

94. Dylan Loeb McClain, "Fugitive Chess Teacher Is Reportedly Caught," *Gambit: New York Times Chess Blog*, December 5, 2009, http://gambit.blogs.nytimes.com /2009/12/05/fugitive-chess-teacher-is-reportedly-caught/#more-2025, accessed March 7, 2011.

95. D. T. Max, "The Prince's Gambit," *New Yorker*, March 21, 2011, 40–49, at 40.

96. Tim Just and Daniel B. Burg, *U.S. Chess Federation's Official Rules of Chess*, 5th ed. (New York: Random House, 2003), 83.

97. Ibid., 21. There is a separate touch-move rule for the visually handicapped.

98. Paul Hoffman recounts a dramatic story in which Garry Kasparov violated the touch-move rule in a game against Judit Polgar and denied it even in the face of

video evidence. Hoffman also presents an example of Bobby Fischer immediately accepting the consequence of his action when accused of a touch-move violation. *King's Gambit*, 194–95.

99. Ibid., 29.

100. Benko and Hochberg, *Winning with Chess Psychology*, 260–61.

101. Viktor Korchnoi, *Chess Is My Life: Autobiography and Games* (New York: Arco, 1978), 17.

102. Danny Kopec, "Steroid Chess," *Chess Life*, October 2007, 41–45, at 45.

103. Jerry Hanken, "Nakamura Rocks Las Vegas," *Chess Life*, April 2006, 12–19, at 12.

104. Dominic Lawson, *End Game: Kasparov vs. Short* (New York: Harmony, 1994), 6.

105. Geuzendam, *The Day Kasparov Quit*, 246.

106. Josh Waitzkin, *The Art of Learning: A Journey in the Pursuit of Excellence* (New York: Free Press, 2007), 58.

107. For instances of cheating, see "Chess Cheating Web Reports," *Chess Life*, March 2007, 21.

108. Goldowsky, "How to Catch a Chess Cheater," 22.

109. See, for example, Evgeny Bareev and Ilya Levitov, *From London to Elista: The Inside Story of the World Chess Championship Matches that Vladimir Kramnik Won against Garry Kasparov, Peter Leko, and Veselin Topalov* (Alkmaar, the Netherlands: New in Chess, 2007), 303–98.

110. Dylan Loeb McClain, "Latvians Say Foe Got Signals from Her Tube of Lip Balm," *New York Times*, January 13, 2008, 23.

111. There is what is called "the Goichberg rule," after tournament organizer Bill Goichberg. Headphones can be used until your record in the tournament is over 80 percent.

Chapter Seven

1. Reuben Fine, *Chess the Easy Way* (Philadelphia: David McKay, 1942), v.

2. Both from "Chess as a Metaphor," *Chess Life*, August 2006, 6.

3. Michael Gelb and Raymond Keene, *Samurai Chess: Mastering the Martial Art of the Mind* (London: Aurum, 1997), 19.

4. Hans Ree, "Rook Six Four Three, Mate!" *New in Chess*, 2006, no. 2, 88–91, at 89.

5. Stephanie A. Colwell, "Devouring December," *Chess Life*, February 2009, 6.

6. Howard Goldowsky, "Geek Gives Chess National Exposure," *Chess Life*, April 2006, 27.

7. Stuart Rachels, "The Reviled Art," in *Philosophy Looks at Chess*, ed. Benjamin Hale (Chicago: Open Court, 2008), 209–25, at 209.

8. Macauley Peterson, "Get Ready for the Next Generation," *Chess Life*, June 2007, 16–23, at 23.

9. Julian Barnes, *Letters from London* (New York: Vintage, 1995), 255.

10. James Jasper, *Getting Your Way: Strategic Dilemmas in the Real World* (Chicago: University of Chicago Press, 2006).

11. Stephanie Banchero, "At Kids' Chess Tourney, Chaos Calls Checkmate," *Chicago Tribune*, March 17, 2007, 1.

12. Other types of tournaments exist, such as elimination (or "knockout") tournaments, in which defeated players are eliminated.

13. David Lawson, *Paul Morphy: The Pride and Sorrow of Chess* (New York: David McKay, 1976); Richard Eales, *Chess: The History of a Game* (London: B. T. Batsford, 1985), 150–51.

14. "Mink," *New Yorker*, June 12, 1989, 38–39; "The Underground Chess Economy," *Chess Life*, December 2009, 38; Fred Waitzkin, *Searching for Bobby Fischer: The World of Chess, Observed by the Father of a Chess Prodigy* (New York: Random House, 1988), 17–25.

15. Chess is a single-player game, in contrast to bridge. In the world of competitive bridge, professionals are for hire as partners, helping less talented players gain master points. See Janicemarie Allard Holtz, "The 'Professional' Duplicate Bridge Player: Conflict Management in a Free Quasi-Deviant Occupation," *Urban Life* 4 (1975): 131–48, at 132–34.

16. Paul Hoffman, *King's Gambit: A Son, a Father, and the World's Most Dangerous Game* (New York: Hyperion, 2007), 60.

17. Alexander Cockburn, *Idle Passion: Chess and the Dance of Death* (New York: New American Library, 1974), 129; David Edmonds and John Eidinow, *Bobby Fischer Goes to War: How the Soviets Lost the Most Extraordinary Chess Match of All Time* (New York: HarperCollins, 2004), 225–26, 308.

18. Michael Gelb and Raymond Keen. *Samurai Chess: Mastering the Martial Art of the Mind* (London: Aurum, 1997), 23.

19. Dirk Jan ten Geuzendam, *The Day Kasparov Quit and Other Chess Interviews* (Alkmaar, the Netherlands: New in Chess, 2006), 53–54.

20. Ibid., 144.

21. Edmonds and Eidinow, *Bobby Fischer Goes to War*; Daniel Johnson, *White King and Red Queen: How the Cold War was Fought on the Chessboard* (London: Atlantic Books, 2007); Boris Gulko, Vladimir Popov, Yuri Felshtinsky, and Viktor Kortschnoi, *The KGB Plays Chess: The Soviet Secret Police and the Fight for the World Chess Crown* (Milford, CT: Russell Enterprises, 2010).

22. For Gulko, see Gulko et al., *The KGB Plays Chess*; Fred Waitzkin, *Mortal Games: The Turbulent Genius of Garry Kasparov* (New York: Putnam, 1993), 119–20; Susan Polgar and Paul Truong, "Cassia's Gentleman," *Chess Life*, October 2007, 14–15. For Korchnoi, see Johnson, *White King and Red Queen*, 244–66.

23. Gulko et al., *The KGB Plays Chess*, 25.

24. Mariano Sana, "When Foreigners Take Over: A Case Study of Highly Skilled Migration," unpublished manuscript, 2009.

25. As of July 2012, aside from Nakamura, two other players born in the United States were on the list (Robert Hess and Sam Shankland), as well as another player, born in Guam, who grew up in the continental United States (Ray Robson).

26. Al Lawrence, "Cold War Post Mortem," *Chess Life*, December 2006, 18–25, at 21.

27. Olim Chism, "Serbs Successfully Challenge UTD," *Chess Life*, January 2007, 16–21, at 20.

28. Michael Weinreb, *The Kings of New York: A Year among the Geeks, Oddballs, and*

Geniuses Who Make Up America's Top High School Chess Team (New York: Gotham Books, 2007), 41.

29. My son's first chess teacher migrated from the Soviet Union in the 1980s.

30. Paul Hoffman, *King's Gambit*, 97.

31. Fred Waitzkin, *Mortal Games*, 88.

32. Joel Benjamin, *American Grandmaster: Four Decades of Chess Adventures* (London: Everyman Chess, 2007), 247-48.

33. Larry Evans, *This Crazy World of Chess* (New York: Cardoza, 2007), 154.

34. Mark Sussman, "Performing the Intelligent Machine: Deception and Enchantment in the Life of the Automaton Chess Player," *Drama Review* 43, no. 3 (1999): 81-96, at 83.

35. Philip Manning, personal communication, 2012.

36. Dylan Loeb McClain, "Wherever You Are, a Game Is Just a Point and Click Away," *New York Times*, March 14, 2010, 21.

37. Robert Desjarlais, *Counterplay: An Anthropologist at the Chessboard* (Berkeley: University of California Press, 2011), 187-93.

38. J. C. Hallman, *The Chess Artist: Genius, Obsession, and the World's Oldest Game* (New York: Thomas Dunne Books, 2003), 29.

39. Edward Tenner, "Rook Dreams," *Atlantic*, December 2008, http://www.theatlantic.com/doc/200812/chess-software, accessed December 22, 2008.

40. Desjarlais, *Counterplay*, 163.

41. Ibid., 169.

42. Tenner, "Rook Dreams."

43. Dominic Lawson, *End Game: Kasparov vs. Short* (New York: Harmony, 1994).

44. D. T. Max, "The Prince's Gambit," *New Yorker*, March 21, 2011, 40-49, at 40. This is true in televised poker as well, where the screen shows the odds of winning for each hand.

45. Macauley Peterson, "Get Ready for the Next Generation," *Chess Life*, June 2007, 16-23, at 16.

46. Gary Alan Fine, *Gifted Tongues: High School Debate and Adolescent Culture* (Princeton, NJ: Princeton University Press, 2001), 260.

47. Maarten van Emden, "I Remember Donald Michie," June 12, 2009, Chess Programming WIKI, http://chessprogramming.wikispaces.com/Artificial+Intelligence, accessed March 12, 2011.

48. David Shenk, *The Immortal Game: A History of Chess* (New York: Doubleday, 2006), 199-221.

49. I. A. Horowitz and P. L. Rothenberg, *The Personality of Chess* (New York: Macmillan, 1963), 345.

50. Hallman, *The Chess Artist*, 30.

51. Feng-Hsiung Hsu, *Behind Deep Blue: Building the Computer That Defeated the World Chess Champion* (Princeton, NJ: Princeton University Press, 2002); Bruce Pandolfini, *Kasparov and Deep Blue: The Historic Chess Match between Man and Machine* (New York: Fireside, 1997).

52. Bob Bales, "He's the Greatest!" *Illinois Chess Bulletin*, July 2000, n.p.

53. Max, "The Prince's Gambit," 47.

54. Garry Kasparov, "Human Malfunction," *New in Chess*, 2007, no. 1, 95–97, at 96.

55. Dirk Jan ten Geuzendam, "Kramnik vs. Deep Fritz: You Lose Some, You Win None," *New in Chess*, 2007, no. 1, 10–23, at 13.

56. Hans Ree, "The Sorcerer." *New in Chess*, 2007, no. 1, 86–91, at 90.

57. Garry Kasparov, "The Chess Master and the Computer," review of *Chess Metaphors: Artificial Intelligence and the Human Mind*, by Diego Rasskin-Gutman, trans. Deborah Closky, *New York Review of Books*, February 11, 2010, http://www.nybooks.com/articles/archives/2010/feb/11/the-chess-master-and-the-computer, accessed March 13, 2011.

58. Ibid.

59. Johnson, *White King and Red Queen*, 234.

60. Quoted in Evans, *This Crazy World of Chess*, 57.

61. Bruno Latour, *Reassembling the Social: An Introduction to Actor-Network-Theory* (New York: Oxford University Press, 2005).

62. Harry Collins, *Tacit and Explicit Knowledge* (Chicago: University of Chicago Press, 2010), 106–13, esp. 108.

63. Andy Soltis, "What Would Fritz Do?" *Chess Life*, March 2009, 14–15, at 14.

64. Soltis suggests that computers are prone to prefer to gain material (e.g., take pawns), rather than choose the strongest position and that they are willing to consider seemingly hopeless positions. Ibid., 15.

65. Gary Alan Fine, *Authors of the Storm: Meteorologists and the Culture of Prediction* (Chicago: University of Chicago Press, 2007), 116–18.

66. Latour, *Reassembling the Social*.

67. Richard A. Peterson and Roger M. Kern, "Changing Highbrow Taste: From Snob to Omnivore," *American Sociological Review* 61 (1996): 900–907.

Conclusion

1. Gary Alan Fine, *Authors of the Storm: Meteorologists and the Culture of Prediction* (Chicago: University of Chicago Press, 2007), 99–134.

2. Eviatar Zerubavel, *Social Mindscapes: An Invitation to Cognitive Sociology* (Cambridge, MA: Harvard University Press, 1997).

3. Michel Foucault, *Discipline and Punish: The Birth of the Prison* (New York: Pantheon, 1977).

4. Ray Oldenburg, *The Great Good Place: Cafés, Coffee Shops, Bookstores, Bars, Hair Salons, and Other Hangouts at the Heart of the Community.* (New York: Paragon, 1989).

5. Nicholas Christakis and James Fowler, *Connected: The Surprising Power of Our Social Networks and How They Shape Our Lives* (Boston: Little, Brown, 2009).

6. Robert Putnam, *Bowling Alone: The Collapse and Revival of American Community* (New York: Simon and Schuster, 2000).

INDEX

PLAYERS AND PAWNS